Pillar
In
The
Temple

Jo Lisa Blossom

*"He who overcomes, I will make him a
pillar in the temple of My God,
and he shall go out no more.
I will write on him the name of My God
and the name of the city of My God,
the New Jerusalem,
which comes down out of heaven from My God.
And I will write on him My new name."*

Revelations 3:12

Copyright © 2023 Jo Lisa Blossom

All rights reserved.

ISBN: 9798389203099

DEDICATION

This book is dedicated to my Lord and Savior Jesus Christ and to my husband and children, who've made me a better person by blessing me with who they are. This book is also dedicated to every victim who said 'enough is enough' and took the courageous, often lonely, road to the ultimate victory of breaking a generational curse to the glory of Christ.

Table of Contents

CHAPTER ONE 10
CHAPTER TWO 20
   My Mother Who Is She? 21
   Writers Group - Sharing Excerpt One 24
      Abuse 25
CHAPTER THREE 36
   Writers Group - Sharing Excerpt Two 38
CHAPTER FOUR 50
   Writers Group - Sharing Excerpt Three 51
      Here's The Church 51
      Go Back 51
CHAPTER FIVE 64
   Writers Group - Sharing Excerpt Four 65
      The Promise Land 65
      Curiosity 66
CHAPTER SIX 78
   Writers Group - Sharing Excerpt Five 79
      I Give Up 79
      How It Is 80
CHAPTER SEVEN 98
   Writers Group - Sharing Excerpt Six 101
      Let It Fly 101
      Who I Am 102
CHAPTER EIGHT 116
   Writers Group - Sharing Excerpt Seven 117
      Sing for Sorrow and for Joy 118

Hope	118
CHAPTER NINE	128
The No Love Shove	128
No Kiss Goodbye	129
Writers Group - Sharing Excerpt Eight	130
CHAPTER TEN	148
Writers Group - Sharing Excerpt Nine	148
Fractured Family	148
Smash The Glass	149
CHAPTER ELEVEN	159
Writers Group - Sharing Excerpt Ten	160
Broken Fixer	160
Dirt Nap	161
CHAPTER TWELVE	169
Writers Group - Sharing Excerpt Eleven	170
To Myself	170
Reprobate	170
CHAPTER THIRTEEN	184
Writers Group - Sharing Excerpt Twelve	185
Bubble Boy	186
Another	189
CHAPTER FOURTEEN	204
Writers Group - Sharing Excerpt Thirteen	205
Garden of Pain	205
Frail	205
CHAPTER FIFTEEN	221
Writers Group - Sharing Excerpt Fourteen	223

    The Plank 223
    When I Die 224
CHAPTER SIXTEEN 245
  Writers Group - Sharing Excerpt Fifteen 247
    Summer 247
    Scribble 248
CHAPTER SEVENTEEN 262
Writers Group - Sharing Excerpt Sixteen 263
    A Clenched Fist 263
    Spirit 264
CHAPTER EIGHTEEN 276
  Writers Group - Sharing Excerpt Seventeen 277
    Lord I'm Listening 277
    Wishful Thinking 277
CHAPTER NINETEEN 291
  Writers Group - Sharing Excerpt Eighteen 292
    Sleeper 292
CHAPTER TWENTY 303
  Writers Group - Sharing Excerpt Nineteen 304
    The Melancholy 304
    End of Story 305
CHAPTER TWENTY-ONE 325
  Writers Group - Sharing Excerpt Twenty 326
    Who 326
    Reject It! 327
CHAPTER TWENTY TWO 337
  Writers Group - Sharing Excerpt Twenty One 339

    Acceptance 339

    The Pedophile's Wife 339

CHAPTER TWENTY THREE 353

    Writers Group - Sharing Excerpt Twenty Two 353

    From Here 353

    Old Things 354

LAST CHAPTER 371

Writers Group - Sharing Excerpt Twenty Three 372

AFTERWARD 378

FORWARD

Stories about people overcoming desperate odds have always encouraged me. So many people have struggled and overcome heartache to find joy at the other side. This story is like that, and I'm grateful for the opportunity to honor God and give testimony to His amazing love.

I've read lots of books written by Christians. Some are not nearly as "gritty" as this one. I heard a pastor once share that there is a reality that is life; and despite the fact that what we most hear about is the *amazing and rare* experiences with God, that is not daily reality. He was making sure that those listening didn't feel like their walk with God was lacking because they didn't have regular, incredible experiences of God's power. He wanted people to know that the stories people tell so dramatically from behind a microphone, are not the most *common* experience. My book is about what happens in between those amazing experiences with God. Sometimes the amazing experiences aren't all at once. *Over time* the experience is amazing…God's love is constant. God's love transcends the grit and grime of this world. God's love is so good. I pray that this story will encourage you, make you laugh and point you to Jesus.

Although this book is largely factual, some events names, places and details have been changed significantly, to protect people's privacy. Most of the main character's current experiences are fictionalized, including in Chapter One where I describe having a panic attack because my son talked me into growing marijuana in the backyard. That was something that I once did when

I was a teen, and I built it into something funny for the book. There are several things like that in the life of the main character, that are fictionalized. The main character was inspired by a baby sitter that we had when we were children. I built her experiences into happy endings, and things I wish had happened in real life. I also built her to be somewhat like me at this point in my life. Thank you for reading my book!

"And they overcame him (satan) by the blood of the Lamb, and by the word of their testimony…."
Revelation 12:11

CHAPTER ONE

"They look like tomato plants, Mom. No one will even know."

"*I'll* know and there is just *no* way, Chuck! And its breakfast! Why are you starting up with me first thing in the morning? This again? I can't take it! Hurry up or you're gonna be late again!" Pouring my coffee, I looked up at my teenage son, the master of the wear down, with milk dripping down his chin. My eyes traveled to his hair, long and sticking out in three different directions. Poor kid wants to be a rock star, and he got my cowlicks. "I think the cow snuck in your bedroom window and licked your head again last night. You need a haircut."

"Whatever, Mom. You know who else has long hair?"

"Idiots?"

"Jesus! Look at that picture you've got of him right there! See it! I'm going for the whole enchilada, Mom. I wanna look like Jesus!" He said it with an almost wistful expression. Undoubtedly learned in the high school drama classes.

I turned to gaze slowly at my favorite possession. It was the most ornate frame I'd ever seen around the old picture of Jesus from Sunday school. He had a point. Jesus did have shoulder length hair. I felt calm come over me looking into the eyes of God. Looking back at my son, shoving his size thirteen feet into his shoes without bothering to untie them, the calm disappeared.

"Whatever. I'm going to get dressed to drive you to school. Look at the time! There is no doubt the bus went by already! You need to retake that driver test on Thursday!"

We were financially stable, but without a lot of extras. Up until about two weeks ago, I had been babysitting four kids every day to make money for things we needed. The kids I was babysitting Monday through Friday were great, but along with the dog breeding and the puppies, and the menopause, it was too much. When I needed a break, I would shoo the kids out the door to the backyard. I would look out the window at the dogs jumping up on them, and trying to chew their little arms. The dogs were wild, and the kids were screaming at them. I would go out and try to train the dogs but they were energetic and I was not all the time. I felt terrible for ever having to shoo the kids out there and I was afraid a neighbor might call somebody, and report that I was putting the kids out there as dog bait. I finally told their mother that she had to find a different sitter. I also planned to rehome two of my younger dogs to a younger, more energetic owner.

Sighing, I pulled the last two pieces of bread out of the sack. Whole wheat. This was the bread those kids' mom brought over. Somehow, I just never remembered to buy bread while she was doing that. "*Bread*", would be there scribbled on my list, and for some reason, I couldn't read my own messy writing. Or I just missed checking that item off my list when I went to the store. Mental block. I just used theirs. I knew it was wrong. I cringed remembering one morning when I pulled out my own week-old white bread, and tried to give it to the kids. The sly, eleven year old took one bite and promptly spit it right back out.

"This bread is stale! This isn't the bread my mother gave you. I won't eat it!" She slammed her sandwich down on the plate and glared up at me defiantly.

I gasped! "What?! I wouldn't do that! That is perfectly good bread. Give it to me! I'll prove it!" I grabbed her sandwich and took a dainty bite, chewing vigorously and trying not to look serious. The crust was a little firm so technically, she was right. Of course, I couldn't let this little food critic know. I was caught, and branded, as a bread stealer in her little mind. I had to think fas,t but now I was a liar too. Darn that slippery slope.

"I'm still not eating it. I'm going outside to starve." She wheeled around on her stool, and headed for the back door. Her siblings just watched with big eyes. Nobody followed her. They thought about it, but they were hungry. They were always hungry, but not always for food. I could see that. The school lunches were notoriously bad, and they needed their sandwich, stale bread or no. The second in command wrapped her little hand around her sandwich, and started to follow her big sister. As soon as she saw the dogs, she turned back. She knew the dogs would jump up, and rip that sandwich clean out of her hand as soon as she hit the yard. I could see her thinking. I could see all of them thinking, and I felt like a jerk. That was the last straw. I decided right then to tell the mom that night when she picked them up, that I had to quit babysitting them in a week. I wanted to at least give her some time to find a new sitter. She seemed like a good mom.

"Hey come back in here, I'll fix you something else." I called out to the ring leader sheepishly. I looked at the kids with regret for my decidedly un-adult, un-Christian behavior. They were good kids. They didn't say much. I knew I couldn't have the poor babies afraid I would starve them slowly with rotten bread. They had already been through too much, and I felt bad for them. Sometimes I got the feeling their stepdad was up to no good, and I wanted to shoot the scumbag. I couldn't prove anything, and even if I got up the nerve to ask, I wasn't sure how to help without making it worse; and they probably wouldn't tell.

All I did was use their bread, but I knew I couldn't keep taking care of them. I was getting morally lazy, and they reminded me too much of my childhood. I was desperately trying to hang on to my joy, and I had become a bit of a slug. Jesus was watching with those peaceful eyes, and I was miserable because I wasn't loving them enough. They spent too much time in the backyard. They would lay out there looking at the clouds, pointing and talking. I knew what they were doing. They were doing what all neglected kids did. They were looking for clouds shaped like animals, faces and giant birds that they could fly away on.

I was fifty-two years old, and tired. I was tired all the time, so the following Tuesday after I took Chuck to school, I laid back down, and slept for a while. Once again, a bread stealing slug.

I slept in until ten, and by noon, after eating pickles, cheese, cranberries, chips, grapes, and an enchilada, I was blankly staring out the window thinking about my life. So many things I needed to get up and do, and I just couldn't get my butt moving. How much caffeine is too much to mix with high blood pressure medicine, I wondered? Lord, help me. I need to weed that yard and get up and go check the mail box. Maybe one out of two isn't bad. Maybe my "big check" will be in there today. I'd been visualizing for weeks now. I just knew God was going to bring me a big check someday soon. I was going to give a big chunk to good causes and then go the Bahamas. Right after I bought a bigger bathing suit.

Closing the mailbox, I looked across the street at the kids in the yard. They look familiar I thought. Holy Toledo! It's the starving eleven-year-old, and the rest of the crew! Their Mom must've talked to my neighbor Maria and she decided to babysit. I hope that works out. I hope her teenage daughter doesn't yell at the kids too much. I cringed remembering the last time I saw Maria, and her daughter screaming at each other in the yard. The whole neighborhood got a glimpse that day. I could hear the yelling, but tried not to listen so hard that I inadvertently heard what they were saying. I was raised not to eavesdrop but sometimes you had no choice. This was the suburbs. I knew the fight was mostly about a boy but I was certain that her teenage daughter also freaked out regularly because she couldn't stand the way her mother breathed. Maria probably said yes to babysitting because those kids were a joy compared to that hormonal bundle of joy.

Chuck bounded up the driveway. Like an explosion he slammed into my daydream.

"Hey Mom. What's up?"

"Oh, nothing much. I see Maria is babysitting those kids now."

I looked down at my shirt with the bits of chips and cheese across the front. "Jesus saves" it says. Hmmmm, I hope Jesus was neater than me.

I walked back inside and sat down on the couch to read the mail. With a new bag of chips, Chuck flopped down beside me. "So, Mom let's talk turkey. You know that entre.., entrevous… entrepeee….. you know that idea we've been discussing? It's really a bit of a business venture. I mean we need money, right? You know, since our supply of free bread is gone now."

I slapped his arm. "I think you meant to say entrepreneurial. Can you even spell that word? And the answer is h-e-double hockey sticks no."

"Well, seriously, you wouldn't even have to know. I could put them on the side of the house and I swear, Roger has some and you can't tell the difference between them and the tomato plants. His grandma had panic attacks, and now she is totally cured!"

"Are you kidding me, Chuck? It's illegal! You are not going to grow pot on this property. I would be a nervous wreck and you know my history! I've never had anyone suggest that crap would help. And what if we got arrested? Who would take care of the dogs? There goes the one source of extra income we have right now. And you need a car."

"That's just what I'm saying, Mom. We would have a second income stream! I could sell a little on the side and give you money every week! You wouldn't have to worry so much and I could get a car." He pleaded with his eyes and tried to sound sensible, but the chip crumbs were on *his* shirt now and frankly they were distracting me from his sales pitch.

"The answer is no! I will figure something out. Now go brush your hair. You look like a hoodlum!"

"Geez you need to chill, Mom, chill!"

"I've got your chill right here, Buddy."

Three months later I was coming to terms with the fact that Chuck had sucked me into his evil plan. I felt absolutely terrible about it. We were now temporary criminals for a stupid jalopy car. To top it all off the alternate income stream was not panning out. I was so broke, that I had to go to the foodbank, *twice*! Beyond that I was still out of my mind every day. Worry over money and breaking the law was making me emotional. As an outlet for stress, I had started to write again. Maybe if I get good at this, I can get paid to write, I thought.

"Guess where I'm going today?"

"Ice skating with a sexy farmer boy?" Chuck giggled at his own joke.

"No, I'm going to a writing group. I'm going to share some of my stuff in public!"

"Awesome! I always knew you could do it, Mom. I'm really proud of you." He smiled and I knew he meant it. I was basking in the moment and in the next, my nightmare began.

Boom, boom, boom! Someone was at the door but that knocking was just too loud. It was startling. It was obnoxious!

"Who is it?" Immediately, I got nervous. "Who is it? Chuck! Look out the window! Is it that Dereck? He never calls ahead."

"Calm down, Mom. Let me look." Chuck marched over to the window and peered out. "Oh no! It's the cops! I'll handle this! You better hide, Mom. Their gonna know something's up when they see you sweating."

"What?! It's the stupid hot flashes! I can't help it!" I started rushing around in a panic.

BOOM! BOOM! BOOM!

Chuck turned around and hissed at me, "Just split, Lady!"

Lady? Who the heck is "lady", now? I ran out the back door. "Get down, get down!" Shoving my dogs away, I headed for the side of the house. Unlatching the gate, I was shocked at the trash cans. They were overflowing. That kid! Why doesn't he do his job? Stepping over the rotting bags, I fell to my knees in front of the plants. I knew this was a bad idea! In terror, I started ripping out the plants. I ripped one out and dirt flew everywhere. I had dirt in my eyes, my hair, my mouth. Frantically, I searched for room in one of the trashcans. Giving up, I yanked a bag of garbage out of one and threw it on the ground next to the others. My hands were shaking as I twisted the plant into a bunch and shoved it in. I dropped down on my knees to yank out another. What was that? I listened intently. Were they coming? Oh God help me! Then as if in slow motion, I saw the sidewalk moving up to hit me in the face. I was dying. I can't breathe! I can't breathe! Is it over? I was sure it was over. In an instant I realized I can't breathe but I can still smell.... garbage! What does that mean? Am I dead already? Jesus forgive me! Save me! Laying on the sidewalk gasping for air, my thoughts raced frantically. I was having a panic attack and I knew it but I was helpless to stop it. I clawed at the dirt trying to reach another plant. I had to hide them! I had to get rid of them! I don't want to go to jail! I don't want to die! Then blackness...

Something was on my face.... crawling. Eeek! Sitting up, my hand flew up to brush the bug off my face. I stared at my filthy hands. Is that blood? I realized my nose was bleeding. But I'm alive! Relief came over me and for a second, I felt like jumping up and down. That was instantly followed by dread. Are they still here? What do I do? Did God save me and now I have to go to jail?

"Mom? Hey Mom!" Chuck was yelling from the back door. He must be all right! Thank God, he's not under arrest! Getting up I brushed myself off and headed toward the gate.

"Are they gone?"

"Yeah, It's ok. They're gone. What happened to you? Is that dirt on your nose? Are you bleeding? Mom! Are you ok?"

Praise the Lord! I thought. Relief rushed over me again.

"I'm ok!" I yelled, lifting the latch on the gate. Turning back for a moment..." Those are out of here today! Jesus forgive me!" I said out loud. Marching up, I hit Chuck with both bloody barrels.

"That is it, Chuck! Get those stupid plants out of here. I want them gone today. And for heaven's sake take the garbage to the curb on trash day. It's disgusting out there!"

"Hey now, let's not freak out, Mom. Chill, Lady, chill!

"I'm serious! I almost died out there wigging out over this stupid crap! And you better not be messing around with that stuff anymore! I will drug test! And if you flunk, forget about the car!"

"Yeah, I almost passed out talking to that cop. I was freaking out on the inside and I already decided I don't want to go to jail. So, I'll get rid of them Mom. It was a stupid idea."

I breathed a sigh of relief. "Thank God! I am so not up to arguing. Don't worry. We'll figure out something for your car."

An hour later, I came into the kitchen freshly showered and in a robe. After that episode, I didn't care about getting dressed today.

With my hair up in a towel and all the dirt washed off, I pulled out the cutting board to make a sandwich. "Honey, you never told me what the cops wanted."

"Hey can you make me one too?"

"Sure, but what did the cops say?" I felt so irresponsible letting my son answer the door, and act like the adult. I used to be so much more mature!

"They had the wrong house. They got a report about Maria shoving those poor kids out in the back yard at five o'clock in the morning when it was still dark. Apparently, they were out there crawling around on the wood pile, and I guess they started screaming and stuff, so they were checking on that. Can you believe that beach?" A small smile crept over my face. Just like his Dad, my son knew right from wrong, and it warmed my heart the way he stood up to injustice for those kids. And he knew how to edit a word so he could keep saying it with immunity.

"I bet it was that older girl. She's tough", he said. I giggled imagining her jumping up on the woodpile to rally the troops.

Apparently, he was imagining something similar. "She probably got them all to scream their heads off to wake up that old man next door. He probably called the cops on that old bat."

"You shouldn't call her that. She's not a "*old bat*". And she's my age for heaven's sake!" I sighed, exasperated. Sometimes I wished I was a younger mother.

Like a radar, he sensed my irritation. He leaned over my shoulder, to bother me some more. "Hey what is that? Are you eating *their* bread?"

Slapping my cheese on the bread, I answered with a smile. "Chill, Chuck, chill." Silly kid giving *me* a hard time when he's the wannabe criminal? That's enough stealing and dealing for both of us, I thought.

CHAPTER TWO

Writers group. Share your writing with others in a creative environment. Be encouraged and critiqued as you hone your skill.

Hmmm……it's the critique part I'm worried about. I stood at the door to the library a second longer looking at the flyer. Shoving the door open, I thought, do I really want to subject myself to that? Some wannabe writers giving me crud about my stuff? I pictured a bald guy with a pony tail, socks and sandals. He means well but he's actually getting his jollies showing up to tell everybody else their writing is horrid. I had met the type, and I knew the trick was to flirt with them for a moment. Then they'd be distracted thinking I might be their girlfriend. But that was tricky when they asked for a phone number. I only made that mistake once.

It was the poetry reading. All that raw emotion made me let my guard down. I remember Andrew. Ugh. He insisted you pronounce his name Ahh-ndrew. He was into theatre and singing out loud while others waited for it to be over, looking uncomfortable. I was just trying to be polite. He seemed lonely and I thought maybe he could go fishing with my husband or something. But he took my good manners as an indication that we were soul mates. I was done for safety reasons but Andrew wasn't.

Two weeks later it was restraining order time. At the police station, the desk sergeant just grinned and shook his head. "Poetry reading right?"

I had been around the stalker block at least once, but this wasn't just poetry so maybe it would be alright. Maybe I could actually meet some serious, published writers. Wouldn't that be cool? Maybe the doors would just open magically for my book. Maybe the creative mind of the universe would just bring it all to me. I knew it was possible but my $800,000 check, the one I'd been visualizing for months, was late showing up. So, I wasn't sure, but I needed something. I needed something to do. I needed an outlet. I needed people who understood the struggle against the darkness, and the yearning for the light. I needed God to help me get out there, and stick to it, so I could finish a book, before I die, for heaven's sake.

Ready to get serious, I went in, parked my backpack in a cubicle, and got out my notebook. Let's see…I feel the creative spark coming on right now! How exciting! Here I am surrounded by the smell of written creativity, and the work of the masters and what comes to my mind? My mother. Seriously? Ugh. I guess I might as well let it out. Maybe someone else will relate. After all, everyone has a mother. With a heavy sigh, I looked at my watch. I only had an hour, and a half, until the first writers' group. Oh well, better go with what I know. I started to scribble furiously…

My Mother Who Is She?

She is the woman who stayed married, knowing her
husband was a pedophile for thirty-five years,
And then crushed me stating that fact
She is the woman who spent forty hours
crocheting a blanket for me

> That I sleep under every night.
> She had Christmas parties with thirty-eight people
> Then stopped calling even one person
> to say Merry Christmas.
> My mother…who is she?
> She is the woman who closed her eyes to truth
> Then wrote a check for my eye surgery,
> so I can see for miles.
> She is the woman who didn't want to be poor
> so she let her children pay a terrible price
> And then bailed us out of debt.
> She is the woman who faithfully visited me in jail
> While helping her husband commit crimes.
> My mother…who is she?
> She is the woman who told me
> that if she goes down to just let her die
> And then made me want to kill myself.
> She is the woman who never, ever said
> "I was wrong and I'm sorry",
> And then I had to forgive her.

Crud knuckles. Why do I have to have this in my life? I think I need a frontal lobotomy or at least shock treatments, like that old country western star. She said they saved her life, and she had such cute hair! Maybe if I just get a couple zaps, I can forget about this junk.

    I mean take last night for instance. My dreams are just too evil! First, I find a half dead body in an envelope. And what is "half dead" anyway? Is that half alive? Is that when the top half of the body is alive, talking like nothing is happening, and the bottom half is dead? The head says, "Oh smoochie, give me a kiss", puckering up while the arms reach out, and the legs disintegrate. Or is it like one side is dead and the other is alive, right down the middle through the crotch of all places? One side is laying on the ground with chalk around it while the other side is kicking and screaming, "Get up! Let's get the heck-o out of here!" I don't know. Half dead. Well, that's how I feel nearly every day. Maybe it's when your brain won't shut up but your body doesn't want to get out of bed. Guess which one is the boss. Lay there long enough, and you'll probably find out which one is in charge all right. All I know is I hate getting older, feeling half dead and exhausted half the time.

Is this creative enough? Sighing, I tried to focus but then out of the corner of my eye I noticed a guy walking by. He had a gray ponytail. Oh no! If that's Andrew I'm going to freak. Just then he turned my way. Oh, thank God just some other poor man who hasn't been to a decent barber in decades, but made it to the library. Ok, where was I….

A few days later, it was time…my first writers' group. It seemed like a pretty harmless group. The blond with the constant giggle was introducing herself. "Well, I just love to write! It makes me feel alive! And it's just fun! It's like vacuuming naked!"

What?! I thought.

She looked around giggling. "But my husband said I needed more. So here I am! I'm so excited to meet all of you." Giggle…giggle and a wiggle. I get it. Smiling at her, I thought, yes and I am unbelievably thrilled to meet you too! Vacuuming naked. Hmmm, I might have to try that. I giggled at her and smiled a little smile. I was smart enough not to show my teeth. Just pleasant, NOT too friendly. You never know what else she's doing naked. No thank you.

Next was the hippie chick. If she would just wash her hair! I was trying not to stare too hard at her dreadlocks. I was pretty sure by her glassy eyes that she had just smoked a marijuana cigarette. I could smell that, and her hair, and it was not good. She's the reason I don't want that junk anywhere near me. I *need* all my brain cells, and I *like* the smell of shampoo. She was licking her lips, and going on. "So, I am just looking for an amazing experience. I have been traveling around this amazing state on my bus and I have seen soooooo many amazing things and been to soooo many amazing places. I know this is going to be totally organically amazing, too. I mean I can't wait to read the expressions of your souls, and I feel like we are all going to touch each other spiritually, and reach a place of peace together. It's going to be soooo beautiful!"

Wow. I'm not sure I want to be part of the touching each other thing, but peace sounds fantastic. Another little smile but luckily the hippie chick didn't see me. She was busy showing the grandma next to her, her black fingernails. Probably hides the dirt from all those treks through the woods, naming the trees. She seems amazing. Sighing, I thought, I really should be nicer. Jesus made her, and I've talked to my squash plants for heaven's sake! I waited for the next volunteer, trying desperately to stop thinking cruddy thoughts about everybody. Love! Think love!

It was my turn. I hadn't shared my writing yet, and now the instructor was telling us we had to. Handing my first pages over to a guy in pink skinny jeans, that I was pretty sure was gay, was nerve wracking. If he wasn't gay, he sure wanted all of us to think he was. Who knows, maybe we're kindred spirits with the same fabu fashion sense. I love pink! Giving him my book pages, I smiled with my teeth, determined to love like Jesus.

Writers Group - Sharing Excerpt One
Genre: Semi-Autobiographical Memoir, Christian
Author: Jo Lisa Blossom

Abuse

A
Tiny
Blemish
On
Perfect
Skin…
Just
An
Insignificant
Scar
On
A
Single
Life
The
Details
Are
Invisible
To
The
Naked
Eye…
But
The
Stripped
Child
Remembers.

    Lying as still as I could, I tried not to move at all. Closing my eyes tight, but not too tight…so he would think I was *really* sleeping. I tried to control my breathing. Slow and steady. My heart was beating, so hard, I was afraid he could see it through the covers. I tried to control my fear and my breathing. In and out…..slooooooowly. If I look asleep, I thought, maybe he will just pass me by. Maybe he won't stop tonight.

I wanted so badly to be invisible. I knew at 10 years old, that I was too big to just hide under the covers. I knew that was silly, but at that moment I would've done anything, *anything*, to be invisible. A moment later, it was too late…he was there with that look on his face and his hand reaching where I knew it did not belong.

Then suddenly…. I *was* invisible! I was up in the corner of my bedroom looking down. Panicking, I thought, what am I doing up here? Am I dead? This is weird… Why am I watching this happen from up here? To me! If I'm down there, who am I up here? I tried to peer around him to see my face, and be sure that it was still me in the bed, but I couldn't see around him. Looking down at the back of his head, I couldn't see past his shoulders but I knew I was being ridiculous. Who else could be there in my bed? It had to be me. But how did I get up here in the corner. It didn't make sense and I couldn't figure it out.

I slowly realized that I wasn't scared anymore, just peacefully floating in the corner. For a moment I actually felt good. Then seeing what he was doing, *knowing* what he was doing, rage began to build. Sort of slow and matter of fact I thought, "I hate him." Then suddenly, I was back in my bed….

"Ok it's time to say your prayers now…" he said. Pulling the covers back up to my neck, I closed my eyes and tried to shut out his face, and think about Jesus.

"Then He said to the disciples, 'It is impossible that no offenses should come, but woe to him through whom they do come! It would be better for him if a millstone were hung around his neck, and he were thrown into the sea, that that he should offend one of these little ones.'" Luke 17:1-2

LIFE IN A BLENDER

We don't need a study by overpaid government scientists to know that being in a blended family is hard; hard on parents, hard on children. We know this and my blended family was no different.

There are verses in the bible that talk about parents being commanded by God to intentionally tell their children history, in order to build their children's faith. In our current culture, few of us do that. Sharing a people's history or a family's history, is what people used to do before books, television and the internet. They would tell stories. Stories about the struggles, and how the Lord faithfully led them through to victory. They gave reasons for why things are the way they are. I want the world to know what the Lord has done for me. I hope this story builds your faith in the God of the universe who saved me.

Unfortunately, in order to share the wonderful things that the Lord has done, sometimes we must also share the sordid details. Those details explain so much and, I believe, allow for more natural compassion, less assumption and less judgment. By nature, when we are hurting, we sometimes unfairly blame or attribute things to people, especially our parents or those who are the closest thing we've got to parents. We have no idea 'why' they are the way they are. Knowing 'why' is so helpful. Everyone struggles with sin and unfortunately, we often judge others by their behavior instead of their *intent*. We judge ourselves by what we intended, but judge others by what they do or how it affected us. Some sins are criminal, some sins are habits in the flesh driven by selfishness, and some "sins" are just misunderstood intent. We can only pray for the grace of God to know the difference, and be willing to first address the sins that we can, in our *own* lives.

Addressing sin in a family breaks the shackles of generational curses. Generational curses are sins that have repeated themselves over and over in a family line. If you are in the midst of breaking those shackles, I encourage you to continue to seek God, and keep reading. Be encouraged! Don't give up!

"O my people, listen to my instructions. Open your ears to what I am saying, for I will speak to you in a parable. I will teach you hidden lessons from our past— stories we have heard and known, stories our ancestors handed down to us. We will not hide these truths from our children; we will tell the next generation about the glorious deeds of the Lord, about his power and his mighty wonders. For he issued his laws to Jacob; he gave his instructions to Israel. He commanded our ancestors to teach them to their children, so the next generation might know them— even the children not yet born— and they in turn will teach their own children. So each generation should set its hope anew on God, not forgetting his glorious miracles and obeying His commands." Psalm 78:1-7

    First, some family history. My grandmother, my mother's mother, got married, at fifteen, to my grandfather. She married young because she had eight younger siblings. My Grandmother, went from taking care of her younger siblings to getting married at fifteen and taking care of my grandfather.
    My grandfather was one of sixteen half siblings because his mother, my great grandmother, was the "town prostitute". My mother said her grandmother was a "sl__t." What?! This was a shocking bit of history. My mother, the non-cussing, non-drinking, never inhaled anything but air, Christian just used *that* word. Whoa! Needless to say, with that one word, I got the picture.

Because of my great-grandmother's occupation, only one child was thought to actually be the biological child of my great grandfather. That child was my grandfather. I don't know for sure but you can imagine what that was like. If my great grandfather's wife was the town prostitute, and she had sixteen children, with only one being his, great granddaddy probably spoiled that boy a little. That spoiled boy grew up to be my grandfather.

My grandfather was charming, good-looking, and very self-centered. He was used to being taken care of without necessarily returning the favor. When he was eighteen, he married my fifteen- year-old grandmother, and she started her lifelong job of taking care of him. When my grandmother died, my grandfather was almost sixty years old, and in all those years, he had never bought himself a pair of shoes. It seems that he went from being a teenager, with an absent, dysfunctional mother, and an excessively doting father, to my grandmother, who waited on him hand, foot and shoe.

My grandmother's ethnicity was almost pure Blackfoot Indian, which was known as one of the fiercest tribes of American Indians. My grandfather was mostly German with a little bit of Spaniard. His ancestors probably came over on the Mayflower looking for a good pair of shoes.

Within a few years, my grandparents started having babies. First a son, then after miscarriages, ten years later, they were blessed with twin girls. When the twins were about twelve, they had one more son. I don't know much about my oldest uncle. He left home early, and never came back. No one ever said why or talked much about him.

My mother's twin sister was far more outgoing than she was. My mother was next in the food chain, and even though they were the same size, she got all of her twin's hand me downs. The hand me down syndrome included not just clothes but also the emotional availability of my grandparents. My mother described the situation by saying, "My parents only had one twin."

My mother told me over lunch one day that when she was five, she got a new pair of purple gloves. Telling the story, she rubbed her hands together wistfully, remembering those beautiful gloves in her favorite color. She loved those gloves, and in the South Carolina winter, she *needed* those gloves. She went on to say that later in the day they went to the theatre and someone stole her new gloves. She was only five but she "got beat for losing those gloves" and did not get another pair until she was thirteen.

She told me another story about a time when she was four. An older relative told her they were going for ice cream. As the day went on, they didn't go. So, like any kid waiting on ice cream, she asked about it. She repeated that someone told her they were going for ice cream. No one admitted saying it, and my mother was accused of lying. Again, she was physically abused. She was teased for a long time about being "taught not to lie." Recalling the horror of that experience, she said, "I thought to myself, you didn't teach me not to lie, you taught me to lie whenever I have to, so I won't get hurt." Thinking back, I think she told me that story for a reason. I think she was trying to explain who she is, and why she has done things like live a lie for thirty-five years. Honestly, hearing that story didn't help me much.

Rule number one, just because your parents did it, doesn't mean you have to. This is the grace of God. Be the first to start something new, and good in your generation. Love your children *more* than you were loved. Take them, (and yourself), to church. Ask God to help you be something better than you had. To her credit and the glory of the Lord, my mother never physically abused us. She broke that generational curse! So, in that way, she was a bit of a spiritual badass.

When she was thirteen, my mother's second brother "accidentally" appeared. Great. Another baby. Now my mother really had no chance to get noticed or loved. But on the other hand, this lonely young girl finally had another human, be it a tiny human, nonetheless, another human, to *love* her. My mother has always had a much closer relationship with her younger brother. As the big sister, I'm sure she was called on to help with him a lot.

My mother was very intelligent, and was valedictorian of her high school. She was smart, and worked very hard to prove herself…quietly. She was also an introvert who liked to fight. Her twin sister, the popular one, refused to walk to school with my mother because she fought so much. The neighborhood boys would start fights with her because they knew she liked to fight. What?! Can you picture that? She was wearing shabby, hand me down clothes, red hair in braids to her waist and bright blue eyes behind horn rim glasses. She would throw her books down in the dirt, and start kickin' butt and takin names. Like a lot of abused children, her rage caused her to win any fight she got in. This was one angry bookworm.

My mother eventually left South Carolina but South Carolina never left her. She struggled with depression nearly all her life. She told me on a few occasions that she first felt depressed when she was "three going on four, leaning against a tree and thinking 'why do I have to live?'" That made me sad, and sounded really odd, but I never really tried to find an explanation. But when she was seventy plus, she finally dropped the bomb.

As a young child, she had been sexually assaulted. It was a terrible thing to hear and, I was stunned. I was aghast, in part because the information would've been so much more useful in figuring out her behavior while I was trying to survive it. It's sort of like the movie where a couple of guys are going through death defying scene after scene, and then one of them finally says 'Hey, I've got this gun.' What?! Are you kidding me?! This was like that…a very useful piece of information that we guessed but never knew for sure. This was something that could've provided vast amounts of healing for a lifetime of hurt, her hurt, our hurt. She finally, as a senior citizen, told us that she was *one of us*.

    This bit of history shed more light, on why she never came out of her shell, and wanted to die as a little girl. And it provides some explanation as to why our lives suffered the ravages of another very stubborn generational curse…sexual abuse.

    When she was five, someone raped her…the "guy down the street, who two days later, went to jail for murder!" She frantically shouted. She didn't elaborate. She didn't need to. This was trauma. It took her over seven decades to tell someone. This childhood experience hurt her beyond repair. As a quiet, "less than" small child, she already felt so unloved, and then at five, she is sexually assaulted by a grown man. As if that wasn't enough, she then came home to parents who didn't comfort her and probably beat her for lying.

    The "guy down the street" was no ordinary pervert. Apparently, he was a cannibal and when he went to jail it was because the mail lady went missing, and they found her dressed like a deer in his backyard. What else did he do to my mother, and her siblings? I would not be surprised if before that happened or in addition to that happening, other things did. How did that grown man have access to her?

    Later when she was eight, a teenage boy down the street "was just curious" so he pulled her pants down, but he "didn't molest" her. What does that mean? Knowing what I know about myself and other victims, I would not call a teenage boy pulling an eight-year-old girl's pants down, "just curious". Maybe labeling it something innocent was her way of coping with more violation.

Minimize: to reduce (something, especially something unwanted or unpleasant) to the smallest possible amount or degree.

I don't believe my mother ever found real healing for her pain. I believe she found Christ and loved Him but she never had the courage to take out that box of deep, deep sorrow and pain, lay it all out on the table, pick it apart, scream, yell, cry, sob and then acknowledge her part in it. No one *wants* to do this exercise, looking closely at the junk, and admitting our sin to others, but often we do anyway because we can see that holding it in is destroying us, limiting the depth of our love and damaging relationships with those we love.

For her, even though she hurt deeply, from what I can see, the circumstances of her life never convinced her that bringing that hurt to the surface was worth it. The excruciating effort it would take to admit the mistakes she made, and then let go of that junk, that burden, that box of rocks, wasn't worth it to her. She chose to carry the grief, and pride, instead. Consequently, my siblings and I struggled with our self-worth. Her emotional dysfunction affected us. We suffered while waiting for her to come to our aid, and later waiting for her to say things we desperately needed to hear.

I could be wrong but it seems like past generations, from the forties when my mother grew up, all the way into the seventies when our trauma occurred, didn't know what a pedophile was. When my mother was a teenager a woman who wore mascara was called a "tramp". Someone wanting to have sex with children was not something people understood. And back then NO ONE talked about their *own* problems. Deny, deny, deny seemed to be the societal motto. Like if you don't talk about it, it didn't happen. No matter what, shut up.

In past generations, women were so financially dependent on men that if they discovered their husband was sexually molesting the children, she would often deny it. This is still a common response but back then it was somehow more justified because at that time, there was no welfare. Women who had no other support system, no parents to go home to, no family to take in them and their children, had to hang onto that bread winner or starve.

There were times when I would've done all I could to help my mother through her sorrow and pain. But she never talked about it. I asked her to tell me more about a few of her childhood experiences once and she refused. She said she was "takin' it to the grave." That was her choice, but from my perspective, it all comes down to a box of dirty, ugly rocks. They look so much more beautiful with the water of life, (Jesus), running over them. But sometimes we prefer to chuck them at our neighbors or hide them in the backyard or carry them around until they become part of our identity.

If you have burdens you've been carrying, I would encourage you to get a real box of rocks, write a burden on each one and then carry them around for a while. literally. Put them in a bag and carry them. Then when you are good and tired of carrying those burdens, take them to a river, a lake or the ocean, and throw them in one by one. Pray over each one. Let God carry those burdens from now on.

"Cast your burden on the Lord, And He shall sustain you; He shall never permit the righteous to be moved." Psalm 55:22

It's easy to ponder it all and wax eloquently now, but at the time, I was a little upset to hear about this trauma from my mother. I could think of literally hundreds of times that she should have talked about that. We wouldn't have been so angry over so much of her inaction. We would've understood on the only level that could've helped. We could've cried together, laughed together, and got well together. We would have finally had the relief of understanding that she was a victim, too. We would've known that she had been hurt, and we would have had empathy for one another. But instead, we suffered for too long, and she carried that burden by herself. When she did finally blurt it out, she wouldn't elaborate. She almost screamed it when she shared it, and there was no sitting down for an in-depth interview. One of my siblings and I stood there with our mouths hanging open in shock. That was all we were getting. But at least we finally got a glimpse of the truth…sad, hard, ugly, beautiful, put your hands in the air and shout, *"Hallelujah!"* kind of truth. A traumatic event had occurred when my mother was very young, and no one helped her. That trauma shaped a woman's entire life and, sadly, some of ours.

***Jesus answered, "I am the way, <u>the truth</u> and the life…
John 14:6***

 # Excerpt End

CHAPTER THREE

As I got older, I became a noisy child. I was the one who talked too much. I was the one who refused to shut up about the important, hard, sad, painful things. I was the one who confronted people instead of accepting b.s. I was the one who got in trouble for laughing out loud in church. Things hadn't changed much, and I knew this because I regularly shot my mouth off. This time I was regretting what flew out of my mouth like a jaybird yesterday.

"My husband was molesting my kids so I kicked him out." The mother of the little bread nazi was at my front door asking me to watch her children again. I was not sure I wanted to do it, until she let that sentence fly.

"What?"

"He's been abusing my kids, and I'm getting a divorce. The police won't do anything, but I'm not going to take any chances that the son of a blank can hurt them again! I've got a lawyer that was molested when he was a kid. He assured me that he would literally bury him if he *ever* tries to be in their lives again. He's their step dad so I feel like we can win in court. Unfortunately, he did adopt them but the lawyer says that won't matter. I don't want to get a gun, and shoot him but I will if he fights to see them." She blurted it all out in a rush and the look on her face was one of total determination. I instantly loved her.

"Holy Toledo! I am so proud of you! You are my hero! Of course, I will babysit your kids!" I was still in shock over what she was telling me and of course, I shared too much information in the moment. "I was molested too. My mother never helped us. Can I hug you?" It didn't seem like a lot to tell this woman but of course, I was worried that I'd made her horrible problem about me. I need to forgive myself, I thought. I have a big mouth but a bigger heart. I wanted to ask her more details but her kids were in the car at the curb. They had their little faces pressed against the windows. They were probably hungry, tired, and ready to go home. "Want to start tomorrow? I'd be happy to start babysitting again tomorrow."

The next day, as I watched the kids file off the bus, I thought, patience and *energy*, that's what I need. They looked tired, and sad, *and* cranky today. Join the club you little rug rats! Smiling, I opened the door and said "Howdy. How's everybody doing today?"

"Just ducky", the little one said. "Can I have a sandwich?" Grinning, I closed the screen door, and looked at the house across the street. Maria and the psycho teenage daughter got fired and I get to take care of a hero Mom's kids. *Thank you, Jesus!*

"A sandwich with a smile, Babycakes. What kind of bread do you want?"

That week in writer's group, the instructor was in rare form. "Today, we are going to share more of our deepest, darkest secrets…oh I mean, our writing." Ha ha very funny. I looked at him sideways. I'm already nervous you butt.

We had just finished listening to our newest member read some of her stuff. She was a woman about my age with perfect blond hair…no gray roots showing on this babe. She had it all together…nails, hair, make up, and her story was perfect too. She shared a piece about her childhood, and I could not believe it was real. I wanted to puke it was so perfect. It wasn't her fault but I usually cringe when people talk about family trees…Some of us just don't have one we are especially proud of, and when I listened to her describe her childhood, I found myself fighting the urge to throw potato salad on her. She seemed nice enough but really? No dysfunction? No drug addicts, co-dependents, molesters or alcoholics? Oh, you poor thing, how utterly boring.

Luckily when it was time to pass out our chapters to share, I didn't get Miss Perfect Potato Salad. This time I got the tree hugger. She made sure I knew she wasn't into my politics. She took my pages and said with a smirk, "Oh, *this* should be interesting." I just smiled. Whatever, weirdo. I love you, too.

Writers Group - Sharing Excerpt Two
Genre: Semi-Autobiographical Memoir, Christian
Author: Jo Lisa Blossom

CHOCOLATE KILLS

My mother, grew up, graduated as valedictorian of her class, went to college, got a degree in accounting, and finally married George. Then the babies began. We were all born about a year apart, and my parents were blessed with five of us by the time they were done. When I was four, my mother divorced my biological father, and married my step father "Arnie", who preferred to be called "Dick". Why? We will never know. Arnie grew up I Alaska with six other siblings.

I remember visiting, my biological father,

George, a couple of times after that. He was already living with another woman who also had five children.... But it felt like ten.

Something that happened during one of those visits has stayed with me for the rest of my life. For years now, I have known what few other humans on this planet recognize...chocolate kills.

"I'm...I'm going to be sick." I mumbled. I was at a birthday party, for one of my bio-Dad's new kids. It was loud and crowded, and as a four-year old without my mother, I felt small and...sick. I ate too much chocolate ice cream, and now I was telling my father that I was going to be sick. He handed me a smelly trashcan. "Puke in this kid." I never did puke, but I still felt sick. Ever since that experience, I have an aversion to chocolate ice cream, chocolate shakes, chocolate cake...you name it.

I tried to enjoy the party but even with all the people, and all the kids running around, I felt alone. I secretly wished that my father loved me, that he would comfort me, that he would hold my little hand, and lead me gently to the bathroom with soft, reassuring words. But he wasn't even looking at me. He was laughing and talking to other people; adults I didn't even know. It was noisy, scary, I didn't feel good, and nobody cared.

If I had been a louder child at that age, I would have stood up on the kitchen table, and yelled at the top of my lungs, "I want my mommy!" It's kind of fun to imagine things like that sometimes.... what we should've done, and said, and how great it would have been to see the look on their faces. All eyes turning to stare at the screaming kid. I'm sure someone would've said, "Hey that kid is having a meltdown, better give her some chocolate!"

I only saw my biological father once after that. It was a school basketball game...going to watch some other kid play, some *other* kid that was important to him.

I longed to be important to him, as I'm sure my siblings did, but I think he found it easier to just let us go. He did give me a stick of gum, and a smile on the way to that game, though. My heart leapt for joy at that small bit of attention. But he didn't hold my hand or carry me on his shoulders. I wasn't the only kid after all. He could've taken turns with all of us but he probably would've thrown his back out. So instead, none of us got that kind of affection. With our little legs, we just walked in the darkness, as fast as we could, trying to stay as close to him as we could.

    I'm sure he did the best he could but when you're four, emotions can feel overwhelming. What can I say, we are needy humans, and some of us never get over it. I don't want to mention any names.

    I know my biological father is dead now and I'm grateful to know he is walking in the light of Christ, so that has to be enough.

"We are hard pressed on every side, but not crushed; perplexed, but not in despair."   2 Corinthians 4:8

DIVORCE IS NOT FOR HIPPIES

    Mom told us stories about why she divorced my biological father. Back then divorce was very frowned upon. You could get thrown out of church for not staying married, but apparently, she had had enough. This was in 1970, and some churches still treated divorce like the plague. You were deemed a chief sinner, and often shunned by other wives. The sexual revolution may have been in the rearview mirror, but for people with a bunch of little kids, what the hippies were doing had very little effect on their daily lives. Divorce did. I'm sure it was a huge decision for my mother to make.

I was told that before the big D, my biological father did immature things that did not help the situation. One story was that when the lawnmower was broken my bio-Dad would mow the grass with it anyway. This was just so he could say he wasn't lazy, and he did something. He didn't care that it wasn't actually cutting the grass. He could tell my grandfather he was being a good husband, and tell my mom to shut it because he mowed the lawn. We were also told that he harassed her to go to work then harassed her for her paycheck. He wanted it to buy a motorcycle. He would keep her up all night tormenting her and she would go to work, and sleep in the bathroom. He told her openly, and often, that he didn't like kids. That makes no sense because he went directly from my mother to another woman with a lot of kids. After hearing all that, I decided that he was more like an oversized kid himself, really. He was annoyed that the mother/woman that he found to take care of him had to focus on wrangling the munchkins, instead of serving him day and night.

One of my few rather clear memories is of my bio-Dad "baby-sitting" us. The operative word here was "sitting". While my mother was at work and a couple of us were still in diapers, he was sitting on the couch watching TV. We were filthy, going in and out of the house, playing in the mud. For a kid, playing in the mud was awesome but to most adults, at some point you have to put a stop to it, and get the kids in the bathtub.

He would leave us to our own devices all day long with no diaper change, no food, no nothing. I don't think people have any idea how a simple thing like laziness can harm children. It's too bad he wasn't watching a good daytime talk show about then. Can you picture that? He's minding his own business, sitting on the couch, completely neglecting his children, and the show comes on. There on the stage a man is crying, "My kids just won't talk to me, they say I didn't care about them! It was just a little mud! Mud! I mean it is natural, right? And I like mud! I thought they did too but now I know the mud scarred them for life! It's all my fault!" It wasn't the mud, bud.

The real Poppy did somehow make a two-story play house in the yard for us. He was probably hoping we would go out there to *our* house while he was in *his* house, and leave him alone. We loved that playhouse. It had a wooden stove in it and windows, and a ladder to the top floor. It was blue, and it was magical. The spell was broken when my mom re-married, and her new husband Arnie promptly tore it down. The excuse for that injustice was probably that it was 'unsafe' or insulting or some other perfectly hideous thing. We cried and decided right then and there, that our new "Dad" didn't know something magical when he saw it.

I don't remember my mother and step father's wedding but I do know my mother got married in a beautiful pink and white suit. I found it later in the attic, and I so wanted to put that baby on! I held it up to myself, and ran my hand over the smooth material. It was 50's stylish and cool! But I was very angry at that point, and it took me only seconds to feel the pain that wedding had begun in our little lives. I stuffed that beautiful suit right back in the box. It was either that or light it on fire.

We were so young when they got married. Sometimes I wish that kids were given a vote. I wish we could say, "Hey, can we pool our piggy bank change to hire a professional think tank to make this decision? Because it feels wrong to me". We were all under eight years old when they married, and then my step father adopted all of us. Even after having older children already, he adopted us. That seems very noble when you compare it to today's world where nobody adopts step kids anymore. Mom said later that she did something "bordering on illegal" to get my biological father to release us for adoption, and leave us alone. Wait, did she just say, "*illegal*?" I marveled at that revelation. Wow! This was my mother admitting she almost *broke the law*. That was saying a lot for a woman who had been reading the bible since she was three, and never missed a Sunday at church. To do something even close to illegal was scandalous in my mind. This is how children think of their parents sometimes. ...perfect and can do no wrong. For her to divorce, the situation must've been just as desperate to her, as it felt to me… a four-year old with no vote.

FLYING LEMONS AND THE WIPE

We lived in a trailer park, across the street from a grouchy old man with a lemon tree. Those lemons were a treat. To little kids, the tree was absolutely huge and the lemons were pure temptation. The lemons dotted that big tree like bright yellow Christmas ornaments. All of us kids wanted those lemons. We didn't particularly like them but they looked so good that we were completely given over to the lust of the eyes. That old man, however, had no interest in giving away his lemons. We thought it was just horribly unfair that he didn't share nicely. Didn't anybody ever teach him that? My oldest cousin, who lived with us then, was the bravest. She was always one to set people straight. "He's not nice", she would say. "He needs to share. That old prune can't eat all those lemons. His face would just pucker up *completely* and we don't want that do we?" We would giggle thinking about that old, wrinkled face, puckering up. Then she would lead us all over to sneak up, and pick his lemons. We would stoop down, and rush over nervously, as quiet as possible. Like a platoon of marines trying to take a hill, we would crouch low, and follow my cousin's outstretched hand signaling us when to go, and when to freeze. The enemy, Mr. Wrinkles, would inevitably spot us.

"Blank it! You blankity blank kids! Get away from my blankity, blank, tree!" He was yelling, cussing, and waving his arms. Never mind trying to watch your language in front of children! Well, that behavior was just another reason to steal his lemons by golly. We would run off scared but hanging onto those lemons! We would run to the back-parking lot and hide between the cars, giggling and whispering. Breathing hard we would stay down, and peak up carefully after a few minutes to make sure the coast was clear. The enemy had retreated. Mr. Wrinkles was nowhere in sight. Then my cousin showed us how to slice them open on a car license plate. She was our hero. She always made us feel like we accomplished something big. We'd pass the lemon around just to screw up our faces, and laugh at each other. Then we'd give each other a salute, march back to base, and wait for our next deployment.

Another mythical, magical thing about that time was the pool. The trailer park we lived in had a pool down the center street. We didn't even mind wearing hideous, uncomfortable swim caps, if we got to go swimming in that sweet rectangle of blue heaven. Afterward, we would get a pop from the soda machine once in a while. It was one of those old machines that dispensed glass bottles, and you had to pop off the cap with the bottle opener in the front of the machine. We learned early, *never* walk away without opening your pop. If you did, you'd have to run back to the machine to struggle with that contraption by yourself, trying to hurry while all the other kids were already peacefully sucking down their fizzy, brown deliciousness.

Besides the pool, our babysitter was also down

the street. For some reason I can't remember much about my mother at an early age, but I do remember the baby sitter. She wasn't the best baby sitter. Every day, after peanut butter and jelly sandwiches, she wiped our faces with a sour wash rag. I would moan, and try to pull away but she was determined to administer this torture. At the age of five, I solemnly vowed, I will NEVER wipe a kid's face with a sour dish rag. It was deeesgusting.

That babysitter was about twenty-five and still lived with her mom. In the living room, her mom had couches, covered in plastic, and some lamps with weird shades. The scary rumor was that her lampshades were made of skin from people that the Nazi's had tortured. Probably that's what gave her daughter the idea for the washrag routine. But besides those gruesome lamps, the house wasn't bad. A beautiful beaded curtain led down the hallway. It was colorful and made such a cool sound when you went through it. It was hippie chic. That curtain and the fancy poodle dog were the only nice things. Every day she would take us kids down there for sandwiches. We weren't allowed to touch anything or do anything, just eat your sandwich and wait for the wipe.

My paternal grandmother lived down the block too. Her trailer was dark, and she didn't seem to want us there. She was overweight, and spent a lot of time in a house dress. Her flabby arms were a detail I don't like to remember. But now, in middle age, as I look down at my flabby arms, it is nice to know it's not entirely my fault. Some of the flab is hereditary. I like to call it what it is, the attack of the flabby arms. Sigh…a housedress is calling.

My maternal grandparents lived a couple of blocks away back then. It was the suburbs. We would walk to my grandparent's house when I was five. I would bring my grandmother empty vitamin bottles that I had filled with tiny rocks and colored water. I still remember how I felt bringing her a new treasure. I felt like I was transporting something so amazingly beautiful. She made me feel appreciated, and special because she gave my collection a prominent place on the windowsill, above the kitchen sink. The sun shining through the bottles was so beautiful, and I could picture her washing the dishes and gazing at them the way I did. At age five, beauty was fascinating. It was especially mesmerizing because I *created* it, and then gave it away for her to love, too. It was our special bond, colored water and rocks. It's the little things you know.

    My grandparents had a beautiful house with a rock fireplace that covered the whole living room wall. In the hallway was a little half size door that led to a closet, kid size. We were intrigued to say the least. My grandfather also had a card shuffling machine and a secret stash of soda that we were not allowed to even look at. He was a self-proclaimed soda addict. My mom said it was just glorified prune juice. That helped with our temptation to take a sip when he wasn't looking.

    At their house, soda was out, but when it came to meat, you'd better eat it. I remember chewing a piece of meat until it was mush. I just could not swallow it. I can clearly see it in my hand just before my grandmother made me stuff it back in my mouth, and chew it some more. Nastyville, USA. Later on, when trying to get my own children to finish their food, I thought about that mushy meat scene. I asked myself, what are children actually *learning* by being forced to eat? Mostly that food, though somewhat delicious looking while on the plate, can later turn into something that will make you want to puke. So, if it's in your mouth, whatever you do, *don't* let it out.

    Nowadays, I don't think it is safe for kids to walk anywhere, but back then, we walked everywhere. We walked to the store, we walked to Grandma's, and we walked to school in dresses that my mother made for us. I remember looking down at one made of shimmery gold material and I was in total and complete awe, thinking 'my mother made this for me.' Wow. I wanted to run my hands over that dress and stare at it the whole way. It was like I was wearing a Christmas miracle. I just wanted to tell everyone how special my mother was, and how special my dress was because she had made it, just for me.

The elementary school I went to for kindergarten was a series of brick buildings set in a square with a courtyard in the middle. The classrooms had linoleum floors, windows in the front and rows of wooden cupboards along the sides. School was exciting and scary at the same time.

The first week of kindergarten, walking to school I saw the worst injustice I have ever witnessed to this very day. We had just crossed the street and were standing on the corner in front of the school when a car pulled up and a kid about seven got out of the passenger side. He closed the car door and turned to walk away but his jacket was caught in the door. The car was a big, tan, two door sedan and there was a man behind the wheel. He and the little boy both had crew cuts but the man looked angry. After the boy hopped out and slammed the door, the driver, I assume, his father, started driving away without realizing the boy's jacket was caught in the door. Instantly when the car started moving, the kid fell and hit his face on the asphalt with his jacket holding him swinging against the car door. He was bleeding and screaming. The crossing guard lady was screaming at the dad to stop the car. He did stop and then he reached over to the passenger door, opened it, the kid fell to the ground, the dad slammed the door shut again, and zoomed off. The kid lay there in the street still bleeding and screaming. I will never forget the look on the crossing guard's face as she tried to console and help that kid. I will never forget what it looked like watching that car speed away while that little boy was screaming on the ground, bleeding. I will never forget how, seeing that happen, made me feel. The shock of that father's lack of caring is still heartbreaking to this day. I realized at that moment that people can be very, very unkind. People, who are supposed to care for you, sometimes don't.

    That day didn't feel very good, but I can't imagine how hard it was for that kid. I have prayed he was able to block out that experience. That would be merciful of the Lord. Unfortunately, I have thought about that incident a lot over the years searching for some logical explanation for that behavior, but like so many things on planet earth, the only explanation is sin.

    I also confess that I have fantasized about all the things that kid could've done to get back at his horrid father. Maybe he could take the old man out for a ride in the mountains. He'd say, "Hey Pops, let's go take a nice relaxing drive…' Then, of course, he'd drive like a maniac and scare the absolute crud out of him.

    After what that father did to his little boy in front of that school, he deserves to be punished. But in truth, we have all done things that were hurtful to somebody, sometime. We all deserve to be punished. Christ died so we can avoid that punishment. What happened to that little boy breaks my heart, but as an adult who's done my own stupid things that hurt people, I hope that father found redemption in Christ. I hope he was able to somehow make it up to his son.

    As for the best thing that ever happened at that school, it was cake! Strawberry chip pink cake with pink frosting that I can still smell when I close my eyes. Ever since then, that has been my absolute favorite because if I have to go to a strange place, with strange people to learn strange things, the very least you can do is give me cake!

Redemption: the action of saving or being saved from sin, error or evil.

 # Excerpt End

CHAPTER FOUR

"No one is listening to a word she's saying. I mean *really*!"

It was writer's group and I was chatting with my new friend in the pink skinny jeans, waiting for class to start. We were sinning, talking trash about someone else in the group. True to form I was shooting my mouth off again. Surely, I'd regret it later but I was simply mortified at the newest member of the group, and I could not resist getting his opinion. It was "hate the sin, love the sinner" in action. "Has she ever heard of an armor bra?" I asked.

"Do tell! What is that?" He turned to look at me with eyes wide with wonder, a sponge ready to soak up every last juicy female secret.

"It's like a bra with padding that hides those nips! Look at those things. They look like they want to reach out and touch someone. I bet you money that all the men in the group have no idea what that last poem was about. Their all mesmerized by round things, including those. They just can't focus on anything else. And she doesn't know it? Pleeease!"

He laughed. "Well darling, I heard every word she said, and that poem was *profound*. But if I was interested, I can see how those things would scare the heebeejeebees out of a man. They are rather protuberous." He said, giggling. "But honey, you know I really want to read more of your stuff." He liked my book. He said there was "a little too much Jesus" in it for his taste but it was "riveting". "Riveting!"

"When's it gonna be my turn?" He half-whined.

"Maybe tonight!" I winked at him as I started forward to join the rest of the class getting a seat. And much to my new friend's delight, I was able to hand him poems, and a few more chapters to peruse as we wrapped up for the night.

"Yay!" He smiled and hugged me. I hugged him back. I thought, Yay for a little more Jesus!

Writers Group - Sharing Excerpt Three
Genre: Semi-Autobiographical Memoir, Christian
Author: Jo Lisa Blossom

Here's The Church

Broken people
Need the steeple
To mend the hurt
They need the church
Not a secret session
Just true confession
Worship with hands held high
Arms around them when they cry
God, please have your way
With the hurting part of us.

Go Back

Sometimes I feel lonely
When I think of you
I wish we could only

Get past things we knew…

Were a fatal blow
To what we had
We both know
That it was bad…

I wish we could
Reach in for good
And feel the way we did
Before we hid…

If we saw each other
Rushing to avoid another
Confrontation with strife
We used to share life…

And now we don't
And we won't
Take a chance or try
Just easier to say goodbye…

We've lost track
Of how to go back
In the end
I miss my friend.

MONKEYS AND BABY SITTERS

"Look at that, the sidewalks are in!" My mother said. My parents had decided to relocate and it was almost time to move. Today we were visiting our future neighborhood. Our track of homes was new, so it was a very clean suburb. It was surrounded by older neighborhoods, all of which were typically middle class.

Most houses had three bedrooms, two baths and an attached garage. The streets were named names. There was Betty Lane, Mark Road and Cindy Place. Total white bread street names, in a neighborhood surrounded by other neighborhoods plagued by Hispanic gang violence. Maybe they were hoping to start a trend…I mean besides segregation and prejudice.

    I was still in kindergarten but on weekends we would go to visit, while the house was being built. The anticipation was tremendous. It was like opening a gift slowly. First there was just dirt, then streets and framed houses and then roofs. It was quite a site. If there was any hint of trouble in paradise with the new husband at that point, I can see why my mother would've completely ignored it. She was finally getting herself and her children out of that trailer park, away from her ex-husband's flabby armed mother.

    After we moved, my mother continued to work but the commute took a lot longer. During that period, we had several babysitters. One of them lived on the corner of a busy street. Her front door was about four feet from the sidewalk, but the house was a beautiful mission style with decorative bushes adorning the front, so it looked attractive. It also had a lot of jungle-ish trees in the back yard. The yard itself was basically dirt but with all the bushes and trees, it felt like it had adventure potential. That was before she showed us the monkey. That monkey had its own room-sized cage out there and he was a very *loud* monkey. We were told not to go near the cage because the monkey could grab us, and really hurt us. It was amazing that we listened to that and didn't lose an eyeball. None of us dared go near that cage. The monkey would scream and jump around, and we instinctively knew that monkey was pure evil. It was a little exciting to know danger lurked out there with us but when she told us it ripped her husband's hair out, we whipped our heads around and took notice. He was *bald*!

When the monkey lady didn't have us outside in the jungle, she would send us up the street, a busy main thoroughfare, to the school for the summer program. My oldest sister, was probably eleven by then and back then kids that age walked everywhere without adult supervision. Now we know that we were too young to be walking anywhere by ourselves. We liked it because the only one yelling at us was our sister and we didn't listen to her anyway. The traffic was a little fast and loud and we could've been run over and killed, but at least we had all our hair, both eyeballs and a free lunch.

My mother has told us that she had to go to the hospital for stomach pains about this time. She said that she would drop us off and be in excruciating pain for hours worrying. We probably didn't help, crying and whining when she picked us up. We are talking about a car full of chatter box children who pretty much weren't afraid to blurt out anything. Soon the stress of leaving her children with horrible baby sitters just became too much.

At that point Mom decided that she needed to stay home with us kids. And when worse came to worse, she got creative and found a way to afford to stay home. I loved her for that. No more cranky baby-sitters! She and my step father became foster parents for the state of Florida.

You have to wonder how my step father got approved. I later learned that this was about the time my mother became aware that my step-father was molesting one of my siblings. She had confided in a relative and they called the police, who then went to the school. They interviewed us but we were deemed too young to testify with credibility. My mother denied everything, of course.

I should tell you that my step father was a nice man to most people. He was social, had friends and worked hard. He was charming, funny and kind. He was also a child molester with no conscience, who grew much more perverse over time. It took me many years to come to terms with the fact that people without a conscience *do* have the capacity to love. Their love is overshadowed by extreme self-centeredness, but amazingly they do *love*. Their version of love is just really different than the rest of us. Without intervention that self-centeredness grows more and more perverse and eventually looks nothing like normal, healthy love.

VAMIRES AND THE BOMB

    "Do you, do you wanna play vamires?" My new little brother was looking at me with a grin on his face. His big brown eyes were peeking out under his black bangs. I was five, and he was four, so even though he was looking at me eye to eye, I was still the big sister here.
    "What are 'vamires'?" I had never heard of this game.
    "Youuuuuu know…they bite!" He hissed at me, showing me his perfectly straight row of little, baby teeth.
    "Oh, you mean, Vampires!"
    "Yes!" He jumped on the bed and said excitedly, "We can lay down and play vamires!"
Even though I was enamored with this new sibling, I wasn't sure about this. I said, "Uh no way, Jose". I refused because it sounded sort of disgusting and I was pretty sure we shouldn't be doing anything laying down and slobbering.
    Besides that, right off the bat, we loved our new brother. He had a sweet nature and could do math like nobody's business. He always excelled in school. I think that was God's gift to him, because he did not have it

easy, for a little kid. From my five year old perspective, the hardest thing was his aunt, who had raised him since birth, because his mother had disappeared from the hospital. His aunt/mom was an alcoholic who had been through abusive relationships and at that point all her children were wards of the state.

    She would call and say that she was coming for Christmas or a birthday or whatever. We would sit with him all day waiting. We would play and run around and then he would go back and sit down and look at the gifts he'd wrapped and stare at the door, waiting. He would dress up in his best clothes and go back and forth between the living room couch and the porch, sitting and waiting for hours, but she never came. Eventually, my mom put a stop to it. She told his aunt that she wasn't telling him anything about her coming anymore, that she would just have to show up to surprise him. But she never came. So, he didn't have any trouble calling my mom, "Mom". He needed one and we were glad to keep him.

    A couple of years later, we got two new sisters! They were six and nine and really nice. We loved them, too. One of them seemed so much quieter and calmer than my other sisters. Truly, she was much kinder at heart. She seemed to have more compassion. That may have been because she had already seen way too much for her age and been through physical and sexual abuse. She and her two younger siblings both lived with us now but they had an older brother still in the foster care system at that point. They had been separated for a few years already.

    My mom wanted all four of those siblings to be together if they could. She set right to work trying to make that happen. In so many ways, my mother was always trying to do the right thing. She was a good, Christian woman with a huge heart of compassion, but then there was the denial of the cancer that was growing and terminal...my step-father.

My foster sister later told us that she had been to several foster homes, and she had been molested in every single one. That just broke my heart. How could a system be so broken that she was molested in *every* home? Even more tragic is that she was molested in *our* home, too. In a home where we never called her anything but "sister", a home where she was truly loved, she still got abused. I feel like we let them all down, even though we all loved each other so much. Those kids were part of our family but we let them down. I wish that our house had been the one where they had finally been safe and protected, but it was not.

"They're gonna blow this place up! You guys are picking me up just in time!" We were looking at our new big brother. He was twelve, tall, skinny and waving his arms simulating an explosion while our eyes were bugging out listening to his story. "You know over there", he was pointing across the street and we were looking, but at who knows what. "Those guys over there said, they are gonna blow up this boys' home *tomorrow*!" We'd never heard anything as wild as this! We were mesmerized...the adventure had begun. We could tell that he had seen more than we had of the rough side of life. He really knew how to tell a story and had a rapt audience just hanging on every juicy word. He enjoyed making us all laugh. He also didn't care too much to do what he was told. We liked him immediately.

Over the years, he proved to be more than a little on the wild side. In the eighth grade he broke his hand punching a window at school. That is a really hard punch for a kid. He went to a different junior high than the rest of us because he got kicked out of the first one.

He taught us how to play 'crack the whip'. This is

where you all join hands in a line and the person in the front runs around at full speed, trying to swing everybody around. My littlest sister wore glasses and she was always on the end. She flew clean off that whip a couple of times to smash her face in the grass or the sidewalk. Mom didn't like that much.

When he was fifteen, my older brother was the master of the 'bunny hop' on a bicycle. All of us younger kids would be outside watching him do stunts on his bike. He jumped basketballs, scooters and anything else he could find. He bunny hopped like a pro…wowing us all. He jumped and jumped with no problems, until one particular summer day. That summer day goes down as a real whopper in the annals of Linda Street lore…

He put a couple of our bikes down on the side walk. "This is how Evil Flyin' Bryan does it on TV! See these are not *really* your bikes. No, what you have here are a bunch of old racing cars. They've been bashed into each other at shows and stuff, so we can put them here to jump and nobody cares. Evil Flyin' Bryan lines up a *bunch* of cars. Anybody else got a bike around here? I don't know if this is enough. Well, I could probably do more, but… Ok let's go!"

He started from way down the block, riding as fast as he could. His pedals were pumping round and round. His hair was flying back and he was hunched down over the handlebars, eyes focused like a laser on that row of bikes. Then whoooooosh! He jumped way up and over. Then at the last moment his back wheel just nicked the handlebars of one of our bikes. My brother flew forward over the front of his bike. It was an endo! We had heard about them but never seen one before. Our mouths dropped open while we watched him sailing through the air in slow motion. He landed hard, face down on the sidewalk. We were frozen in shock until a horrendous sound broke all of us out of our trance.

"Mmmmooooommmmm!" Our hero was screaming. We all ran over and stood there breathlessly.

"Are you ok?" we all asked at once. Then we saw his wrist and we knew he wasn't. Broken for sure. I scanned the faces around me. We looked at each other not knowing what to do. We just stared at our super hero brother who was laying there bleeding and yelling, at the top of his lungs. Finally, somebody went and got Mom and she helped him up. His face was bloody and his wrist was askew, but he was ok. At that moment he was completely oblivious that something terrible had happened; besides the blood and broken bones. I was glad he was going to live but I couldn't help thinking that his stellar reputation as a bicycle stunt man had just gone down the tubes in a split second. It wasn't the accident. Even Evil Flyin'Bryan munched it once in a while. But the screaming for Mom. That was *not* a Flyin' Bryan move!

When my big brother was in his late thirties forties, he called me crying. He was weeping and describing what had happened to him in foster homes before ours. He was absolutely distraught at the surfacing of memories that had been blocked out. He was so upset because they not only abused him but then they tried it on the other kids in the home. He was beside himself with pain. It is no wonder, that he later died in the prison system, shackled to the bed. Just when he might've been able to overcome his past and stay clean and sober, he remembered more of the reason he started using in the first place. He also knew that he was guilty of some of the same sins.

Have you ever wondered about what you can't remember? That conversation with him scared me. When he was crying and telling me about the memories that were surfacing, I was thinking that I was definitely in for it. I knew that I had blocked out large portions of my childhood. To this day, I can remember so little about my parents *inside* the house. I have a total of about five memories of them. Why?

I know why, and I am grateful to God for the incredible invention of our minds. He designed us with automatic protection mechanisms and He is merciful in what He allows us to remember and when.

Repressed memory- a condition where a memory has been unconsciously blocked by an individual due to the high level of stress or trauma contained in that memory. Even though the individual cannot recall the memory, it may still be affecting them unconsciously.

"And the God of all grace, who called you to his eternal glory in Christ, after you have suffered a little while, will Himself restore you and make you strong, firm and steadfast." 1 Peter 5:10

TATTOOS AND TUBES

When he was in his early forties, we got a call that he was dying. He had collapsed in prison and become incoherent. They had removed a brain tumor the size of a lemon. Now he was in the hospital being kept alive artificially.

Unfortunately, my big brother spent most of his adult life in jail, and that is not a shock if you consider his beginnings. His heart was so big that I don't think he ever got over the hurt. He was a junkie that liked to write poetry. Most of his arrests were for being on drugs but, like most of us, there were other things he did that went unpunished.

He was the ring leader for things that went on

under the roof of our home that never should have been. As a seven year old, there were times when I sat at the breakfast table in my flannel nightgown and wanted to die. Even though I didn't participate, just because I was invited to, I was so ashamed. I was overwhelmed with the desire to literally light my nightgown on fire. The corruption that he brought in as a twelve-year old was horrific. But he was only twelve. The adults in the house should have done more to monitor the situation but unfortunately in this case, the adults were corrupt, too, so the children were unsafe.

  The crimes my older brother did get caught for were enough to take over his life. He was on parole and once you are on parole, it is very hard to get off. Especially if you still like to get high, and ride your bicycle around at two in the morning bunny hoppin' stuff.

  It seems like our family was the perfect storm for victimization. I have learned that the abuse is much wider and deeper than I imagined. Is that normal? I hope not but when I think about the prevalent 'sweep it under the rug' policy of the seventies, it is possible that many people are still recovering from multiple abusers in one family. Of course, the out of sight, out of mind, sweep it under the rug policy, doesn't work. Next thing you know you have to crawl over the big lumps in the rug and then shortly after that you are like 'rug? What rug? All I see is a room full of junk.' Alas another book emerges.

  When I was twenty-one, I found myself trapped in a hotel room with a cocaine dealer. I knew I was close to death and I only had one person to call that I knew would show up no matter what. It was my brother. I had been doing coke for over twenty-four hours and this was not cut coke, this was very pure, powerful, knock you on your butt coke. I was not a chatty party girl. I was sick and about to die. I wanted to leave but could not physically drive or do much of anything. I was hurting so badly that I probably should've gone directly to the hospital.

I said, "Hey Bro, can you come get me because if I don't get out of here, I am going to die." He was there within an hour. He didn't accuse me or ask a bunch of questions.

He just said, "I'll drive you home." That day he was there to rescue me and I have no doubt that he saved my life. I was so sick and I could not stop and I could not leave. He took care of me like a big brother should.

A couple of years later, when I was in rehab, he was the only sibling who came to see me. He arrived with a roar on his cool black motorcycle. It was likely stolen or borrowed from someone upset that they had loaned it to him for "a quick trip around the block". But he showed up because he cared. He didn't try to sneak me any drugs and he went out of his way to be there and encourage me. I felt loved. The rehab was a three-hour drive for anybody who wanted to visit, and he was the only sibling who made the trip. I don't know why that is. Probably because everyone was busy with their own lives. Maybe rehab was a scary place nobody wanted to visit. I guess he was the brave one. He had survived a boy's home on the verge of an explosion, terrible abuse, jail, and prison by this time. Rehab was probably like Camp Snoopy.

Seeing him in a coma was hard but knowing he was almost free, was not. I could not even bring myself to cry because I knew that he was one "peckerwood" who went from this painful life, directly into the arms of Jesus. He's not in prison, and he's not in pain anymore. He'll never have someone try to break his knuckles with a hammer over drugs again. He'll never be dirty, stinky and homeless again. He'll never have to go to jail, get arrested or report to a parole officer again. He'll never again find out that is best friend in prison is getting a divorce and feel sad because he didn't even know he was married. He'll never have to feel like a failure again. He'll never feel like he's dying if he can't get a fix again. *He'll never hurt anyone again.* He'll never hurt *himself* again. He'll never hear and believe the lies of demons again. Because of the love of God, he is finally free!

 # Excerpt End

CHAPTER FIVE

"Hello, Ladies and Gentlemen! Tonight, we are *officially* assigning poetry writing. I don't always assign it, but some of you have been including them, and let me just say that I've been very impressed with what you've all done so far." One of our instructors, Jeff, was at the front of the class walking back and forth in his penny loafers with a real, shiny, copper penny tucked in the front. He was a throwback to some other time. I just hadn't quite put my finger on the exact era yet. But tonight, he wasn't wearing a blue fedora with a peacock feather swinging around as he walked. A shiny penny was actually a minor distraction in the big scheme of things.

"Do we have a volunteer?' Instantly, my hand shot up. I was one of the guilty over achievers who'd been including poetry. I love poetry readings, especially when no wannabe stalkers had my phone number or home address.

"All right! Come on up and remember the instructions were to read three poems, and each one has to be a different style. Read with emotion and direct eye contact with the audience as much as you can. Be proud of what you've written. And don't forget before you leave tonight to share another excerpt with the person seated directly in front of you. Doesn't matter if you know them on not. Be brave and confident! We enjoy peeking into each other's souls, don't we?"

He started clapping and as I reached the front I thought, my *soul*? Holy cow, now I'm really freaking out.

Writers Group - Sharing Excerpt Four
Genre: Semi-Autobiographical Memoir, Christian
Author: Jo Lisa Blossom

The Promise Land

Another brother made it
to the promise land
He got to the gate
Jesus said it's not too late

You finally made it home
No longer have to roam
Or run to the mountain top
And wait for the painful drop
To the valley below

Another brother made it
to the promise land
He knelt at the altar
Jesus took him by the hand
"Son, you're free
You finally found Me

Another brother made it
to the promise land
"Lord please forget my sin
and let me in"

Jesus pulled him up to stand

Took him by the hand
Another brother made it
to the promised land.

Curiosity

One
Eye
Large
And
Blue

Peeking
Through
The
Hole
In
The
Fence

Lashes
Brush
Against
Old
Peeling
White
Paint

While
Searching
For
Greener
Grass.

I WANNA HOLD YOUR HAND

      I looked over at my sister and narrowed my eyes. Why does she have to have a hand? We were heading into the store to go shopping for groceries. This was a once per month trip, and I knew we would eventually have two carts full of groceries, and neither one of us would get to hold my mother's hand. I was nine and my mother meant so much to me. My sister and I would each get a hand when we went places, but I wanted BOTH hands. I would get mad because my sister was holding her hand too. I wanted to be the only one my mother loved. I wanted her all to myself. Is it possible that when Cain killed Able it was because Cain wanted the Lord all to himself? Is it possible that he, at one point loved the Lord so much that he was angry that he had to share him with Able? I know that Cain killed his brother out of jealousy but what causes such rage? I think I know. We are built to want relationships, significant relationships. And when those don't happen right, and of course they don't because of sin, we struggle. In the saga that is life, the first relationship we crave is a mother and a father. And being the selfish, fallen creatures that we are, we do not want to share.

"Adam knew his wife Eve intimately, and she conceived and bore Cain. She said I have had a male child with the LORD's help.

Then she also gave birth to his brother Abel. Now Abel became a shepherd of a flock, but Cain cultivated the land. In the course of time Cain presented some of the land's produce as an offering to the LORD. And Abel also presented [an offering][1] – some of the firstborn of his flock and their fat portions. The Lord had regard for Abel and his offering, but He did not have regard for

Cain and his offering. Cain was furious, and he was downcast.

Then the LORD said to Cain, why are you furious? And why are you downcast. If you do right, won't you be accepted? But if you do not do right, sin is crouching at the door. Its desire is for you, but you must master it.

Cain said to his brother Abel, let's go out to the field. And while they were in the field, Cain attacked his brother Abel and killed him." Genesis 4:1-8

    It was Christmas time and I was nine. My parents had gotten all of us bikes and mine was a bright yellow ten speed. "I love it, I love it, I love it!" I knew I would have to wait for the snow to melt to ride it, but I didn't care. I was in love.

    After saving all year, they always made Christmas special for us. With so many kids it was not easy but we always had several gifts under the tree. Like most families, some of those gifts were practical. Socks seemed to be a favorite among mothers.

    One very special sock was a long, white tube sock with a red racing stripe around the top. His name was "Joe Cool". Under the tree, my little brother's sock doll was on duty. He would guard the gifts from intruders. The morning they wheeled in all the bikes we had almost convinced our mother to let us go outside in the snow to ride our new bikes. We were busy telling her how our jammies were actually excellent snow gear, when my brother screamed.

    "Oh nooooo!" It was Joe Cool. He had been tossed aside and fell face first onto a Christmas light. Now his little cheek wasn't white anymore, it was light brown and burnt. My mother examined him.

    "He looks like a misshapen roasted marshmallow. He'll live", she said, handing him back to my brother. He looked satisfied.

"Maybe I can tie him to my handlebars! Joe Cool wants go, too!" It was off to the races in our jammies, socks and all.

That Christmas morning was good, but most Saturday mornings were not. As a pre-teen sleeping was heaven and sleeping in on the weekend should've been the highlight of my week.

"Good morning! How many eggs do you want?"

I sighed, rubbing my eyes. "I don't want any today, Dad."

"Come on, yes you do. How many?" I knew there was no point in refusing.

"Two." Every Saturday, my step father would wake us up to ask us how many eggs we wanted. He made breakfast every Saturday, and in a normal family that would be awesome. But in our family, most of us always wanted the same number of eggs- exactly ZERO. But he would make a point of waking us up, on the one day we could sleep in, to ask. Even though he knew we didn't really want any eggs, he would barge in and ask us. No knocking of course…in case we were dressing. It was as if he was making sure we knew that he was in control. He had the power to barge in to our private area, and force us to get up and interact with him. Heaven help us, if we didn't get out there, and eat those eggs while they were warm! It felt like he was pretending he was doing something nice but, really, he was reminding us that even on our one free day a week, he was in charge. We couldn't do a thing about it, and if we *could* do something about it, he seemed to relish the fact that we were *unable* to. We were kids and he was an adult. It was not a fair fight so we would just answer, "two" and then lay there and fantasize about screaming at him to take those eggs and shove them where the sunny side up don't shine.

By nightfall, we sometimes had a much bigger problem.

"Who's out there?" Peering out the window, I could see someone outside.

"Guess who", my sister said.

I sucked in my breath. It was Dad. I had just taken off my bra and realized he was watching us change our clothes, getting ready for bed. There he was in his white underwear, watching again. No curtains, no blinds just Mr. Peeping Tom out there making us want to march out there and strangle him with his own skivvies. Why didn't we tell my mom? Why were we afraid? He had the power. He had the house, the car, the money, the food, the eggs. Bleh! We were just the hungry kids. How do you fight someone who is constantly reminding you of how weak you are?

"You kids come here!" This time, we heard him yelling and came into the living room to meet the new friends my parents had over. "Stand over here, oldest to youngest." He lined us up and began introducing us. "Well, this here is 'big ears'" he said pushing my hair up to show my ears. "And this one is 'big mouth' and I call this one 'cry baby'", he laughed. I don't remember what else he said. I do remember the shocked and embarrassed look on the couple's faces.

One of my siblings cussed under their breath, as we shuffled out. He was being just plain mean and at that moment, like every moment, we were powerless to do anything.

It was times like that which eventually made us look at one another and band together like a platoon of soldiers. We had a common enemy. We were forced to work together because if we wanted to survive, we were going to have to beat him. It took a while for us to come to terms with the fact that our commander had to go. For a while we did what we were told and took the orders. That's what good kids do right? For a while we didn't realize his behavior was wrong. Then we slowly realized that his behavior was also wrong to other people. We saw their faces. We saw the pity in that couple's eyes. They never came back to visit. We began to realize that it was not something wrong with *us*, but with *him*.

I wish that couple had said, "Hey you jerk, don't talk to your children like that!" I'm sure they figured if they said anything, we would have it worse. They were right. Sadly, my mother didn't say anything to stop him. She was fast becoming the queen enabler. I have seen the damage enabling and denial does. It is just as bad to be abandoned by your mother as abused by your father. Neither one is any good.

I believe a demon is in charge of that lack of response. That demon has a name: E-N-A-B-L-E. Are you enabling anything today?

Don't be afraid to say "I reject you satan, you and every demon trying to harm my family….in the name, power and authority of Jesus Christ of Nazareth who came in the flesh! Get out!" Then go get some help and stop enabling. Act stronger than you feel in the face of what is wrong. Don't be an enabler anymore. Ask God to help. He always does.

Enable-to make able; give power, means, competence, or ability to; authorize…

MR. CATS ON A STICK

"Don't worry about him. Let's walk over here", my sister said, taking charge of our group. We were at the park. We went there a lot. It was within walking distance of the house and our favorite hang out in the summer. They had activities in the community center, basketball and baseball. When there was no soap carving, or a Carrom game going on, it was fun just to go there, and play on the playground. But sometimes there was an older guy that would show up, and he scared us. Now he was headed our way. My sister sprang into action and led us the other direction across the park. We were afraid because he would run around screaming and out of control. We were always worried that he would start running after us. He was loud and would yell but didn't make any sense. We had also heard the ugly rumor that he was a cat killer.

One of the other kids at the park told us, "He eats cats! Then he puts their skins on sticks in his backyard!" We were horrified. We'd never heard of this brand of crazy. As a coping mechanism my older sister explained to us younger kids that he *really* was crazy. That made sense and we felt a little sorry for him but not enough to hang around when he was there. As kids, we had no idea what really crazy people were capable of. How do they think? Why do they yell? We did our best to avoid him and lucky for us, he was always yelling so we would usually hear him coming. When he was on one side of the park, we tried hard to be on the other. It was decidedly gruesome but to cope with the fear, we joked about it. We called him "Mr. Cats on a stick".

"Mr. Catsonastick, he's over there yelling again. Mr. Catsonastick here he comes. Mr.Catsonastick, he looks hungry. Better hide fluffy!" And we would run off as fast as we could to the playground to climb up to the top of the rocket. We would pretend we were soldiers in our secret hide out. We would shoot at him with our imaginary guns and watch him yelling and screaming at the people below. We felt safe looking down on him from our third story perch. Mr. Catsonastick couldn't get us up there.

Later that night, at dinner, we had even more

excitement.

"I can't stand this disgusting liver! This blank stinks! I want to go and you know what Dad? You can't stop me!" My older foster sister was cussing and complaining because my step-father had just told her that she wasn't allowed to go to the movies with her boyfriend. It was at the dinner table and like typical pre-pubescents, pre-teens and teens, we were mouthing off. We hated liver and would take turns feeding it to the dog under the table. But now we were mesmerized by the scene unfolding in front of us. You could've heard a cheese puff drop.

"What did you say?" He stood up and cranked his arm back getting ready to back hand her. We had seen him knock a toddler out of his highchair once with the back of his hand. I was still traumatized from that incident. Now my heart was beating out of my chest. Screeeeeeech... my mother's chair scraped along the floor as she stood up, turned and looked him straight in the eye.

Without raising her voice, she said slowly, "Don't you *ever* lay a hand on my children." We were all holding our breath, but we gasped when she did that. I know I wasn't the only one in pure bliss at that moment. I mean it was pure physical bliss. A warm feeling of joy came over me that is hard to describe. *She finally told him how it was*! We all knew she was scrappy and strong and could probably knock him out. We were overjoyed. She finally stood up for us! She finally *did* something! For a moment we had hope that she would throw him out of the house! I, for one, had fantasized regularly that she would divorce him and finally choose us over him. She had the power to do that and we did not. But alas, she didn't whip out any divorce papers and slam them on the table. She didn't say another word. He glared at her, threw down his fork, left the table, and that was the end of that. For me, I lived on that blissful shred of hope for literally years. Suddenly the liver tasted like chicken.

By morning he had lulled her back into full on enabling. She told us that he cried, and said he wanted his kids back. Was it manipulation or the sincere pain of a tortured man who doesn't know how to stop being an abuser? I don't know. I guess it didn't matter.

That night as I lay in bed, I knew he wasn't coming to touch me. He was in trouble. I was elated. My sister looked over the side of her bed.

"What are you smiling about?"

"I think Mom's gonna divorce Dad."

"Yeah, maybe." My sister wasn't so sure. Maybe she was afraid to hope. My mother's resolve was fleeting and nothing more happened. When he cried to her, she gave in to denial once again. We still had no one to help us against his nightly rounds, emotional abuse and lewd comments in the light of day.

It took me years to realize that denial and co-dependency was the favored coping mechanism that I *learned*. It took me years to recognize that even though I was actively seeking truth, the devil doesn't want us to embrace truth, because that would be embracing Jesus himself.

"Jesus answered, 'I am the way and <u>the truth</u> and the life. No one comes to the Father except through me.'"
John 14:6

On this dirty blue ball in the sky, truth is hard to face sometimes. Jesus is the remedy but until we fully embrace Him as our solution, it is hard to accept the truth. It is hard to accept that others are damaged, broken humans. And so are we.

BEAR CAMP

"You're going to be alright." I was going to summer camp. I threw my suitcase in the car and climbed in next to my mother. We were headed to the church, and I would be on my way to my first real adventure away from my parents and home. I was so nervous I felt faint. I wasn't sure I wanted to go. I wasn't sure if I had the flu. I wasn't sure if I'd packed my toothbrush. I wasn't sure about anything, but my mother was. When we got there, I was still wobbly legged and holding her hand for dear life. She walked me over checked me in and next was the bus.

I leaned over and threw up. "Mom, I'm sick." She just looked at me. She saw how scared I was.

"You are going to be alright. You'll see. You'll live." Of course, I will. I'm not dying. She was a smart mother. I didn't have the flu. I was just nervous. She put me on the bus and waved goodbye while I took a seat and tried not to toss anymore cookies.

I loved camp but I still felt like something was missing. I felt different. I wanted what the other people at camp had, but I felt dirty. They seemed peaceful and joyful. I felt sad and alone. My best friend from church was there. That should've helped but for some reason, it didn't. Apparently, we were both struggling emotionally because after lunch one day, we got into a physical fight. We were alone and we just fought. I think we both had unspoken frustration and pain. We were still friends after scratching and slapping each other. Neither one of us knew why it happened. We couldn't verbalize why. Things were wrong in both our lives, and we couldn't figure out what to do about it.

Besides the way I felt inside, the adventure of camp was awesome. Sleeping in teepees, and being in the woods was wonderful. We got to pick our own Indian names, and make headbands so we could all remember everybody else's name. We went horseback riding and swimming. We got up early and had scrambled eggs at long picnic tables in the woods. One morning we got up in the dark, and hiked to the top of a hill with flashlights so we could see the sun come up. It was an assembly line of French toast and forest. I loved it.

I was making amazing memories, and started to feel better but then one night I woke up, and didn't know where I was. I knew it was very late because except for the stars, there was no light. It was *dark*. All I could hear was a bunch of faint snoring and my own breathing.

It took me a second or two to realize I was in a bush. I was sort of laying in the bush, and I didn't know why. As my eyes adjusted to the darkness, I started to look around, and could see what looked like my teepee, a couple of hundred feet away. It was across the dirt road, but there was something else, big and black in the middle of the road. Whatever it was, I slowly realized that it was between me and my teepee. It was between me and safety. The counselors had told us about bears living up here in these woods. As I tried to get a handle on my situation, I came to the obvious conclusion that there was a huge bear sleeping in the middle of the road. That *bear* was between me and the teepee! I listened intently, and I could hear louder snoring coming from that blob, and it sounded more animal than the other snoring noises. It was a bear!

In the pitch blackness, I did not move. The 'spirit of fear' had come over me physically. I had a sensation of shivering on the inside of my body but my outside was completely paralyzed. I had never been that scared for that long. I was afraid that if I moved or made any sound, the bear would wake up and attack me. I stayed alone, and petrified in that bush for literally hours. I was so cold, and so scared I could not move, or sleep or scream for help. Finally, the sun started to come up, and the spirit of fear left me. I slowly untangled myself from the bush, and started creeping ever so slowly towards the road. What?! I could finally see that the bear was fuzzy and blue and looked familiar…I crept forward….what is it? It's…., it's ….my blanket! That's embarrassing.

    That experience is amusing now but, in reality, it is really similar to my life, the big adventure. For years, I was in the dark, afraid and paralyzed by the destructive spirit of fear. God has freed me, and as I seek Him, more and more light has come into my life. I'm not afraid anymore. I know what's in the road now. It's still warm and fuzzy…it's Jesus.

"God has not given us a spirit of fear but of power, love and a sound mind." 2 Timothy 1:7

Excerpt End

CHAPTER SIX

"Wow Mom, you've been really busy with that writing class. I'm proud of you." Propping his feet up on the coffee table, I noticed he had a hole in his sock. His big toe was trying to make a break for it.

"Thanks, Chuck. It has been great to get all that stuff from my life, good and bad, out there. I like writing. It's therapeutic."

Grinning, he asked "Have you written anything about me yet?"

"Well, I can't tell you that, Son. Some of what I write is just too juicy to repeat. I mean what would I say…'handsome teenager whose socks are so holy he can only wear them on Sunday, really needs a job…'"

"Whatever, Lady. You know I'm the apple in your fruit basket."

"I know. Now take off those socks. I'll put one in my purse as a reminder to buy you some new ones. Leaning forward I started to pull the sock off his foot myself, and then felt the hair in my nose starting to catch on fire.

"Oh, my word! Chuck, your feet stink! That sock is not going in my purse! I'll just have to write it on the list."

"Oh, you mean a shopping list like *normal* people? Who needs a whole sock as a reminder? Oh, that's right. My crazy mother!"

"That's it, Buddy! No socks for you! "Leaning over, I kissed his cheek, and headed out the door to another weekly writing class. This week was going to be a good one.

Later that night, as I handed a classmate my newest excerpt, I was nervous. She had become a friend and I was worried she would read my sarcastic thoughts, along with my checkered past and judge me. It was too late to make the excerpt seem all- American and apple pie-ish. It was her turn to read my stuff and part of me hoped she wouldn't read it. Do all literary geniuses worry like this? I wondered.

As I handed her the pages, I said, "Enjoy", like an idiot. Literary genius slash total dork. Smiling, time to be brave! I thought.

Writers Group - Sharing Excerpt Five
Genre: Semi-Autobiographical Memoir, Christian
Author: Jo Lisa Blossom

I Give Up

Another white flag
of surrender
to the Lord.
I tried but
I give up
again.
You're in charge, God.
It's all you.
I can't crawl
another mile
back to safety.
I'm lost in the jungle
of heartache.

Going in circles
with no direction
or hope.
I'm exhausted and out
the strength.
Come get me, Lord.
I give up.
Help me
back to where
You are.

How It Is

I don't care
What people think
Life's not fair
And I'm on the brink
Of being attacked
All over again
The odds are stacked
They've always been
The truth is not
Easy to hear
It's all we've got
But the fear
Anger and sorrow
Are all together
Yesterday and tomorrow
Today and forever.

WAKING UP TO DARKNESS

"Our little brother almost died last night!" My sister was standing in front of me with her hands on her hips. She looked a little mad at me but I couldn't figure out why. I was just waking up and rubbing my eyes, trying to catch on. Then it all came out.

"He had a seizure, was puking up green stuff and you slept right through it!"

"What?!" I asked, now sitting straight up and wide awake. We were at my aunt's house visiting for the weekend. I was sleeping in a room that smelled like baby and something else, I couldn't quite put my finger on. But all of that didn't matter now that this had happened.

"There were fire trucks and an ambulance! Dad had to slam him over a chair because he swallowed his tongue!" She was still talking and waving her arms around. Part of me was hanging on every word, the other part was wondering, what's a seizure and how on earth do you swallow your tongue? I licked my lips, thinking she must've made that tongue thing up.

"His wrists swelled up this big and he was puking green stuff." I stopped her, suddenly struck with overwhelming fear…I had almost forgotten that she was talking about one of my beloved little brothers.

"Who? Which one? Is he ok? Where is he?"

"Oh, he's fine now but I still can't believe you slept through that! He almost died!" I ran from the room to find my brothers and look for the green one. I needed to hug that little booger butt. Green puke or weird acrobatic tongue, he was my little bro and I had to see for myself that he was ok.

Besides the vivid descriptions by my sister, the one thing that struck me about that night was what my step father had done. He had slammed my young brother over a chair. That sounded so violent and distressing but that *saved* my brother's life. For a long time, I viewed my step father differently. He was a man. He made a decision at a moment's notice and probably scared the crud out of the others in the room. But because of his quick thinking and determination, my brother was *alive*. Thinking about that made me realize how different adults were. They knew what to do in an emergency. My step-father was strong and brave. I was in awe of him and for a while, he was my hero.

My brothers brush with death had me thinking and the next Sunday at church I made a big decision.

"Do any of you want to make Jesus Lord of your life?"

"Yes." A chorus of voices answered the Sunday school teacher She had just explained that we were sinners if we ever thought a bad thought about anyone.. I knew I hate my siblings sometimes. They just made me so mad! She then said that we couldn't get into a perfect, holy heaven with a perfect, holy God if we thought like that. Jesus could fix that, but we had to admit that we had those bad thoughts or had done bad things, like lied to our Mom. She told us that we had to ask Jesus to forgive us in a prayer.

"Ok, well close your eyes and repeat after me and you will be saved. 'Dear Jesus, thank you for dying on the cross for me.'" We all slowly repeated every word. "I know that I am a sinner. Please forgive me and come to live in my heart. Please be the Lord of my life from now on. Amen." We all finished the prayer and opened our eyes looking around at each other smiling. This was good stuff! Jesus loves me and now He lived in our hearts! It felt good to have made such a "big" decision and to know I would be going to heaven. I was glad.

A few weeks later I had made another big decision, along with some of the other children. I was taking the plunge.

"Come on, honey. It's your turn." I moved slowly forward down the steps into the warm water. The gold baptism robe flowed around me, and then stuck to my legs, as I nervously kept walking toward the pastor's outstretched arms. I had gone from a being six years old singing, "Jesus loves me, this I know, for the bible tells me so...." to now, and I *did* know. God *did* love me. I was grateful, and glad to stand up to say, that I loved Jesus back. I looked out at the church, full of people. Then back to the pastor, and time to grab my nose.

"I baptize you in the name of the Father, the Son and the Holy Spirit." I heard him say as he held me and leaned me back into the water. I was one of several children that morning, who were dipped in the warm, clear water to have our sins washed away. I remember how refreshing it felt. I remember feeling really happy.

Soon after that, I started seeing things I'd never noticed before. Sitting in the pew at church, I noticed my step father with his arm around my mother. I had mixed feelings. On the one hand it looked so right. He looked like he loved her, and I wanted her to be loved. On the other hand, they never closed their bedroom door at night. From what I saw, the arm around her, a few hugs, and quick pecks here and there, was all the love she was getting. People their age still had sex, didn't they? Weren't they supposed to? But looking at them, I started to think maybe the arm around her was for show. I started to suspect that he was somehow controlling her with that little bit of love. Did she feel loved? Was that enough? I didn't think so. What about what he was doing to my sisters and me? How did *that* fit in? Did Jesus approve of that? Why did it *feel* so wrong?

I was looking at things around me with a critical eye and even though I was always pretty sure God was real, I wasn't so sure he was "everywhere". I felt like someone should be able to see that something was wrong with our family. I wondered why God didn't let anyone see. Eventually, I felt like church might be a waste of time because my parents didn't seem to be good. I mean, he was doing nasty things to us during bedtime prayers. How could that be 'good'? Aren't people who go to church supposed to be good?

Even at school I was reminded that things were not right at home.

"Next word, hypocrite." I sat at my desk, with the other fourth grade students, looking down at my list. The teacher read the vocabulary words for the week. "H-y-p-o-c-r-i-t-e – a person who pretends to have virtues, moral or religious beliefs or principles that he or she does not actually possess, especially a person whose actions are not in line with stated beliefs."

When she read that word and the definition, the word seemed to glow on the page. I didn't hear anything else the teacher said. Hmmm…I think I know one of those. In my mind, I saw my step father's arm around my mother in the pew at church.

"What sorrow awaits you teachers of religious law and you Pharisees. Hypocrites! For you cross land and sea to make one convert, and then you turn that person into twice the child of hell you yourselves are!" Matt. 23:15

In spite of what was going on at prayer time, and the doubts I was wrestling with, I liked church. I felt peaceful learning about how much God loved me. I believed in God. I wanted more of Jesus but, in the years just after I was baptized, the devil attacked me full force.

My older siblings were at the height of their teenage rebellion, and the rest of us just followed them. One Sunday morning, I started to think maybe I didn't fit in at church. Maybe I didn't want to go. I only had one friend there. I didn't go to school with her or any of the kids there. They didn't live near me. I noticed that they seemed to know each other but they didn't know me.

As my parents walked toward the sanctuary, and we walked toward the classroom buildings, one of my older siblings suggested we ditch Sunday school, and walk to the convenience store on the next block. I went along without thinking twice. I was picturing slushies. Then the pot came out. We stood back there by the dumpster passing a joint. My brothers in their matching vests and ties. Us girls in our matching dresses. My mother had made us all outfits for Sunday, and now we were getting high in them. It was beginning to feel like there was something *really*, *really* wrong with us. We weren't good enough to be in church anymore. We didn't belong. We all knew we were dirty, misfits. We didn't talk about it but we were ashamed of what was happening to us. Ashamed and resentful. We were dirty and everyone at church was so clean. They were so happy, and I wasn't anymore.

I was getting older, and now I felt bad almost all the time. I was not comfortable in my own skin anymore. My step-father's abuse, and my mother's lack of help made me feel so powerless, and alone. Drugs made me feel bad, and at the same time they helped me forget how I felt about everything else for a little while. I was more, and more, confused about right and wrong. Then it got worse.

"Tonight, we are going to that presentation at church about abortion." My mother said, and I had no idea what she was talking about.

"What's abortion?" I asked as I pulled up my knee socks.

"You'll find out", she answered.

The special presentation was in the secondary building. We took our places on the folding chairs, and someone turned the lights out. The film began with a man sitting on a four-legged stool talking about "abortion". I had never heard that word before, and I still wasn't clear on what he was talking about. Then they showed us. I remember the blood, and the body parts. This was 1978. Abortion had been legal in the United States for a few years by then but for me, it had just begun. I was in shock. People *do* this? To babies? Why? By the time the night was over, I understood. This was injustice. This was horror, and it was legal. It was wrong so how could it be *legal*? Driving home that night, I asked my mother, incredulous.

"Don't you mean *illegal*? It's *illegal* right? You know, *not* legal?" She shook her head slowly, back and forth.

"No." Her face looked grim. Suddenly, I felt sad. Is this what growing up is all about? This horror? People doing this to innocent babies? In the silence, I watched out the window as the street lights were going by. Dark, light, dark, light, dark, light. I sighed, and thought, there is just not enough light in this dark world.

WHO'S MY DADDY?

That year, I started to have a longing to know my biological father. I needed a hero to save me. My stepfather's hero shine had completely disappeared by then so I was on a mission. This was way before the internet so, in my quest, I had to do it the old-fashioned way. I started looking up people with the same last name in the phone book. I was making my way through the list asking if they knew my father. I only had his first, middle and last name and the color of his hair and eyes. One phone call made me just want to give up.

A man answered and I told him the name I was looking for. "No that's not my name." He said.

"Well do you know or have any relatives with

that name?" I asked, still hopeful.

"No, I don't. Why are you looking for him?"

"Well, he's my real Dad and I haven't seen him since I was three. I'm eleven now and I'd really like to meet him. I know his name and he had blue eyes."

"Hmmm, I don't have blue eyes," he said.

"Oh ok." I couldn't hide the disappointment in my voice. I had a man with the same first and last name as my father on the line. I was surprised when he started asking *me* questions.

"What color are *your* eyes?"

"Sky blue," I gave him my standard answer.

"Oh, and how old did you say you are?"

"Eleven"

"You sound pretty."

"Thank you." I answered, smiling a little.

"I bet you like boys by now. You probably dress cute, too. What are you wearing right now?"

"What?" A boyfriend had asked me this question once so I understood this question was not an innocent one. His voice was suddenly hoarse and insistent.

"What are you wearing? Do you have a tight little shirt on over your little……"

I gasped and hung up. Shaking, I just sat there and cried. That was the end of that. I was afraid to make any more calls. Why was he so gross? I felt dirty again and now I had another problem. What if my biological father was a pervert too? I had never considered that he could be anything but perfect. That horrid man convinced me that it wasn't worth the risk. What if I found him and he talked like that? What if that was really him and he was lying? Sighing heavily and wiping my eyes, I walked back to the kitchen and put the phone book back in the drawer.

"Ok here you go." My mother handed me a pair

of mittens she had knitted for me. Today was a treat. It was the first time we had come up to the snow! She waxed our mittens to keep the snow out. I pulled them on as fast as I could and ran out to join the fun. It was cold but the snow was awesome! We sledded down the hill and threw snowballs at each other until we were soaked through. We went back into the camper for a quick hot chocolate break. Then it was outside again. Several families were near us and everybody was having a great time. Snowmen and sleds were everywhere. Even my step father was busy building a snowman. My older brother was putting the finishing touches on his. It was small and a little crooked but he was diligently trying to smash a rock into the face for a nose. I walked around to the front of the one my stepfather had made, to see what he was using for the face. His snowman didn't have a face but it did have a large set of boobs.

"It's a snow woman!" He exclaimed, laughing. I was instantly embarrassed. He had even put a pine branch for the pubic hair. I looked around nervously, hoping none of the other families noticed. I wanted to crawl into a hole I was so embarrassed. I was mortified, but to him, it was funny. To me, it was a reminder that the fun only lasted so long and, then we had to go back home.

DO SOMETHING

"I had a weird dream last night." I said quietly.
"You did? What was it?", my foster sister asked groggily. With her head still on her pillow, she was waiting for my answer. I felt sick thinking about it but I knew I had to tell her. We shared a room. It was a big room, with our bunk bed on one side. I was on the top bunk and she was on the bottom. I was looking over the

side of the bed at her face, thinking about what to say next.

The walls of our room were pale pink and lavender and our curtains were lace with tiny pink roses. It was the perfect little girl's room, which annoyed me because it felt babyish. But none of that mattered this morning. I lay back onto my pillow again, trying to find the words and remember what I couldn't forget. Sometime in the middle of the night I had woken up with something in my hand. I was half asleep but soon realized that my step father was standing on a stool next to our bunk bed. He had taken my hand, and put it on his private parts!

For a moment I didn't know what to do. Scream? But this was so embarrassing. What would I say if my sisters woke up or my mother came running? Would they believe me? Was it *my* fault? I quickly jerked my hand away, pulled it under my blanket, and turned toward the wall. My heart felt like it was literally pounding out of my chest and my mouth was dry but I desperately tried to breathe slow and deep. I slowly scooted as far as I could away from him. I was facing the wall, and my eyes were still closed but I was wide awake. I was trying so hard to move slow enough, and breathe deeply enough so he would think I was sleeping and leave me alone. I felt vulnerable, and for a moment I was afraid he would touch my back side.

"God, please make me invisible," I prayed. He stood there for a couple more minutes but it felt like an hour. Finally, he left. I was still awake when the sun finally came up.

"I dreamed that dad was standing on a stool next to our bed naked, and he put my hand on his private parts." I said softly, embarrassed. I felt sick even saying it. I had somehow been protected mentally from what had been going on in the same room with the her and the other girls, for years at that point. We switched siblings sharing a room every year or so, and he was doing things to them that could not be hidden, and I could not have slept through. But it was as if I was not fully aware of it, until the night when I woke up to his penis in my hand. He had been treating them like his wives on a daily basis but my conscious mind simply didn't allow me to *know* it. But that day, at dawn it was the *first and only* thing I could think of.

"That was no dream." She said with a mixture of disgust, and sadness. My eyes were opened, at that moment, to the pain they had been enduring. It was not a dream. It was a nightmare. Shortly after that, the police showed up.

"Ok Dear, you go with Officer Lathrop now." As directed, I moved toward the black leather couch in our living room. I sat down next to a policeman. Now it was my turn to be interviewed. Another policeman was on a chair facing me and he started talking. They both looked nice. The one talking had light brown, short hair and big brown eyes. He was doing his best to help me feel comfortable. But truly I was a bit enamored with the police at that moment. They were here to help us! Yay! Finally, help had arrived. It was surreal. And there was no stress at that moment. There was no worry about matching stories or keeping lies straight. The single conversation with my foster sister was the only time any of us had talked about it. I was nervous with these strange men, but I sensed that this was a good thing. I felt relief. I could finally tell someone the truth. Finally, someone cared! Someone would *know,* and help us. There was no real anxiety as I told my grimy, embarrassing story. It was embarrassing but I looked him in the eye and calmly told the truth, the whole truth. It was all we had.

Those nice male detectives interviewed each of us, separately, in the living room. Then those men, with crew cuts, slacks, white shirts, and ties, took my step father outside on the sidewalk and yelled at him. I could see them through the window. Officer Lathrop was waving his arms, and yelling in my step father's face. The other policeman stood behind him glaring at my stepfather. He pointed his finger, and shouted a couple of times. They were really giving him heck, and he just stood there taking it. Then that was it. They all piled back in their unmarked police car, and left.

The detective with the big brown eyes looked back at us, looking out the big living room window, as they left. He didn't smile. He looked angry, and sad. Soon that's how we felt, too.

It slowly dawned on us. They weren't coming back to take my Dad away. He came out of the bedroom from talking to my mother in hushed tones, with a little smirk on his face. He looked prideful, and gave us the look like, 'See I won". We went back outside. He did not make a habit of hitting us but we were afraid he would then. He couldn't yell or hit us if we were in the front yard. The neighbors would see.

I cannot tell you how it feels to have those who are supposed to help, abandon you. Those nice policemen, looked us in the eye, heard our story, got angry, and then got back in their shiny police cars and left us there. They left him there, and they left us there to face him… a bunch of scared kids, and a completely silent mother.

That was the beginning of my rage at the local police department. Why didn't they arrest him when they had *all* of us telling them what he was doing? Nobody was helping us. Not my mother, not the police, not anybody.

The police did not even call the state social

worker for the foster kids. But not long after that, someone took matters into their own hands. I suspect it was my oldest foster sister. The social worker, got the call. She showed up, and looked mad. She looked like she meant business, with briefcase in hand. I thought, *this is it!* She's got important papers in there. She's going to stop him! She talked to my mother, and wrote things down. Then she put the papers back in, and snapped her briefcase shut again. Within minutes, we realized that this last brave attempt to get justice, had only brought more pain.

      Instead of having to say goodbye to our abuser, we were crying and helping our foster siblings pack their belongings. My sister went to the bathroom to get toothbrushes, while I started folding my foster sister's clothes with tears streaming down my face. We were all crying, going around in circles not knowing what to do. I sobbed, as we hugged our brothers and sisters, goodbye. My step-father was nowhere to be found. My mother sat in a chair looking like a zombie, and the social worker tried to reassure us.

      "It's going to be all right. They'll call you when they get settled." Where were they going? When would they be back? No one would give us an answer.

      Standing there on the sidewalk, watching that car drive away with half of my family, something turned off inside me. My older sister was yelling at my mother.

      "Do something! Why don't you do something?!" The neighbors were watching, and I didn't care. With a ragged sigh, I wiped my tears with my sleeve. Suddenly, I didn't feel like crying or screaming anymore. I didn't feel anything. I felt dead, and dead people don't feel anything. Lifting my chin up, I turned around, headed for the house, and walked back into hell.

YES I MEAN NO

In fifth grade, I made an appointment to *really* kiss a boy for the first time. "Behind the building" meant we were meeting, and we weren't playin'. It was me and Ceasar, also known as "Bongo Lips". They were big, luscious, and very distracting to fifth grade girls. The other couple going through the French kiss gauntlet were Betty and Rick, also known as Betty and Rick. At recess, we snuck back there. Us girls put our backs against the building while the boys took their positions. I, for one, was petrified. The only tongue I'd had in my mouth was my step-father's and that was NOT the same. This was about love, and to say I had 'butterflies' would have been an understatement. I put my hands behind my back, and closed my eyes. Ceasar wasted no time, and started slobbering all over me. At one point, I opened my eyes long enough to peer sideways at Betty and Rick. At that moment I realized that I still had my hands behind my back. I was surprised to see Betty was using hers like she was blind, and had to figure out what color Rick was wearing. She was busy. A minute or so more of wet, disgusting, pre-pubescent love and it was over. Ceasar stepped ped back smiling at me, like a matador that had just slayed a prize bull. I looked at him and smiled back. I wasn't sure if I wanted to marry him or bring a bib next time, but we were in love…messy, beautiful, young love.

    Ceasar and I didn't last long. His reputation as an amazing kisser got around, and so did he. Apparently, I had a reputation too, and by sixth grade, I had another boy inviting me to sneak off during recess to his house. I only went a couple of times, and we only kissed but it felt like I was headed down a path I didn't really want to go. I was sort of over the slobbering. The mystery had worn off, and it had begun to feel wrong to me. Plus I didn't want to get caught.

When a child is being abused, they feel overwhelmingly alone, and powerless. There's no choice in the abuse. It is so shocking, and shameful, that most kids are paralyzed to fight back at all. Going along with whatever a stronger, more aggressive, or assertive person wants becomes a habit in the flesh. But I was tired of feeling dirty at home, and now I felt dirty, and ashamed at school. I couldn't do anything about what was going on at home but I was determined that I could do something about it at school. So, I stopped going along with whatever boys wanted at school. I made excuses, and tried to hang out with really shy boys that I thought would never get up the nerve to kiss me. I was right some of the time. Some of those little wall flowers had a one-track mind…. kiss or be kissed.

Next was junior high school, and it was a pivotal time. I went from elementary school, and some loss of innocence; to Jr. High and complete corruption. The devil began luring me into rebellion and bad decisions. My older siblings introduced me to all the sinful substances they could, and I had no desire to "just say no". I remember the first time I smoked pot with my two best friends.

"Do you want to try this?" I asked.

"I don't know…" Lauren said, hesitating. Lauren and Sandy were two girls that I had met that year in seventh grade. We had walked up the street to Sandy's house after school. Now we were standing in Sandy's backyard, and discussing the marijuana cigarette that I was holding, and about ready to light.

"Look you guys", I said, "this is gonna be fun. My sister gave it to me, and its good stuff. It won't hurt you. I've done it and I'm fine." Next thing you know we are all completely stoned, and the devil had free reign with our twelve year old souls.

"Wow! I feel fantastic!" Lauren said giggling.

"I, I can't believe how funny everything is!" Sandy was laughing so hard she was crying.

"What time are your parents coming home?" I asked.

"Heck, I don't know, and I don't care!", she answered gleefully. We all fell into uncontrollable laughter. Then the devil kicked the door down.

"Hey you wanna play with the Oujee Board?" Sandy asked.

"Sure, let's do it!" I said, like an idiot.

"Let's see if we can talk to the dead!" Lauren added. We thought it was a big joke but then we actually talked to something. A demon was moving that thing around, and answering us.

Looking back on that experience, as a parent, I am outraged to think those things are still on sale at nationwide toy stores! When will we learn that the devil is real and there is nothing entertaining about evil? I'm glad to say that even at that young age, we learned that lesson quick. We never played with that thing again. It scared us and I noticed that we weren't laughing anymore.

"I gotta go home." Lauren was the first to bail out. We learned that if you want to ruin a good time, just whip out the Oujee board.

"For our wrestling is not against flesh and blood, but against the principalities, against the powers, against the world-rulers of this darkness, against the spiritual hosts of wickedness in the heavenly places." Eph. 6:12

"Listen Ladies and Gentlemen, settle down. Today we are going to be talking about something very important, drugs." Puberty was rearing its ugly head, and all of us seventh graders were trying to focus. In the dark gymnasium that smelled like tater tots and sweat, they showed us a film about drugs. There were photos of heroin addicts with black arms. This was the seventies. Society was just starting to understand that the sixtie's philosophy of sex, drugs and rock and roll was actually destructive. Kids could die from that stuff! Wow. Who knew? Although this film was gross, it wasn't convincing me. Those black arms, and skinny people with no teeth, didn't look like reality to me. At least not *my* reality. I just wanted to get high, and forget I cared about anything. Most of the time drugs and alcohol were still fun. We laughed at this attempt to scare us straight. My friends and I, we'd never get that bad. After school, before walking home, we went across the street, and hid under a tree. We smoked pot, laughing about the film.

"That blankity blank was so stupid." Sandy said.

"Did you see those black arms? I've never even heard of that before. I think that was fake. But I'm never gonna shoot anything in my arm anyway. You'd have to be out of your mind to try that."

From an adult perspective, we were the "bad" kids. I was selling pills, and my friend was stealing liquor from her parents. But we didn't feel like we were that bad. We didn't have the brain capacity to think through our stupid decisions, but we weren't hurting anybody. We were just trying to get away from our own emotions. I never felt like there was any other path for me. I was smart but I was in so much pain, I couldn't make any plans for the future. Just make it through the day.

My parents didn't help scare us away from drugs either. My step father was non-committal about it all, and we suspected he drank and smoked pot with my uncle. My mother didn't seem to have a clue. She never talked about drugs but she did tell us "Keep your pants on".

Then the guy down the block died from a drug overdose. We heard something was going on so all of us walked down the sidewalk to check it out. Now that was a shock. I learned that you never, never, never get high naked…Why? Because you might get carted off that way…wrapped up in a puke covered sheet with your bare back side hanging out. Nothing glamorous about that.

    I am grateful to those who made a valiant effort to at least talk to us, as young people, about the evils of the day. This was an improvement from the previous generation when it was a "big no no" to talk about problems. I mean you could judgmentally say a quick, "Oh he just can't stay home" or "She takes a few too many trips to the corner market", but you could never and I mean *never*, sit down over coffee and discuss, at length, social ills on a *personal* level. Nobody ever said, "Hello, my name is Fred and I am an adulterer" or "Hi, my name is Sandy and I am an alcoholic." Family problems were nobody else's business and for that generation, it was better just to avoid them all together. But some days that just didn't work….

 # Excerpt End

CHAPTER SEVEN

"Hey girl, how you doing today?" I sat down on the back porch, next to the oldest girl I was babysitting. She was twelve and in junior high. That alone was enough to make a person crazy but today she looked down.

"I'm ok." She answered.

"Are you sure? You look like something is bothering you today and you know I care about you kids. If there is something you need to talk about, you can." I felt bad that these kids were going through so much. Their mother was my hero, leaving their child molester father, but it was a lot of change for them.

"Well, I heard my mom arguing with somebody about money, and I think she doesn't know where we are going to move to. I told her anywhere is better, away from Dad, but I'm worried." She confessed.

"I understand, but you know those are adult things, and your mom is smart. She can take care of it. You should worry about school, not things like that. Those are adult things. Your Mom can handle all that. Everything is going to be all right. You don't need to worry, but I know it's easier said than done." I tried to assure her putting my arm around her for a side hug.

"I remember being your age. I used to get sooooo upset about things at my house. I used to throw pots and pans at the fence because we were so mad. It was silly but it helped. Do you want to try something?"

"What?" She turned to look me in the eye.

"Well do me a favor, pick up about ten rocks over there and bring them to the porch. Make them about this big. You know big enough to throw. I'll be right back." I used to hate those rocks. I wish I had the strength to gather them all up and take them somewhere. Now they were coming in handy. I went inside to grab a box of markers. I joined her and picked out some rocks and we put them on a pile on the back porch.

"Ok, I want you to write something on each rock. It doesn't have to be a lot of words. It can be one or two words that are something, or someone you are worried about. Or it can be something that makes you mad or sad." She was eyeing me suspiciously and by now her little brother had wandered outside. I sent him off to pick up a couple of his own rocks.

"You don't have to show them to me." I said quietly. "This is for you. Just between you and God. He can see us right now under His sky and He understands how you feel. He knows what you are thinking and it's ok. He understands. *Whatever it is, it's ok*. Just pick a word for things that are bothering you and write it on each rock." She took a marker and started to label her rocks.

The five-year old came up with an armful of rocks. "I got mine."

"Ok buddy. Is there anything or anybody that makes you mad or sad or worried right now?"

He frowned, thinking. "Yeah, probly."

I was distracted by his cuteness. He had blond hair, bright blue eyes and lips that were bigger than most. When he talked, he sort of had to maneuver those big lips. It was adorable.

"Well, I want you to take a marker and write a letter or a little picture, like a frog or a cat or something that reminds you of that problem. Do you understand?"

"Do I have to tell you?" They both were carrying shame. I could see it on their faces.

"No this is between you and Jesus. He knows what we are sad and mad about anyway but if you put the mark on the rock for those things, then we are going to do something to make you feel better about that stuff. Ok?" He took the marker in his little hand and made a mad face on his first rock.

Pretty soon, their sister wandered out and followed suit. When they were done, they each stood by their little pile of rocks, on the edge of my little backyard pond. "You guys did a great job! Now comes the fun part. Let's hold hands and say a little prayer first, ok?" I squeezed their little hands in mine.

"Father God, please help us to give you all our problems. Please let us throw these rocks as hard as we can and Jesus will you please catch them under the water? We know you can handle all these hard things and we can't. We don't have to, anymore. Please take these rocks and all these things that we are mad or sad or worried about. As we throw these rocks, we are giving you these problems, God. We are letting you have them so we can be happy. Thank you for taking this stuff, Lord. Help us feel better every day and remember that you are bigger than all our problems and you love us. We love you, too. Thank you. Amen." The little guy looked up at me with a little smile. I looked at the girls and I could see their shoulders relax under their long brown hair. Already they felt relief.

I looked them each in the eye, "Now I want you to throw those rocks as hard as you can. I mean throw them and those problems right outta your mind. Go!" They threw those rocks with all their might and by the end of our rock chucking session, everyone was smiling. I hugged them each tightly and wiped away my tears so they wouldn't see me crying for them. So much for such little people.

"Let's go get a smack! Oh, I mean snack!"
Laughing together we walked back inside a little lighter.

"A time to scatter stones and a time to gather stones…."
Ecclesiastes 3:15

That night at the writer's group, all I could think of was their faces. I was so distracted I didn't hear who I was supposed to give my excerpt to. Luckily, someone put their hand out and I knew what to do. This is the kind of class I need. Easy, peasy, auto-pilot can still fly the plane.

Writers Group - Sharing Excerpt Six
Genre: Semi-Autobiographical Memoir, Christian
Author: Jo Lisa Blossom

Let It Fly

Sometimes we fight
with words.
Sometimes we fight
with a
fist in the face.
Pray, pray, pray
and then
ball it up
and let it fly
into the face
of
evil.
Back it up
in the physical.
Back it up
in the spiritual.

Either way
we mean business.

Who I Am

It's "who I am" he said
I know it's strange
I can't change

It's who I am
But only
When I'm lonely

It's what I do
But truly I
Don't know why

I could get well
And tell, tell, tell
But it's too hard

I'm sick
But the trick
Is to believe there's no hope

It's who I am
Even if it's wrong
The lure's too strong

I can't fight anymore
Just embrace it
Never face it

The devil lies
And I'm his slave

What I hate, I crave

I cry sometimes
Over my crimes
I've hurt so much

The truth is
I'm in pain
It's insane

Avoiding the past
Abuse
It's no use

It's who I am

CAN IT!

"I am sooooo loaded!" My siblings and I were laughing and stumbling our way across the front yard. A wannabe rock star rented a house around the corner with his band. For us, they were the ultimate in cool. They were older, had long hair, their own house, electric guitars, drums, you name it. We would go over there and get stoned every chance we got and today was a doozie. We stumbled into the kitchen. My mother had about thirty canning jars upside down drying on the kitchen table. She ignored us but one of us tripped into that table. Glass jars are falling all over. Crash, bang, crash, clatter. Pretty hard to ignore that.

"What's wrong with you?" My mother asked frantically. She looked right at us with our blood shot eyes, crawling around on the floor trying to pick up the jars and giggling. She had to face the fact that we were intoxicated.

"I, I, I'm sorry Mom", a chorus of our voices said. In the epitome of hilarious, my mother glares at us and yells, "Can it!" The fact that she was actually canning and yelling 'Can it!' was not lost to us. We were trying to stop laughing but with no luck.

She roared, "I'll clean this up! You go to your rooms!" We sat in our rooms coming down at a rapid pace and tripping out on what the punishment would be. Amazingly, that *was* the punishment. It was becoming clear that my mother did not know what to do about us, or my step father…She did nothing. She chose the non-confrontational route. She said nothing.

But other people were talking. This was the beginning of the day time talk show era. What a blessing to the planet. We would ditch school and come home to smoke pot and eat peanut butter and jelly sandwiches. We would sprawl on the couch, stuffing our faces and watch in complete awe as all those secret problems, that nobody ever talked about, were on TV! People were baring their souls in broad day light and *anybody* could watch!

Those talk shows were refreshing to my soul because as a family, we were all signed on to the "don't talk about it" policy. We were pretending there was nothing wrong. I didn't realize at the time that victims rarely talk to each other. Unfortunately, victims are usually so overwhelmed with helplessness and shame that they assist the abuser by not revealing their secrets, even to other victims.

At the time, I thought we were all just pretending. I didn't want to but I felt like I was the only one that didn't want to pretend. I had a strong desire to rebel against this false picture but I had no idea how to get the words out of my mouth. I didn't know *how* to share my feelings. I just knew that we were not the normal, big, happy family, that we pretended to be on Sunday at church. We were more like the people on those talk shows. We were leading a "double life". On Sunday, my siblings and I would all pile into the old, brown station wagon with my parents and go to church. Pretending again. Hurting sinners marching in, hurting sinners marching out.

"Ok, it's your turn. Just breathe deep and hold it." My older brother and my girlfriend from school were in the garage sniffing paint. We had become bored with playing pass out, smoking pot and drinking beer and had decided to try the 'hard stuff'. It is scary what kids experiment with when young, dumb and desperate to change how they feel. We were in the garage, which was attached to the house, with a paper bag and a can of purple spray paint. We were huffing away like idiots when suddenly our exceedingly foolish behavior was interrupted. On the other side of the garage door, a car pulled into the driveway. Instantly, we knew it was my step-father coming home from work.

The surreal thing was that at the *exact* moment that the car pulled up, my very tall brother passed out. He is falling backwards in slow motion and my friend and I turn to look at each other, "Oh no!" I whisper. I am petrified. All I can think about is how am I going to explain why he is laying on the garage floor unconscious, with purple paint smeared on his face. Then a miracle occurred! My brother pops back up and as if by instinct, he runs out the back door. In less than a second flat we grabbed the paint, the bag and our sense enough to follow him out. We got away but I'm pretty sure we left some of our brain cells behind.

The whole reason we were engaging in that stupid behavior was to escape. That day we successfully avoided a disciplinary encounter with my step father but many other times we were not so lucky. Looking back, I believe people who molest children are mentally disturbed by a split personality that is led by the demonic. My step- father would get an entirely different look on his face when he was harassing, abusing or "disciplining" us. If he caught us with our elbow touching the table at dinner, he would stab us in the elbow with his fork. His demeanor and personality would change. He was mean.

But sometimes he was nice, and I wanted a father so badly. What young girl doesn't want her daddy? I didn't know then, that we are built to want a father, and that father is God. At the time, I would try over and over to fit the picture…the pretend picture of a happy family. But no matter how mean, or nice, my step-father was, I knew in my heart, I did not have an earthly father. I often felt like I also didn't have a mother.

The more I abused drugs and alcohol, and told my friends what was going on, the more I was beginning to realize that my mother was not protecting us. I began to really grasp that she was *supposed* to protect us. I slowly realized how abnormal this was. She was not saying anything at all when these things occurred. She was walking by the open bedroom door when he had his hand in my jammies. She was not yelling, screaming, throwing him out. It dawned on me, that she was making a choice. She was choosing denial and she was choosing *him*. She was choosing this sick, disturbed man who would not stop chasing us around the house. She was not choosing her children.

I thought my mother wouldn't help me with my step father because I was not worth it. Some part of me began to think that if I was just good enough, maybe she would choose me. I worked hard to be the "good kid" when I was at home. I helped make dinner. I cleaned the house. I did everything I could think of to ease the burdens of my working mother. I tried to be good while at the same time becoming a slave to my own bad choices.

"Enter by the narrow gate. For the gate is wide and the way is easy that leads to destruction, and those who enter by it are many. For the gate is narrow and the way is hard that leads to life, and those who find it are few." Matthew 7:13-14

ROCKIN & ROLLIN' GRANNIE STYLE

"Man, Grannie can smoke!", I said. My sister and I were lighting our own cigarettes, down the block from my Grandparents house in Georgia. They lived in the second to the last house on a dead-end street and bare, wild hills began where the sidewalk ended. It was beautiful. You could see for miles and miles. Looking over those hills at all the places we could explore, I was excited because our visit had just begun. We were breathing deep and taking it all in. "Tomorrow we are gonna have to climb down there." I said. "And did you notice Grannie has a pack of cigarettes, lighter and ashtray in like every room? She even has them in the bathroom!"

"I know that is crazy!" she said.

I marveled that my grandmother was such a committed smoker. She had been smoking for over forty years and exhaled through her nose like a steam engine. It was all very gruesome but we still loved our grandma. She spent all day, every day in a house dress. "What's a house dress?", you ask. Well, it's really just a glorified night gown that somehow older women in the seventies were able to wear anywhere. Apparently, Grandma didn't own a smoking jacket and being comfortable was rule number one.

Sadly, the first day we got there, we also took notice of her pill collection. We decided to try a few, without asking of course. The top of her refrigerator was literally covered with prescription pill bottles. There must've been fifty up there. It was a smorgasbord of stupidity of us to risk our lives with. Back then there was no internet to look up what each pill did or *could* do to kill you. We had to rely on what we heard about at school. So naturally we picked the ones that didn't kill us and because we didn't want to get caught, and we were careful not to take too many.

In case you don't realize it, let me just assure you that drugs don't make you smarter or more aware of anything except how stupid you're capable of being. After rolling joints on the table one day, we accidentally left one right there, smack dab in the middle of the table. It was there throughout dinner and my grandparents didn't even notice. It was all normal run of the mill chit chat at dinner.

We didn't talk much because we were petrified. But neither of my grandparents said a thing about the doobie in the middle of the white, eyelet tablecloth and dinner dishes. We, of course, were much too afraid to grab it along with another chicken leg. What struck me most was the way that no one said anything. They were old but not blind! It was denial extraordinaire. My grandfather didn't notice. My grandmother didn't notice. Her excuse could've been the medication but I have no idea why he didn't notice. We couldn't get our eyes off of it. It just laid there the whole time, in the middle of the table, between the chicken and the mashed potatoes. When dinner was over, we offered to clear the table faster than you can say zig zag.

My grandmother did get out of her housedress to go to town. We would go into the bathroom while she finished getting ready to go. It smelled like baby powder and wrinkles. Baby powder was a bathroom staple at that time. She sprinkled her pits and then was on to the next big task, adjusting her bra. She was very well endowed and we were just getting started. When she struggled to get all her stuff into her bra we just stood there with our mouths hanging open.

"What size is your bra Grandma?" I had to know.

"What? Well, heck." She was getting irritated as she was literally trying to stuff her stuff into the top of her bra. My sister and I glanced sideways at each other. Undoubtedly, we were thinking the exact same thing. Were ours going to get that big? I looked down and tried to imagine. I wondered if maybe I should try some of that magical powder.

"Ok girls, lets hit it!" Grandma was ready. We had waited while she put on bright red lipstick, polyester slacks and a frilly blouse, then off we went. She would drive down the hill at mach one in her American muscle car. Those nights, we weren't eating chicken with a side order of rolled stupidity, we had Mexican food. While at the restaurant, much to our surprise, Grandma really enjoyed the margaritas. She had a couple and drove us home again, while we held on for dear life. Grandma was scary but she was cool! Clearly the roots of many of the sins of the flesh that we were engaged in, ran deep. We stole her pills and went roller skating. She took pills, drank, and drove her souped up car home like a maniac. I hung on for dear life and tried not to toss my taquitos in zero to sixty seconds.

A few years later, when I was fifteen, my grandmother died of lung cancer. That was unexpected and felt like a huge loss to the family. It was at her house that all the Easter egg hunts happened. My grandparents didn't have a large house, just a three-bedroom, middle class home. But once a year about thirty-five of us would cram in to celebrate Easter and enjoy each other. We would sit and eat our dinner on whatever flat surface we could find, including handy metal TV trays. Then all of us kids would go out into the backyard looking for the hidden eggs.

    I loved those parties, but in the last couple years, I started to feel really emotional on the way home. I would leave those parties and feel extreme regret because I didn't express my love for my family. This really started to bother me. A year earlier I had met a girl from Arkansas. She was a new girl at our high school, and we became fast friends. She was warm and hugged people she cared about, including me. She had no hesitation or shame about hugging people. She just did it! I'd never experienced that, and now I had a strong desire to hug my family when leaving those family get-togethers. I knew I wouldn't see them again all year long and I loved them. It took me a couple of years to work my way up to actually hugging them. Do you know how that feels? Have you ever missed a moment to let your heart show? I invite you to take charge and join the revolution to be who you really want to be...a major hugger.

    Back at home, I realized we were not poor. My parents provided well. We were very middle class. My mother had gone back to work by then and she made dinner every night no matter how tired she was. And I know there were times when she was very tired. With so many children growing into adolescents and teenagers, she didn't have much peace. A few years before she would send all of us out to weed the garden and we would inevitably end up in a dirt clod fight. Somebody would accidentally, or intentionally, flick dirt on somebody else, and it was on. She would come out an hour later to find dirty, sweaty, complaining children and weeds still in the ground. We weren't much more helpful as we got older. But I soon began to take on all of my mother's problems. I would make dinner and clean the house and generally do whatever I could to make her life easier. I became a rescuer and a co-dependent enmeshed in her emotions, instead of my own.

I wonder sometimes about her spiritual walk. Did she read, "Love covers a multitude of sins" and decide to excuse what my step-father was doing? Did she hear Jesus say, "forgive him seventy times seven"? Did she believe that as a Christian woman her job was to be submissive to her husband? Did she pray for him? I don't know and I may never know. That has to be ok. God knows and I trust Him with those unanswered questions.

SURFS UP AMIGA

In eighth grade, I made an unexpected friend. Her name was Mary, and she was the most popular Latino girl at my junior high school. In that part of the suburbs, we had a mix of African Americans, Anglo Saxons (whites), Mexicans, Asians and who knows what. But Mary was Mexican. She was long haired, very pretty and very tough. Her older sister was known to have slammed another girl's head against the curb during a fight. Nobody messed with her. She was the best fighter and meanest Chola in the eighth grade and her little sister, Mary, my new friend, was the most feared and respected Chola in the eighth grade. I was the typical, white girl, full of herself, seventh grader. I was having fantasies about being a model, and having the whole world tell me how beautiful I was. That is embarrassing to admit but I'm sure I'm not the only one who had these ridiculous thoughts. I look back on that and can see how it is a tool of the devil to get us to focus on physical attributes that have absolutely nothing to do with who we really are, or our real worth. To make matters worse, I was very popular and successful at school. I had a lot of friends and a lot of boys who wanted to be my 'friend' too. Yeah, right. I had also labeled myself a 'surfer' although we were hundreds of miles from the ocean, it was the 'in' thing. We had the surfer shoes and clothes and feathered hair and we were "cool". If you recall, junior high is all about the cool. To prove ourselves, first we started with how we looked and then eventually moved on to who could kick who's butt. I was very good at shooting my mouth off, and I said that Cholas weren't so tough when they were alone. In a group they could fight but alone I was pretty sure I could win.

Next thing you know, I'm in the girl's locker room, and here comes Mary.

"Hey, blank, I heard you think you can kick my blank." Well, I just took the opportunity to clarify. Not many people stood up to Mary but I sure wasn't going to run. I had enough things making me angry at home, and older sisters that had been pulling my hair and picking on me for years, so I was ready to give it a go, verbally at least.

"No, I didn't say that. I said that I didn't think Cholas were as tough alone as they are in a group. I didn't say I could kick *you're blank*." Apparently, my answer was good enough for her because she immediately just started talking to me. She basically told me that I was right. Some of those girls weren't so tough, and not everybody likes to fight. I got the impression that Mary *had* to fight for many things in her life but she didn't want to. We became close friends immediately. At lunchtime, both groups of our friends were aghast that we would sneak off campus together, just the two of us to smoke pot. They would stand there with their hands on their hips and their mouths hanging open.

"Where you goin'?" one would ask, glaring at her.

"That's blankity blank you hangin' out with her you know," another would say.

"She's just a white blank." Three voices and six eyes giving me hard looks but we just kept on walking. Both her friends and mine expressed their distrust of the whole situation, but we were enjoying our new friendship. It felt different. It felt real. It felt good.

We would laugh and talk about everything. I would complain about my siblings. She told me about her older sisters all having babies as teenagers and dropping out of school and that she didn't want to do that. She wanted to finish school and go to college. She was only thirteen but had already decided that she wanted to be different than her sisters. I knew *exactly* how she felt. We would go back to school, to our separate groups, feeling like we had something special. Truthfully, in the midst of the height of peer pressure, we did. With each other, we were authentic, and didn't have to put up a front or be anything else. We were from different worlds but so much of how we felt was the same….it was refreshing.

A couple of years later, Mary did drop out of school and have a baby. My heart ached for her. I knew that she didn't get her dream. I went to visit her at her house and then my heart ached even more. The house had no flooring, very little furniture or decorations. No drapes or anything to make it look pretty. It looked poor. She must've seen the look on my face when I walked in because she started to explain. She said that her mom was working all the time that's why she wasn't home at seven o'clock at night, and her dad was an alcoholic. He even wandered through. His nose was red and misshapen. She said that was because he was always drunk and falling down.

My heart grew a new kind of compassion that day. I was face to face with what children of addicted parents endure. They are expected to get up and go to school without "cool" clothes. They are expected to visit with friends in a tiny room, with cockroaches running across the bed. I wondered how she slept there. It couldn't have been easy. The house was not dirty. There was so little in it that I could see that. I'm sure that food and gas were knocking the exterminator off the monthly budget, and that was that. My friend's family was undoubtedly struggling financially and her father was forcing her mother to be absent all the time. One sick parent, one absent, by necessity, equals one child without hope. She was talking about her boyfriend, and her little baby boy. I don't know where her baby was but he was not there. She was explaining to me how things were going but she had a sad look in her eyes. She remembered telling me about her dream and now she was trying to smile while telling me it had died. I told her about my step father molesting us. Then we did, what all tortured, young teens do, we made some bad decisions.

    This time we weren't smoking pot, we were smoking PCP. That is elephant tranquilizer that you sprinkle into a joint and smoke. There was a Cholo across the street, that was a little older than us, and he asked us if we wanted to smoke it. I had never done that before and didn't really want to but he was insistent that I buy one of his laced joints. So, I gave him the money, and he pulled out a joint to smoke. Then he did most of the smoking. I was really nervous so I was taking tiny hits and never felt anything. He was taking HUGE hits and trying to smoke the whole thing without us. I'm grateful for that now because the next thing you know he is literally 'flying' around the front yard. He's got his arms out flapping up and down. He's running around in circles, just flapping those skinny arms like mad and he starts squawking also known as screaming. His parents come out, and then their screaming. It sounds funny now but it was really rather shocking and scary. It was a bad scene, and gave me a glimpse of what Mary saw every day on her block. It was no wonder she didn't get her dream. I don't think many people around there did. You would have to be so focused that you couldn't even look around for fear of seeing something so discouraging it could take you off the path. Or seeing something so abnormal it would be funny if it weren't real. Like a grown man flapping his arms, pretending he's a bird while his parents are chasing him around waving their arms, and yelling at him to stop.

That visit taught me many things. I learned that my friend was more than where she lived or the clothes she wore. She was a beautiful, funny, sweet girl, and nothing else truly meant anything compared to that. Her worth was not measured in her home life or her family heritage.

When I hugged her goodbye, I wished I could've just taken her out of there. My home was bad but hers felt worse. My heart broke for her, and I learned not to judge people too harshly. We have no idea what they face every day.

"He has delivered us from the power of darkness and conveyed us into the kingdom of the Son of His love…" Colossians 1:13

Excerpt End

CHAPTER EIGHT

In writer's class that week, my friend was telling me about her boyfriend and I started remembering when I met my husband. It was in a room almost like this, I thought. I was going to twelve step meetings and had noticed him. Every week, I did my best to sit as close to him as possible. Unfortunately, I wasn't the only woman there who thought he was the cat's meow.

I remembered the first time we really connected. "Hey Lady, how are you?" He had snuck up behind me while I was daydreaming about him. How awesome is that? He looked at me and smiled, and man he was charming. I sucked in my breath.

"I'm great. How are you?" He was so attractive in his jeans and muscle shirt; I was having trouble focusing on his words. Then I couldn't get my eyes off his big, beautiful lips.

"Well, I was hoping you might be interested in going to church with me this Sunday?" Was this guy for real? Church? And he's this cute? It was all over. The answer was "Yes!".

Later in the week, I was simply ecstatic waiting for Sunday.

"Oooh you are singing!" My co-worker looked at me like I was a very annoying alien living on her planet.

"Sorry, I'm feeling fantastic and you can't stop me."

"Well, what's so great?" She was peering at me, and then spun me around to look at my face. She gasped as it dawned on her. "You're in love!" She smiled at me and tried to peer into my soul to confirm her suspicions.

"Oh, stop it! It's just a date. He invited me to go to church with him on Sunday. Do you want to come as the chaperone?" This wasn't a serious question so I didn't expect her answer. She went straight into Mother mode.

"Yes! As a matter of fact, absolutely yes! I need to do an inspection, and if I have to do it at nine am on Sunday, I'm there. Where did you meet this guy anyway?"

I put my hand up to stop her. "He's from the twelve step meetings I go to, and if you're coming to church, you better get your butt out of bed on time. I'm not gonna be late waiting for you. I really, really like this one."

"You know what, girlfreind? Asking you to go to church is either awesome or he's secretly a pervert cult leader trying to brainwash you, and by God we're gonna find out!" She raised her pointer finger to the sky in determination. I chuckled remembering, and now my friend in writing group, realized I hadn't been listening to her drone on about her boyfriend.

"Have you been listening to me? Now, I'm gonna have to start all over." No, please no, I thought. Lucky for me, class was starting and by the end of it, when I handed my excerpt over to a newbie, I hoped, in my daydream, I hadn't drooled on it.

Writers Group - Sharing Excerpt Seven
Genre: Semi-Autobiographical Memoir, Christian
Author: Jo Lisa Blossom

Sing for Sorrow and for Joy

Relationships are hard
We want to cut and run
We're already scarred
And to just be done
Sounds so easy after all
But to be like Christ
We have to go, have to call
And pay the price
Of hauling our pain
Back into the ring
We fight to forgive to gain
True joy as we sing
Praises of reconciliation to our God.

Hope

In the suffering
We are refined
It is how
We are designed
We need the hurt
Our face in the dirt
So we figure it out
What the healing's about
God is there to show us
What we need to see
He will grow us
Until we are free
To love and give
Without the sorrow
In Him we can live
With hope for tomorrow.

BAD TRIP

"Your father didn't molest you!" I said, staring at my friend in disbelief. We were back to the routine of walking up the street after we got out of Mr. Pinkston's seventh grade math class to my friend's back yard to smoke. "I know he's a jerk, and he smokes a disgusting brand of cigarettes, but *really*? Did he *molest* you? Because if you are joking, that's not funny!"

My best friend was serious in her answer, "Yes! The sicko is and I'm sick of it! My mother won't do anything. She's like a quiet little mouse that I just want to pound. I know exactly how you feel and I just want to beat the crud out of both of them." She lit her cigarette, well not hers exactly, but one of the disgusting brand, that we had stolen from her equally disgusting father. "Well," she said, "screw them both!" How common is this? I thought. Now I knew I wasn't the only one. But what to do? I had no disgusting idea.

"You can't go!" It was about a month later and this time my best friend was fuming. My step father wanted me to go on a business trip to California with him. I was young, and even though I was scared to be alone with him, I loved the beach. He told me how nice the beaches are, and said he'd be gone at work all day so I could just hang out on the beach. The hotel was right on the beach and it sounded great. I didn't really want to go by myself but my mom said it would be ok. My friend objected strongly more than once. In my twelve-year old mind, I foolishly thought she was jealous. Like most young people, at that age, I felt immune to the danger. I was lured into a tropical fantasy, so I went.

It was my first time on a plane. It was also my first time in a strange place with no adult supervision all day long. I was nervous a lot but I really loved being able to walk around wherever I wanted, and peruse the gift shops. It was a cute little coastal town and I loved it. The beach had very few people on it. Thinking back, it must've been in the off season, but it was still warm to me. The sand was beautiful and white. It was a special treat that there was a thick layer of tiny sea shells all over the beach. During that week long trip, I was a victim waiting to happen. But God kept me from even being approached by a stranger with ill intentions. My problem checked in with me.

 He took me to a different restaurant every night and some of them were very interesting. One was huge and looked like an old plantation building with pillars and shiny marble floors. They served a plate with mostly plate. The rest was small portions of delectable food. I still remember those five peas! They were amazing!

 The next night, we went to a dark little place with a woman from another country dancing on stage to music I'd never heard before. She had a sexy, colorful dress, and I'd never seen a show like that. It felt like I was soaking in some foreign culture, but by the time we ate dinner, I was barely speaking to him.

 He had held me down on the bed the night before, and scared me. He laughed at my fear, and I thought he was going to rape me. I knew then that he had intended to hurt me on this trip. But I was on my period, and I had made sure he knew it. I am convinced that is the only thing that saved me. I'm sure he didn't want any blood or screaming bringing attention to our room. In his arrogance I'm sure he believed he could manipulate me with all the nice dinners. He already knew I would be paralyzed, and unable to fight back, but he must've had doubt about being away from home, and me finding a way to tell someone. Or the maid asking about a bunch of blood on the sheets and a twelve-year old girl with an older man in the room.

 By the time we went home I was thoroughly done

with the tropical fantasy. I was back to the hard reality of being treated like a spouse when I was just a kid. The constant physical contact, flirting, lewd comments and surprise "just a peck" tongue kisses, and I was ready to explode. By the time we drove to the airport, I didn't even want to look at him.

SOMETHING WILD

Even in the midst of extreme dysfunction, there were many wonderful memories of childhood and specifically, things my parents did to bless our lives. I have been to many states and one other country. My parents liked to go on road trips. They showed us adventure and for that I am truly grateful.

In a campground on the rim of the Grand Canyon, we slept in sleeping bags, on cots, in the snow. Then we got up in the morning, and took cold showers in the campground showers. Little brown buildings with cold white tile and plastic shower curtains. We would gather our tiny bottles of shampoo, conditioner, bar soap in a plastic box and a towel. We would rush over hoping for hot water. Standing there, in cold bare feet realizing that there was no hot water, we quickly decided washing our hair was a luxury we would do without. A rinse would have to do. My sisters and I would rush through shivering with excitement at being somewhere new on an adventure, and freezing from the cold. Coming out of that bathroom with our long hair still dripping wet over our shoulders we would rush over to the sunny spot on the path and stand there waiting for the sunshine to warm us up. Our arms loaded with toothbrushes, towels and dirty clothes, we wore shorts under our sweatpants, anticipating more sunshine. Luckily, later that day, we got some. It wasn't enough to melt the snow but it felt good.

Amazingly, when we hiked down towards the bottom of the canyon, it got steadily warmer. It was fourteen miles down but it felt like less. The trail was well worn under our tennis shoes. It was dusty reddish brown, and the center of the path was ground into dust while the sides were covered with bigger and bigger rocks. The walls of the canyon were hues of red, orange and gold. The sky was incredibly blue with the sun beating down on the sage brush and cactus. We would almost run at the steeper places, and then once in a while we would find ourselves on both knees with our palms in the dirt, grinding us to a halt. Our knees would just give out because of the constant downhill travel, for so many miles.

We did not prepare for this hike. There were no months of training for this marathon. We just went because our parents said we were, but we were loving it. In the beginning we talked and talked, all about this fantastic adventure, and what our friends at school would think of this. This was amazing. Then slowly we began breathing harder and talking less. Then talking about how a donkey to ride on would be so awesome! Those people ahead of us riding on donkeys had no idea how lucky they were. Next time we'd have to talk our parents into that! Then bam! Down into the dirt again…our knees giving way to gravity. Our palms were skinned, our knees were burning and our legs were getting scratched up by the scruffy bushes along the path, but we marched on.

We finally made it all the way to the white sandy beach at the bottom and eighty-degree weather! No snow down here! It was dreamy! It was so beautiful down there. The river water was blue, and the beach was so clean leading up to the majestic, colorful walls going up, up, up to the clear, blue sky. We felt like Indians in an old western movie. We were there.

"I get the top bunk!" My sister shouted, throwing herself down on the bunk in front of us.

"I'll take this one!" Came the next voice.

"I'm over here!" And the next as we staked out claims.

The cabin was well worn. It had rustic wooden plank walls, wooden plank floors, and peeling green and brown paint. The windows had screens over them that were unusually dense, and we later learned that was to keep critters out. Critters! Yes! We wanted to know if we could bring some of our dinner back to the cabin. We wanted to put it on the window sill and call them over. No. Ranger Rob scared us straight right then and there.

"Listen, Campers, we've got a little problem down here with bears and raccoons. You can't leave any food out *anywhere*. We have to use mules or a helicopter to get anything and *everything* in or out of this canyon, so supplies are sparse. We'll feed you a good dinner but please don't feed the wildlife. Unless you want something wild and fuzzy sleeping in your cabin with you, please don't try to open the windows or sneak any mashed potatoes back for a midnight snack." He was standing at the front of two rows of picnic tables, outside, in the little clearing under the trees. The cabins and trails were surrounding this area and we could smell the dinner cooking. We looked at each other and smiled from ear to ear. This was major adventure time. Bears! Raccoons! We couldn't wait to get a glimpse of something wild. As if reading our minds, he then let the real cat out of the bag.

"I know some of you think 'Ah, those critters must be hungry. One little french fry won't hurt.', but let me tell you, these are *wild* animals. They don't know the difference between french fries and fingers that *smell* like french fries. Those critters have teeth, lots of 'em and claws. The last kid who fed one, lost part of his finger!"

Then he showed us his finger, bending it and making it look like it was missing a section. Okay. We got the hint. On this adventure you never knew what appendage you might need, so we got over wanting to feed anything.

After a long day of hiking, I was totally distracted smelling dinner cooking. I was sure I was literally starving. I imagined my stomach shriveling up. I quickly decided I was going to feed myself every last morsel.

"That raccoon can forget it. I'm not sharing!" Apparently, we all felt the same way because at the end of dinner nobody shoved a french fry in their pocket for the bears.

Later we got on our bunks but we could barely sleep watching that window screen and waiting for something furry to try to break in. I was worried I hadn't washed my hands enough, and the critters would gnaw my fingers off while I was sleeping. I was so tired, but I wasn't sure if I would sleep through it. Hours later, I woke up and I'm pretty sure I heard something scratching but I rolled over and went back to sleep. I figured it was probably just my brother with a wedgie.

We were very fortunate kids. We had a string of adventures. We got to catch fish with pieces of cheese tied to the end of string in the Samtee River. After we caught several and refused to throw them back, my sweet Mother dutifully fried them up for us to eat on paper plates. We got to water ski and make silly sand on the banks while we were still young enough to really, really love that. We survived a wind storm at Lake Weahu. That was one adventure I don't want to repeat.

I was thinking about that windstorm, and fingers, while watching the dust poof up under my tennis shoes as we hiked out of the Grand Canyon. That sandstorm snuck up on us. We were on the gorgeous, white sandy beach next to the Samtee, and it was very hot. I mean *very* hot. I was about seven and, all of us kids were just hanging out on the beach under the canopy eating barbequed chips and drinking root beer. We swam and swam. It was awesome. Then the wind began to blow…and blow and blow. In a matter of minutes, my parents started yelling and panic struck. Our stuff was flying away. I grabbed a raft and tried to hold onto it. This was back when rafts were made of canvas and had ropes around them. Those ropes grabbed around my fingers and the wind blew the raft in circle after circle squeezing my fingers tighter and tighter. The twisted rope was threatening to tear them off!

    My mom was yelling at us to get into the camper while my step father grabbed the dog and threw him in the boat. He took off while we scrambled for cover in the camper. By this time the sand was in our eyes, our mouths, ears, noses, hair and stinging our skin. We were terrified and all of us were crying. My fingers were bloody but attached. My sister had grabbed the raft and stopped the twisting just in time. She helped me untangle my fingers and then we started running for the camper. Nobody cared about the rafts anymore.

    "Get on the floor! All of you kids get down on the floor! Lay down on the floor!" My mother was yelling at us rapid fire. My mom was so smart. Many R.V.s flipped that day, but because she had us get onto the floor, ours did not. We were safe because of her quick thinking. I don't recall ever going back to recover our gear but I think it's safe to say some of it blew away never to be seen again. My fingers not included. Thank you, Jesus.

    A few years after the Grand Canyon, the family went to a little tourist spot in Nevada. Unfortunately, by this time we were not 'good' kids anymore. We were confused, angry, and we stole things. We just didn't care about being good anymore. I still feel bad about the jewelry we stole. I wish we would've gotten caught.

Once we almost did. My older brother wore a red bandana around his head, and I think with the long hair, the shop keeper decided to watch him. He got thrown out of the store while the rest of us acted like we didn't know him. The shop keeper threatened to call the cops but when my brother told him we were camped 'way over that hill', he decided to let him go with a shove in that direction. It was all very scary.

    We got back to the camper and laid out our loot of earrings and necklaces. We liked them but it was impossible to really like them. We felt like bad kids but we didn't want anybody to know that we were bad kids. The shove by that shop keeper signaled the end of our petty theft crime spree. Our collective conscience was no longer being seared into submission. We were ashamed.

    I am a firm believer that it is a great and glorious thing when people get caught; especially when they get caught as kids. This interrupts the downward spiral into sin. As corrupt humans, consequences are what we *need*. Guilt makes it possible to just do a "bad thing" and not become a "bad person". Repeated sin leaves an open door for the devil to exploit us. With repeated, unchecked sin, sooner or later, we believe we are a "bad person" and there is less and less room for repentance and change. It's too late.

    On that summer trip, for us, we decided not to ignore our guilt and fear. We were much too afraid of getting caught again. Sterling silver earrings shaped like tiny buffalos just didn't feel worth it.

"Then you will remember your evil ways and your deeds that were not good, and you will loathe yourselves for your iniquities…." Ezekiel 36:31

    The next day, we had another off the beaten path adventure, also known as a "cave tour". We went where few children had gone before. We walked, hiked and then even crawled on our bellies into the bowels of the earth. Complaining about claustrophobia, or screaming that the walls were closing in, was useless. There was no turning back. First of all, no one wanted to be called a chicken. Secondly if you stopped, and everyone else went on, you would be in the dark *alone*! We marched on, scraping our knees, getting dirty and wondering where in the heck we were going. We finally reached the end of the line. We were crowded in a cavern about the size of a living room with twelve-foot ceilings.

"OK Folks, you made it!" The tour guide was talking, and all I was doing was panting. I was starting to wonder if we were going to get a gold nugget or *something* for making it all the way into this filthy rat hole. But alas, no.

"Hold your candle cans up to your faces and blow out your candles." What? Is he out of his mind? I hesitated until my sister blew mine out for me. Apparently, this was the highlight of the tour. "Do you notice how incredibly dark it is?" Ranger Bob asked.

"Whoooooaaaaa. That's rad!" My brother crooned. Figures a boy would think this was cool. We had put our cans right up to our faces and couldn't see them. Then the tour guide told us to put our hands up to our noses and shockingly, we couldn't see those either. Then he relit our candles and it was back to squirming on our bellies in the dirt. We'd walk, then climb then squirm through the holes in the rock. It was petrifying and grueling at the same time. We survived, and lived, to tell about it. More importantly, now we know why earthworms crawl in packs. It's a lonely, scary, cold and *dark* world living in the dirt. No thank you.

Excerpt End

CHAPTER NINE

It was writer's group poetry reading night again. I tried to think Godly thoughts while I listened to others share. I was already feeling a little dark. But now it was time for Eddie to read. He liked to call himself "AKA Eddie A. Poe Reincarnate". Because I had functioning nostrils, and eyes in my head, I knew he was living up to his self- proclaimed title. If he *was* the reincarnated Edgar Allen Poe, he was once again here as a depressed alcoholic who had no running water and rarely bathed. I had been praying for him so in spite of my dark expectations, I was relieved that his poetry turned out to be kind of fun.

The No Love Shove

Your caboose is cooked
Yeah, tender and ready to go
get the bucket
You licked clean of tears and spilt milk
The time's right
Your bird's been plucked
Dry of feathers and pain
Your sass is grass
Waiting to grow
On your grave

So go ride
Up the creek
Without a saddle
Grin and barely
Get where you're going
That's the only way to fly
A knot at the end of your rope

No Kiss Goodbye

I suppose I am getting
Just what I deserve
All the pain I've inflicted
Is now hitting me in the face.
I suppose I'll get over it.
The anger surfaces and turns
Into an ugly sort of determination.
I'm going to leave here
And when I do I will
Never turn around
And I surely will not
Kiss anyone goodbye.

    I could totally relate to his last poem and I figured he's letting it out, so he might be scary but I think he's going to be ok. I took a deep breath, and held it as I gave him a big hug and a smile. Then I handed him my latest excerpt. In the back of my mind, I hoped my writing wasn't too depressing, and he heard Jesus calling him out of the dark side into the marvelous light.

"But you are a chosen generation, a royal priesthood, a holy nation, His own special people, that you may proclaim the praises of Him who called you

out of darkness into His marvelous light."   1 Peter 2:9

Writers Group - Sharing Excerpt Eight
Genre: Semi-Autobiographical Memoir, Christian
Author: Jo Lisa Blossom

CASHING IN OUR CHIPS

"She's lying! She did this! This is her fault!" My stepfather yelled.

It was the last trip we ever took as a family, and it started with a bang. Sixteen hours earlier we had all piled into the camper excited about going across country. In the midst of all the unrest, we needed a change of scenery. We were on our way to see family in North Carolina. We were told it was green and lush and peaceful. Excited, we packed our sleeping bags, our toothbrushes and climbed in the old blue camper with the flowered curtains and cushions. We laid up on the overhead above the cab and talked about the injustice of it all. We were forced into a small space all together and the results were not what my parents had planned. Our little committee meeting turned into a mutiny. By the time we got to the hotel with the big red neon 'vacancy' sign we were nervous but determined. We had voted.

"Let's tell Anthony."

Anthony was a family friend who seemed trustworthy. He was sort of like an uncle to us. He was warm and friendly. Later we realized that he was mostly friendly with the girls and had his own issues. But at that point, we needed *somebody*. An hour later, here we were. All of us kids were huddled on one end of the hotel room with my step father on the other. Anthony was glaring at my step-father, who quickly realized that he was on his own in this confrontation. He was pointing his bony finger and yelling. His eyes were bulging in the middle of his beet red face and he was *mad*. He was trying to take out the leader, blaming one of my older siblings. No admitting anything. Nothing but a wagging finger, in the face of a sixteen year old, who was already taking the brunt of the abuse. In our first group act of defiance, we stood strong, and ready to pounce. But we never got the chance. My step father knew better than to resort to violence against this miniature mob. He did not want the police called.

So there in this little gambling town in the desert, we had just cashed in our chips. But there, standing on that hideous green carpet, leaning against a dark paneled wall, I felt so scared, and then hopeless. We came to realize that our bravery didn't help us hit the jackpot, like we had hoped. We were still fighting this fight alone. We had counted on Anthony but he wasn't the obnoxious hero we wanted him to be. No one was admitting anything, and clearly there was no adult who was going to get up in my step father's beet red face. He yelled and the other two adults in the room let him.

"We are telling the truth, Dad!", "She's not a liar.", "You know it!", "*You're* a liar!"

Our chorus of small voices were met with a loud, booming, "You better watch your mouths!" as he made two steps towards us. We were already in a corner, and the only one who stepped up to meet him was my brave older brother. To our surprise, my mother had already lost her cool with my brother one day, and beat him into the corner. He never lifted a hand to fight my mother that day but now it was our dad. He was daring the old man to make a move. For a moment, my step-father stood there with clenched fists and eyes ablaze, but then he just stormed past us, and out the door. We looked around at each other. We were in a strange city, a strange room, and had just experienced a horrible disappointment. My mother sat on the edge of the bed, with Anthony's arm around her. She looked like she was in shock but she was still silent.

The elephant in the room got some attention but it wasn't nearly enough. No one said they were sorry. No one admitted anything. No one demanded change. No one threatened or promised divorce. No one got arrested, and no one was dead. No one was going to save us.

"C'mon let's go." We headed out the door into the dark night. Even then God was comforting us. We were not alone. We had each other.

"Bear ye one another's burdens and so fulfill the law of Christ." Galatians 6:2

Later that night we went back to the hotel and made our way to the hot tub. We were on vacation, right? I was told years later that Anthony had a heart attack, right next to me in that hot tub. Apparently, he had to be pulled out of the water and 911 called. He was taken by ambulance to the hospital. I was incredulous to hear of this.

"Don't you remember? You were right there!" my sister said.

"No, I don't remember." I answered. I've tried to remember that but to this day I have no recollection of that part of the night. It was not the first or last time that the emotional trauma proved to be too much. God protected me by allowing me to completely block it out. It was a gift so I could go on. A person can only take so much, and my Father God decided when I'd had enough. I am grateful for that.

The next day none of us were talking much. We were like zombies headed east. We packed our suitcases, only half brushed our teeth, and hung onto our pillows. Where we were going on the map and as a family, we had no idea. We found out soon enough.

    Next, we stopped at the home of a distant relative that we'd never heard of before. That was an eye-opening experience. We lived in the suburbs, and we had never really been in this much nature before. This was real country living. We were several states away now and it was amazing to me that people lived in such a beautiful place. Their house was the only one around in sight! It was white, two story with pillars and French doors. The upstairs bedroom was long and narrow, with beds in little alcoves, in the walls. The carpet was old swirly floral patterns and the whole house felt southern. I loved it. After lunch we tromped through a huge corn field to come out right next to a bubbling brook. We walked through a meadow full of little white flowers and over beautiful green rolling hills. We saw a red fox and walked through the deep green woods. For us suburb kids, it was exhilarating.

    A few days later was our real destination, another relative's home in South Carolina. It was my mother's great uncle, and I remember when we arrived. It was late and way past dark. We pulled up in the driveway, and a big man came out of the front door. Apparently, he wasn't sure who it was. I don't think his wife had told him we were coming. He came up to my mother real slow, peering at her in the dark. She just stood there smiling and waiting and when he finally recognized her, he bellowed. "It's you!" We watched out the window of the camper as he picked her up in a big bear hug, spinning her around before putting her down. I've never seen my mom smile so big. After all she'd been through in the last week, this was worth the trip. A long-lost relative loved her, and was simply thrilled to see her. God had not forgotten her, and neither had her great uncle.

    We made it through that trip by smoking a lot of

pot with our new found cousins and listening to rock music on an old cassette deck over and over for hours. It was such a beautiful place that it was easy to forget the mess we were in. They had a picturesque barn that looked just like the old pictures. On the top floor it actually had a hay loft with a rope swing. Wild bunnies lived underneath the barn, and we squealed with delight when the cute little baby rabbits hopped in and out. They had pasture on one side of the road, pasture on the other and deep woods everywhere else. The road was dirt and there was only one other house in view, and it was our second uncle and aunt once removed or whatever. They had a son in his twenties and he had HUGE pot plants in the backyard. I had never seen one and this was like a Christmas tree farm but it was weed. His parents were very elderly, and probably had not walked back there in years and if they did now, they couldn't see well enough to realize those weren't regular backyard bushes. I don't think they had any clue that they were engaged in illegal activity.

That trip was the one and only time I've ever seen my mother drunk. She left with her cousin and came back sloshed. She found a fly swatter somewhere and proceeded to smack us all on the head with it.

"You all need a swat! Just a bunch of bugs!" Laughing she thought this was a fun game. We couldn't believe our mild-mannered mother was drinking, much less totally sloshed.

By the time we got home from that summer trip, it was more of the same. That one-time drinking binge didn't make alcohol "liquid courage" for my mother.

"You're pretty!" We were standing in line for an amusement park and my stepdad turned to me and told me I was pretty. He said it like he'd never noticed before. How could that be? I still don't know. The abuser is so demon driven that I think they rarely 'see' their victims as the human beings they are. They are so caught up in the self-centered drive to meet their own perverse need, that they are blinded to their own humanity. Classmates and other people had been telling me I was pretty for years. Under different circumstances, that compliment would've made me feel good about myself, but in that case, I just stood there with my mouth hanging open wondering why he'd never noticed before. Like every young girl I longed to be loved and admired by my Daddy.

Before the transformation of Christ occurs, the abused person wants so badly to be loved, wants things to be right, that we put amazing amounts of energy into denial of truth. As I got older, I would waffle back and forth between the rage and the romantic notion of a dream that just wasn't. I'd go from the hate one moment to the desire to be loved the next, and neither one felt good. The blind desire to be loved and the hate don't last. While I waffled back and forth, the dark powers of the world continually put thoughts into my head, telling me "You're a failure" or "You're weak". I instinctively knew that I wasn't well. Perhaps this is why the Lord tells us not to be 'double-minded'. Waffling back and forth is not healthy. In order to work up the courage to act we need to be absolutely sure about why we are doing what we are doing. In order to hold a boundary, border or hang onto our faith, we need to be sure. We need the confidence to stand for what we know is truth and reject the falsehood the devil tries to distract us with. It's better to accept reality, even when it's hard.

"A double-minded man is unstable in all his ways."
James 1:8

I did not have a "Daddy" on earth and I never would. I also did not have an emotionally healthy mother. Neither could truly 'see' me. I was more than "pretty" but they could not see any of it. They were emotionally unavailable and caught up in their own problems and demon driven desires.

As I grew, I found that I also had to accept that I had made many mistakes on my own. I could not blame all that was wrong in my life on my parent's issues.

Standing in the kitchen, my mother was looking out the front window at the neighbor's house. "They are dealing drugs over there. That's just way too many people hanging around all the time", she said.

At fifteen, I sensed it was time to confess about my own drug use. "Mom, I've been doing cocaine." She turned and looked at me and then slowly turned back to cutting up the chicken.

"I don't want to know", she said. What?! My attempt at shock and awe had failed. My attempt at shaking her out of her stupor of denial, went unsatisfied. I wanted her to tell me to stop. I wanted her to turn to me, grab me by the shoulders and hug me tightly. I wanted her to look me in the eye and tell me she was proud of me for confessing. I wanted her to ask me what she could do to help. I desperately needed her to love me and pray with me and be a healthy, spiritual leader at that moment. But she never prayed with us and usually advice was limited. At that moment it was clear she didn't have anything else to say. She wouldn't even look at me. So the only thing I got was callous indifference and shame.

She wouldn't tell me to stop destroying myself, but who told me to start? I had to accept the truth that *I* was responsible. If I wanted positive change, it was up to me. At that moment, my mother showed me that she was not available to help. I realized that I was doing "adult" things, and I was on my own. I was growing away from my parents and realizing my choices to do wrong were my own. I realized that I may once have been able to go to my mother for help for some things but not the hard things. She may have helped me buy school clothes or get a car, but she wasn't there to help me out of the pit of my sin. She wasn't there to talk to about it. She wasn't there to hold my hand and pray. She wasn't there to ground me or put me on restriction. She wasn't there.

Later I read an excellent book about sexual abuse and what it does to people emotionally. If you've been the victim of abuse, read the bible. Then read a book about sexual abuse and it's affects. I learned what I already knew but didn't understand. Victims feel overwhelmingly powerless and alone. I devoured that book. I was so relieved to be understood. I was no longer alone and in fact I was "normal". I was doing what every normal victim does. But I refuse to be a "victim" forever. There is a movement against being a 'victim' in today's world. But what if you *were* a victim? Do you just act like you weren't? No, you admit that yes, what others did to you is wrong, it hurt, and denying it won't help. It is essential to admit the truth, work through the pain and then decide that being a 'victim' is not going to *define* you.

As for the perpetrator, in my experience, molesters don't always happen overnight. For some it may take a long time before they give in to what must be a relentless temptation. It probably takes most of them a long time to get to the point that they actually hurt a child. I believe molesters have all been molested but those who continue the pattern are those who have had too much hurt happen in their lives. They suffer more abuse by more people or they grow up and get their hearts broken by grown women. They are damaged emotionally so their attempts at long term, successful relationships fail. Eventually they give up trying and give in to just *taking* what they need, to numb their pain. They also do not pursue God. Perhaps they feel unworthy. Their only real hope they have of breaking the pattern of abuse is a relationship with Jesus Christ. No amount of behavior modification therapy can address the spiritual need, and help them heal. Their soul needs God. He and His Word can help them see themselves and other human beings as having value and being worthy of love and respect. They can forgive and love themselves again. They can defuse the demonic influences and have self-control.

"But the fruit of the Spirit is love, joy, peace, patience, kindness, goodness, faithfulness, [23] gentleness and self-control. Against such things there is no law. [24] Those who belong to Christ Jesus have crucified the sinful nature with its passions and desires. [25] Since we live by the Spirit, let us keep in step with the Spirit." Galatians 5:22-25

Without seeking God's help, sometimes an abused person will, without conscious effort, gravitate towards another abused person. Sometimes that abused person takes the opposite, but equally abusive route of becoming an enabler of their sin. Because of the enabler's own brokenness, they lose, or never had, any resolve to protect their children or themselves. The enabler regresses to their own abuse, and cannot stand up to the manipulative, aggressive, deceptive abuser in their house. The abuser engages in pornography addiction, and other things that over time cause their conscience to be "seared". Their compulsive and impulsive behavior takes over, and they lose all self-control. The enabler may, or may not, put up protest for a while but eventually instead of taking a stand, they give up completely. They may be sinking deeper into a depression over time, and of course, this helps the abuser. The abuser may also become hopeless and depressed. So, the abuser and the enabler, who are both "victims" go unhealed and eventually commit crimes and create more victims. They become the person they hate. They become the abusers.

"Now the Spirit speaketh expressly, that in the latter times some shall depart from the faith, giving heed to seducing spirits, and doctrines of devils; speaking lies in hypocrisy; having their conscience seared with a hot iron…" 1 Timothy 4:1-2

"Can you stop that please?" I was in the bathroom, putting on make-up, and my stepfather had reached in and flipped the switch. Reaching out I turned the light back on while he laughed.

"What's the matter you can't see your sexy self in the dark?" Ugh. I hated his games, and he was relentless. He did this one with the light switch every chance he got. He laughed but it was never funny. In the face of my tormenter, I was unable to really fight back. He would do juvenile things for attention, and it was emotional abuse. Every time it happened, I would feel like I was four years old and unable to speak. My unexpressed rage would deepen with every incident. Turning off the light might seem petty but when it goes on over, and over it becomes abuse. He knew that I was holding onto a lot of anger, and was paralyzed by unnatural fear. He seemed to be trying to push me into expressing it, and enjoying the fact that I couldn't. He could get away with everything. He knew, and I knew and the demons knew. They just kept whispering into his mind while they were screaming into mine.

Later that year, I was surprised when I walked into our

garage.

"What is that?" I asked. I looked down and saw that my foster sister had a needle and she was digging into her flesh with it.

"It's a star and it means that when I'm fifteen, I'm going to commit suicide."

"What? That's not right. You shouldn't be doing that."

"It's just a symbol. It's just a reminder. I feel like that's going to happen and I need something to remind me of it."

"I think you should stop it." She looked up at me irritated for a second and then went back to scratching.

"Doesn't it hurt?" I asked.

"Not really. Do you want to try it? Do you want a tattoo?" She tried to entice me to join her and I foolishly took the bait.

"Well… I do like butterflies."

"You can try it after me. You can put a little butterfly on your ankle or something."

"I'll do it, but it's not going to have anything to do with committing suicide. I think you should stop talking like that." This time she didn't answer or look up, she just kept digging that needle into her flesh making another triangle on her bloody star.

We were self-destructive and we had discovered home-made tattoos. We knew we were supposed to be using indian ink but we didn't have any. We didn't know where to get any. We just used a needle and some ink we'd found for a fountain pen. Somebody said it was indian ink but we didn't know. And we started making symbols on our skin. It could've been beautiful. It could've been art. It could've been just another decoration, but it hurt. We bled. In reality it was just another reminder that we were alive. We could still feel physical pain. We acted like we couldn't really feel it, but we could.

With all that was going on we had become numb to a lot. We spent a lot of time using and drinking whatever was in front of us to try to stay numb. We were trying desperately to forget what was happening. We felt so helpless and powerless. But this little needle and this little symbol and this little thing of ink reminded us that yes, we were alive. We could still do something rebellious our parents wouldn't like. They didn't have complete control of us. We could decide what was good and bad and we decided digging into our flesh with a needle was good. But in reality, it was just another symptom of the unworthiness we felt. We were just garbage. Nobody really wanted us. Nobody really fought for us and we just didn't want to feel anything. But this reminded us that we still could. We had a little bit of hope somewhere that we could do something about something. We could choose when to hurt and how much. We could create the scars. We could be in control of what happened to our bodies.

KISS ME GOODBYE FOREVER

"Bye Mom."

"Bye, Baby." I reached over to give my mom a kiss before I left the house. She was sitting next to my step father on the couch, so next I leaned over to give him a kiss. Our lips met and he shoved his tongue into my mouth. I lurched back in shock. This was not the first time he had done this and each time I responded the same way. Disgusted I quickly got away as fast as I could. I felt physically sick. I didn't look back and I didn't look at my mom. I just kept my head down and kept walking towards the front door in shame.

*"**Fathers, provoke not your children to anger, lest they***

be discouraged." ***Colossians 3:21***

For many people who knew my step father, this book will probably be a shock. My heart goes out to them, but the truth is the truth. I would have done almost *anything* to have a better father, a well father. I spent years desperately trying to have just that. I would pretend everything was ok because everybody else was acting like it was. This kiss goodbye scenario happened over and over. I would be mad for a couple of weeks and refuse to give him a kiss. Then somehow, I would rationalize and be so hopeful and so full of longing to have a "Dad" that I would try again. I never understood how he had the nerve to pull that, in front of my mother. It never occurred to me to ask her why she never did anything about it. At that point, I had not 'woken up' to my mother's responsibility in the situation and I just accepted my mother's lack of action and her inability to do anything. She needed us to handle him because she couldn't. I was waiting for her to help me and at the same time making excuses for her. So, I blamed him…and myself.

Insanity- extreme foolishness or irrationality, doing the same thing over and over and expecting different results

Thirteen was the year of the complete loss of innocence. We had told on our step father, started smoking pot and felt completely out of place everywhere. I was lost. I had the good side of my life, and I had the bad side trying to completely take over. This was the seventies and deck shoes in different colors were the rage. Pooka shell necklaces and hanging roach clips with raccoon tails off the back of bell bottom pants was rock and roll. Feathered hair and roller skating was the highlight of our week. But eventually being Editor-in-Chief of the school newspaper, popular and pretty wasn't enough to distract me from my home life. I was lost and in pain.

I had a boyfriend I loved for about seven months. It was an all- out record. We broke up because he wanted me to sleep with him and I said no. But by mid-summer, I was a multi-substance abuser. Whatever everybody else was using, I was using, no questions asked. The sexual sin at home had opened the door for the devil. It didn't matter that it was not *my* sin or that I was the victim. Sexual sin opens the door to shame. I was carrying around shame that didn't belong to me but I didn't know that at the time. This is why victims don't talk about it. The devil, that the bible calls 'the accuser' will put thoughts in the victim's head. "This is your fault. You made this happen. No one is going to like you if they find out what you've done. You should've known better." Sometimes the abuser actually manipulates the victim with similar statements. In that case, it's the double whammy. The 'accuser' and the abuser unknowingly work together on the victim's state of mind. The victim doesn't realize they are a victim. They think they are responsible and see themselves as guilty participants.

Accuse- to charge with fault or offense, blame

Abuse- to use to bad effect or for a bad purpose; misuse

For me, shame was a constant companion. In the morning I would get dressed and act normal. But when I went out with my older friends, drug and alcohol use made me vulnerable to whatever came by. One night an older guy who liked me somehow had me alone, in a dark bedroom. I let him have his way. It was early in the morning, after drinking alcohol and taking LSD. He wanted what he wanted, and I really didn't even object much. All my usual defenses were nearly non-existent. But on the way home, in the light of day, in the back of my friend's car, I almost puked. I was so ashamed that I was literally sick. I knew I had sinned. "Sin" wasn't the word I was hearing in my head but that's what it was. I knew that I had done terribly wrong, and there was no going back. I knew that waiting until marriage is what decent people did. The only thing my mom ever said was 'keep your pants on'. Simple. And I failed.

    As a young girl who thought she was grown up, I didn't make the connection between being abused, and letting that boy have his way. I felt like this time I was completely at fault, and I was mad at myself for not telling him no. The boyfriend I had really loved, before this one had pressured me to have sex for months and I finally broke up with him over it. This was different than being abused. I wanted to remain pure until marriage with a boy I loved. Wasn't that the "right" thing to do? I separated what was being done to me against my will and what I chose to do in a romantic relationship. For me, there was no connection between the two. I knew what was happening to me at home was wrong and I wanted to do what was right. Now drugs and alcohol had become part of the mix and I had no fight left. I didn't know how to fight in the here and now. I could only object verbally to a boy but if he was physically in front of me, I never learned how to say "no". I was conditioned by the abuse to just go along with it.

    Needless to say. I got over my disgust and continued to see that boy. Maybe he would marry me someday, right? It was similar to second grade when my 'boyfriend' blew milk through his nose laughing at the lunch table. I was mortified at first but as I wiped the milk off my cheek, I noticed how cute he was when he was laughing really hard. From that moment on, I was mesmerized. I overlooked a lot so I could always have one of these mythical creatures, that females have been enduring gut wrenching hardships to find, and bring home, for centuries…I had to have one….a boyfriend….

This boyfriend who had taken my virginity was a couple of years older than me and he really did like me. We would spend hours on the phone talking about everything. Then when I was in the height of adolescent love, another bomb went off. He turned out to be bisexual. He was a hair dresser, a high school drop-out, and had several past relationships with gay men. I did not know this at fourteen. I felt like we were in love. But somehow our intimate encounters were less than what I thought love was supposed to feel like. I was there but I wasn't being loved.

Later he began treating me very badly and cheated on me with another girl in our group. One day, I built up the courage to ask him about his Jeckyl and Hyde routine. I asked him, "Don, why do you treat me so good some days and so very badly the next?'

'Guess', he answered.

I did without thinking. The words just came out of my mouth. "You're in love with Eddie."

"Yes", he confessed. He admitted what in my heart, I already knew. He didn't love me. We weren't getting married just because we were having sex. He wasn't my soul mate. I had crossed the line that all the girls in my group had already crossed. There was no going back. We were all lost and trying to change how we felt inside. Sex was the same thing drugs and alcohol were, another failed coping mechanism. Sex didn't really mean forever. It didn't even mean an entire summer. It pretty much meant nothing as soon as someone more interesting came along.

I can see now that he was the first of several intimate encounters that could have had deadly consequences for me. This was not many years after AIDS was discovered. Gay people were dying. Now I'd had sex with him unprotected. Woops.

Years later I saw that guy again. It was late at night in a diner. He was with another guy who was dressed just like him in red and black leather. He was mute and quite obviously under the control of the guy he was with. His eyes looked bloodshot and sad. His face was blank and I could see that he was very thin. He was not even allowed to wave back or respond to my conversation. They left their half-eaten meal behind as his 'boyfriend' literally shoved him out the door, back into the night and away from me with my mouth hanging open, waiting for a response. My friend Eddie, (of all people), and I just looked at each other in shock. "What was that?", I asked.

"That was sad, man, really sad." Eddie, who was never bi-sexual and had confessed that he'd always been in love with me, looked down and shook his head. "Wow. I guess he's not in love with either of us anymore."

JOIN THE RESISTANCE

"Get in the car young lady!" My friend's mom was yelling at her daughter in my front yard. It was my freshman year of high school and my parents were out of town, so the party was at my house. Her mom had somehow found out where her daughter was and had come to get her. She was not happy. I was standing on the porch feeling tipsy, rebellious and mouthy. I was about to yell at that old lady to take a chill pill, but before I could express myself, my friend got in the car, and her mom slapped her across the face. That hurt. Suddenly I was speechless. I realized at that moment that I was the "bad kid". I was the person her mom had warned her about. She *hurt* her daughter because of *me*. I was the bad influence, the troubled girl, the person nobody's mom wanted their kid to be friends with. I felt bad for my friend and I felt bad for me. "What a blank!" With no coping skills I turned on my heel and went back inside cussing and complaining.

    I had my first brush with the law about a year later. "Get out of the car young lady!" Oh great. The police were shining their light, in the back window, on my new boyfriend and I. We were in the backseat of his car and in the midst of making some bad physical decisions. It was dark and we were parked on the street about a mile from home. Eventually the police called my stepdad. How ironic that the person modeling exceedingly bad moral decisions showed up to be the "responsible" party. I would've laughed out loud except I was pretty sure they would slap the cuffs on me just for effect. That would happen later.

Rebellion- resistance to or defiance of any authority, control, or tradition

Excerpt End

CHAPTER TEN

It was Wednesday and I really needed to get my excerpt ready for tonight's class. Man, I've got to focus!

"Honey what are you doing?" My husband had just come up and slithered his arms around my neck for a side hug while I was click clacking on the keyboard, paying no attention. Now I felt guilty for ignoring his obvious need for affection.

"I'm so sorry, do you need a hug? Come here, give me a two-armer."

"No Sweetheart, I was trying to choke you out just to see if you'd notice." He said with a big smile.

This week along with the regular excerpt of our book that we had to share, we also had to share a "faith statement". A thoughtful, reflective statement about your faith. Easy peasy, I thought. I love Jesus and Jesus loves me.

Writers Group - Sharing Excerpt Nine
Genre: Semi-Autobiographical Memoir, Christian
Author: Jo Lisa Blossom

Fractured Family

An eye like broken glass
Sees the past and is shattered
Circling the iris and the drain with our pain
Father, mother, sister, brother

How do I get you out of my head
So the vision is mine again?
Maybe that's not how God wants it
Maybe He wants us to love each other
Forever…broken, beautiful and blessed.

Smash The Glass

How do you get past the past?
I don't know.
How do you see the glass
Half full or half empty
Dirty or grimy
Polished or shiny?
I don't know.
How do you break the hold
That sorrow has on your heart?
I don't know
She's The King's wife
Waving her wand in anger.
You can feel the danger
Of buying into the ploy
Crushing the joy
Is the by product
Of her playing the victim
We all want to help
Make it all better
When there is no effort
From her on the throne
Just lots of casual talking
About how grand the kingdom is
When really, we are all crying
dying or dead.

Free Tokens

Why are you
the way
you
are?
Why do
you scream
and cry
and forget
dignity?
Did someone
hurt you
so bad
you cannot
reason?
Who
gave you
permission
to talk
like that?
Who said
it was ok?
Did the
Lord?
Did I?
No.
Forgiveness
is
yours
but
the
free tokens
you
had
are gone.

BACK STREETS TO BIKERS

"Hey let's go to Ken and Shawn's'. My best friend was trying to talk me into going out. It was Friday night and during this phase of life, I spent a lot of time hanging out with my best friend. We were bored and lonely so we ended up out partying somewhere every weekend. The majority of that summer we spent hanging out with a couple of biker friends. They were nice enough. They were typical middle-class, middle age bikers. They were middle-age to us. Looking back, I think they were in their thirties. Pretty harmless. They had jobs and were somewhat ecstatic to have a couple of young cute chicks hanging around. One biker was a little scary. When his teenage son mouthed off, he used a stun gun on him… a standard biker parenting technique. Besides that, these guys were ok. They weren't in an official gang, but they were living the biker dream. They would park their hogs in the living room, brag about scraping the stucco off the ceiling, bagging it up and selling it as high-grade meth to low IQ drug addicts. They always had meth and had been using so long they were smart enough not to snort or inject drugs. No, they were functional addicts and onto the more sophisticated methods of using, namely putting meth in their morning coffee. Breakfast of champions? Uh no.

At first the roaring engines and the cool place to hang out felt great. It was exciting to have the wind blowing our hair back and roaring around. We were always welcome and it was fun. On top of that, there were no parents showing up and making us feel bad about corrupting their daughters. Eventually though, my feelings began to turn.

"Nah, I don't want to go."

"What? Come on they are going to the canyons to see a band and want us to come."

"We won't be able to get in", I replied.

"Got it covered! They know the owner and he already said he'd take their word for it that we are twenty-one", she looked at me smiling. It looked like I was the only party pooper.

"Ok, but this is it. I just don't want to stay all night. I've got stuff to do tomorrow." I didn't have anything to do except recover from my hangover, and I knew my words meant nothing. For several weekends my resolve had failed. I wanted to be wanted, and I sure didn't want to stay home with my step-father lurking around, but my problem with these bikers is that I didn't want to go there anymore either. But somehow, I would find myself back on their couch drinking a beer, snorting a line, over and over. I started to get physically ill just thinking about it. The problem was that I hated, and I mean *hated* staying up all night. The feeling I would get when the sun was coming up AGAIN, and I was still awake, was the epitome of my self-loathing. I failed again. It signified my lack of control, my lack of hope, my spiral into drug addiction that I could no longer manage. It's hard to pretend you are still doing ok, and can quit anytime, when you just stayed up all night *again*. We would party all night, and wonder why we felt like walking death the next morning. I know how Paul of the bible felt. Even though the thorn in my side was self-inflicted.

"So the trouble is not with the law, for it is spiritual and good. The trouble is with me, for I am all too human, a slave to sin. I don't really understand myself, for I want to do what is right. but I don't do it. Instead, I do what I hate." Romans 7:14-15

THE BIG LIE

The lie I began to believe as a young girl was that I was "not worth it." I was not worth my mother fighting for us. I was not worth my step-father going to counseling. I was not worth the police arresting him and protecting us. I was not worth it to myself since I could not avoid self-destruction.

It is a scheme of the enemy of our souls, satan, to lie to us. If he can get us to believe a lie about ourselves, he can lead us down to destruction and eventual suicide. The lie can feel like it is part of us. It can make us believe something false about the core of who we are. Couple that with the fact that we are made of dirt and drawn down to hell instead of up to heaven and we barely stand a chance. We have to fight against the lies of the enemy. If what we believe is not something good then it is a lie. Such a simple test for every thought. Is what I'm thinking about good? Good *for* me? Something good *about* me? Good for my life? Good about others?

Ask yourself, "What lie do I believe right now?" Wait for God to tell you and then reject it! Say out loud, "I reject the lie that says "…..", in Jesus name!" Determine never to believe another lie. For every thought, use the simple test…*is it good*?

"... He, (satan), was a murderer from the beginning, not holding to the truth, for there is no truth in him. When he lies, he speaks his native language, for he is a liar and the father of lies." John 8:44

DOCTOR VOODOO

There were many years that I wanted to make both my parents pay for the pain we endured. At that point, I had no understanding whatsoever of my mom's lack of action. I blamed her as much as I blamed my step-father and for a while the drive to make them pay almost consumed me. I was so determined to stop the hurt that I thought, like many of us do, at some point, that if I just got the truth out there loud enough, they would change. If I made them feel the hurt that I was experiencing they would have to change. I was wrong. I have come to realize that the only time people truly change is through the transformative work of the Holy Spirit. Only God can cause major change in a person. He does it all the time. He has done it in me.

No one will ever change because we want them to or we present a good case or even irrefutable evidence. Only God changes the hearts of humans, and He does it in His time. We can plant seeds of information, and if we do so with love, they may take root, but how the crop comes up has nothing to do with us. They can choose not to water the roots. I know that now but back then I was determined that I could cause change. I was desperate to cause change. My methods to cause change were not loving. They were angry and ineffective.

One of the ways that I tried to affect change was to make up posters that I hung around my parent's neighborhood, up and down the driveway of their church and at random places they went. One of the posters had a photo of my step-father, with his arm around my siblings and I, as children. lying in bed with him. This could have been an innocent thing. Lots of people snuggle with their kids but unfortunately, this photo said it all for me. I added big text. "Warning This Man Is a Child Molester".

Another poster named my mother as an "Accessory to Child Abuse". I was brutal in my campaign and it was the result of years and years of pain. The boiling point had arrived. For months and months, I would hang flyers.

Part of the motivation and justification. for

'sounding the alarm', was to try to protect more potential victims. That was a good thing at face value but looking back, I have no idea whether I was successful in that. I can imagine that in some cases, I was the one viewed as the problem, not the perpetrators. Even though I was right, and telling the truth, I now know that you can't be seething with rage and expect people to take you seriously. Hair, perfect. Make-up, perfect. Clothes, cute. Anger, a little distracting from the cause.

Revenge: a harmful action against a person or group in response to a grievance. be it real or perceived. It is also called payback. retribution. retaliation or vengeance; may be characterized as a form of justice.

"Dearly beloved. avenge not yourselves. but rather give place unto wrath: for it is written. Vengeance is mine; I will repay. says the Lord." Romans 12:19

    The "insane" thing was, that it was during that time, my mom was paying for me to see a therapist. Of course, she was. At least somebody would go. She wouldn't, and my step-father wouldn't, but the stupid, drug addicted daughter would. She would send me to therapy, whine to rest of the family about how "mean" I was and go around taking down flyers every week, without confronting me. What?! It's almost funny when you think about it...almost.

    My tormented mom wouldn't have been paying that therapist if she knew what kind of a spiritual wacko that "Christian" therapist turned out to be. She was not a Christian in the traditional sense. In other words, in not one of our sessions did she point me to forgiveness, or biblical truth, or prayer. She let me talk and talk and then would tell me I was putting my anger exactly where it belonged. "Just hang the flyers", she said. What did that do for me? It made me feel guilty. It made me feel sad and frustrated. It made me angrier that I even cared how my parents felt. Why couldn't I just "put my anger where it belonged" and *feel* better? Why weren't they held accountable by anybody but me? Why weren't the neighbors and parents that lived on their street calling me and thanking me for warning them? Why wasn't the leadership at their church calling me, and telling me they were stopping my step-father from going on camp outs with the youth group? Or on mission trips to Africa with all those very vulnerable children? Why did I feel like I was screaming, and no one could hear me? Why were my parents free to hurt other people, and nothing I did was working? Why was my father allowed to go overseas to help missionaries who had little girls in the house? Who was protecting the innocent kids around them, and if that was my goal, why did it feel so bad, trying so hard, to do good?

    This voodoo "therapist" hypnotized me once, and I have no idea if the marijuana in my system helped or hurt the process. I know what I felt and saw. I now know the first time my step-father put his tongue in my mouth. I know I was six. I know he held me down, tickled me and then did that. I know all of that but I also know that having that information did not help me get better. Perhaps I did not express my rage eloquently enough for this woman to understand what she was digging up. I was already having fantasies about shooting both my parents, and going to jail for the rest of my life seemed like a viable option. Who cares if I lived or died? I was miserable.

    At one point, I was so desperate to see my step father caught and stopped, I was willing to do anything. I had hung the flyers for months. I had talked to the police and spent hours searching for information about what I could do to hold him accountable, and still he was walking around free to hurt more children. I was at my wits end. I called a lawyer. I knew that suing would make me look like I was trying to get money but I didn't care. I was desperate, and very angry. I was truly driven by rage.

"I want to make them pay!" I told the attorney on the other end of the phone line. "I don't want the money. I plan to donate it to charity but I want them to pay. This has gone on long enough. They need to be stopped!"

He was kind and felt for me. I could tell. He softly said the words I was afraid to hear.

"The statute of limitations is up for those crimes. I don't think you have a case."

"What do you mean I don't have a case! That bastard chased me around at my sister's wedding, right in front of everybody and that was only a year ago!"

"Yes. but did he sexually assault you then?"

"Well, I'm grown up now. He can't *assault* me in front of everyone, but he was abusing me mentally and emotionally. He knew what he was doing!"

"I'm sorry the court won't see you as a victim anymore." Bad, bad words came to my mind, and then I took a deep breath. I knew he was right. I remembered my manners. It wasn't his fault. I thanked him for his time. Another brick wall, but I was determined to find a way to climb over…"Sooner or later", I thought. "I'm going over the wall, and this pain is going to stop."

Fret- verb, to be constantly or visibly worried or anxious, cause (someone) worry or distress.

"Fret not thyself because of evildoers, neither be thou envious against the workers of iniquity." Psalm 37:1

Eventually I gave up because my campaign, of

revenge and community awareness, was only hurting me. I was the one that needed to change, and not by going deeper into anger and vengeance. My goal of protecting other children was noble, but for me to survive, I needed to forgive. That therapist did not encourage or even bring up forgiveness. Maybe she figured just focusing on the junk for as long as possible is the best way to keep cashing mommy's checks. I forgive her.

God does not direct us to be focused on self for a reason. That root of bitterness and self- pity became a tree that over shadowed my life.

My therapist did invite me to a 'group session' once. I declined but not before I got a glimpse of the group. They were praying but not to Jesus. They were asking a "spiritual force" to join their group. I consider it purely the grace of God that kept me from joining that group, and opening myself up to further demonic activity. A demon of anger already had me by the throat and my mother was paying for me to be told that hating her was ok. I would send my parents articles from the paper about child molesters getting 156 years in prison. I sent poetry about shooting myself in their yard, and having my brain matter spread all over the front lawn. Clearly the therapy was not working.

Excerpt End

CHAPTER ELEVEN

"Ok folks, tonight we are sharing our regular book excerpts, and poetry, but I have a special assignment. Art! Along with your excerpt I want you to draw, paint or color with a crayon, a therapeutic piece of art." Oh, here we go I thought. Here comes the psychobabble, weirdness.

Roger the guest instructor continued. "I know what you're thinking, here comes the psychobabble, weirdo stuff." What? Wow! He almost pegged me verbatim. Can this guy read my mind? Oh no! I immediately worried about the bad thoughts I'd had about his very unprofessional choice of paint-stained sweatpants. He was the guest instructor! I was busy justifying my critical spirit, and then he looked right at me and said, "But no worries…here's the instruction sheet, and keep in mind, this exercise is all about how YOU feel, so if *anybody* is a weirdo, it would have to be you!" Throwing his bald head back, his ponytail swung back and forth as he laughed at his own joke.

He continued, "Also as a side note, I wanted to let you know that every Tuesday at the community center I have a free, therapeutic art class. It's free, it's fun, and you can take all that junk on the inside, get it out, and make something beautiful at the same time. Please think about joining us!"

Uh, that's not gonna happen, I thought. But

maybe I could take my menopausal irritation, and slap together some nice splatter paint. Throwing paint at something actually sounded fun. And hey, I could wear sweat pants!

Writers Group - Sharing Excerpt Ten
Genre: Semi-Autobiographical Memoir, Christian
Author: Jo Lisa Blossom

Broken Fixer

When am I trying
to fix?
Constantly.
Why can't I
just listen?
Advice,
Advice,
Advice.
Do I really
know so much?
Am I special?
Why do I
care
with compulsion?
What am I trying
to fix?
There is
an answer
I
don't
have.
A question
that leaves me
quiet.

Why am I trying
to fix?
What good
am I really doing
offering up
with no permission?
Do I seem
Prideful?
Do they feel
Insulted?
Ugh. Sorry again.
Who am I trying
to fix?
Me.

Dirt Nap

Can't we just lie down in the sweet, sweet earth?
Can't we just close our eyes on the cold, hard dirt?
I don't want to live like this anymore
I don't know what my life is for
Pain is dragging me down
Pulling me into the ground
I just want to sleep
So God can sweep
Soft green grass
Back over me.

VINDICATED

      When I was twelve and we had just "told on" my step dad, one of his relatives called and I blurted out. "Dad's been molesting us."
      "What?" She asked incredulous.

I took a breath, and repeated. "Dad's been molesting us."

She didn't miss a beat. "I don't believe you." I laid the phone on the counter, and went to get my mother. There was no arguing with an adult. I barely had the guts to get that out. I wasn't going to get the details out, and I knew it. She wasn't going to listen. She shut me down, and I gave up. I'm not sure what I was expecting, but it sure wasn't that. It sure wasn't to be called a liar. I was hurt for a long time over that.

There is an old movie, and one of the characters in the movie feels like he is getting the short end of the stick continuously. He feels like no one really believes him or can see what is truly going on. He is tormented by this. He wants people around him to 'get it'. At one point in the movie, they finally do. His reaction is exactly how I have felt a couple of times in my life. He gets this look on his face of complete joy, and defiance. He raises his hands in the air and yells, "Vindicated!" I had that feeling about this time when another one of my step-father's relatives came over to visit.

We hadn't seen each other in years and for me, most in depth conversations at that point in my life eventually gravitated, towards my great source of pain. This conversation was no different. I didn't want to shock her but I wanted to know if she had also been molested. I was hinting around, working my way to the real question, but to my surprise. I didn't have to say much. She looked me right in the eyes and said pointblank, "Yeah, he likes to put his tongue in your mouth." At that moment, I threw my mental arms in the air and jumped up and down shouting, "VINDICATED!" It was terrible truth but I was elated and relieved. How horrible to be happy to hear that someone else was abused but I was so excited because I finally felt *understood* by a part of the family that I longed to connect with. I felt less alone. But that sick joy was short lived because almost immediately grief took over. I looked at her and knew that she was burdened just like me. It didn't appear that others in her family had ever experienced what she had. She had been bearing this burden entirely alone. Maybe they didn't believe her either. We never did delve further into that subject because we didn't need to. What we needed, at that moment, was to stuff this pain as far down as we could and try to forget. Another failed coping mechanism.

  I found out later that every victim feels like they are alone. For some reason, humans who are victimized feel two things - overwhelming powerlessness, and utterly alone. She was not alone. I was not alone. Victims also don't do much talking to each other. Carrying your own pain is an immense burden and makes it nearly impossible to even imagine asking about the depth of someone else's pain. The pain is just too heavy. It was gratifying to know she understood and didn't think I was a liar. Vindicated was my new favorite word. Right next to idiotic.

Vindicated- to uphold or justify by argument or evidence

SANTA WILL RESCUE ME

  When I was eighteen and trying to figure out what was wrong with me, and why my life was such a mess, I went to a shrink. He looked like Santa Clause with a buzz cut. His office was mostly dark wood, and the carpet was decidedly orange. It was next to a beautiful park that you could see out the window from the waiting area. It gave me a beautiful, peaceful feeling until I walked into his office, he closed the door and it was just me, him, and the orange shag carpet. He had white hair, and a kind heart, but the whole thing still wigged me out. I wasn't comfortable with a man his age, in a room with the door closed. I had to fight my urge to bolt but I was desperate for answers, and Santa was my only hope in that moment. I only went there once but he helped me in a huge way. He put a technical term on one of my problems. Within about five minutes he said, "You are a 'rescuer'".

"What does that *mean*?", I asked him.

"That means that you are trying to save others even at your own expense. Your tendency is to put yourself last, and in this case, allow yourself to be abused, trying to protect your mother from having to deal with this."

"Isn't it good to care about other people more than myself? If they need my help?"

He looked me in the eye, and softly explained, "You are not helping others in a healthy way. You cannot let yourself be harmed so others don't have to address their own issues. You are rescuing to the point of self-destruction. You are giving away your coat when it's freezing outside. That is not healthy, and you won't truly help anyone by taking on burdens that aren't really yours. You have to stop taking on other people's problems to the point of your own pain. You deserve to be healthy and happy, and when you are, you will find ways to help those you love. But what you have been doing has to stop for you to get better."

He chuckled, "In reality you could freeze to death without your coat. And then someone will have to rescue *you*."

"Rescuer"….wow. I left his office, with my mind over the hills and far away.

For years I had put up with way more than I should with regard to my mom. But why was I doing this? Why was I trying to protect her from 'dealing' with my step father? Why wasn't I able to put myself first in the situation? I was an adult now. I was no longer being molested but I was being abused mentally and emotionally every time I encountered my step-father. I concluded that I was trying to "rescue" my Mom. It is interesting how we were all so screwed up, we eventually enabled each other to continue the patterns of abuse without even realizing it. She enabled my step-father by never addressing it in a serious, I'm gonna stab you in the throat sort of way. I enabled her to continue with that by protecting her and never threatening to hurt somebody if they didn't stop abusing me. And so the circle just continued….until that therapist called me a 'rescuer'. I realized at that moment that I was trying to rescue my mom and possibly a couple of boyfriends. I felt sorry for her. I didn't want her to have to hurt by seeing the truth of how bad it actually was. But I think she knew and so her defense was denial. Mine was trying to make everything ok for everybody when I should have been up in somebody's face freaking out with a sharp object of some kind.

    Resorting to violence and possibly sharp objects is the human response to pain and it is interesting to note that Christ was crucified with just such things. He took on unbelievable abuse and pain on my behalf. And *yours*. He paid the price for us, you, me, my mom and my stepfather, everybody. I wanted to hurt someone so my own pain would stop, and violence was the last thing that would actually work. Only the pain that Christ endured healed the situation. Christ didn't stab anybody. He was the 'stabee'. He took on the anger of the abused on the cross. He took on more than just our sin. He took on our flawed human response to pain. Our response to hurt others in the face of our hurt is why my step father was a molester. Hurt people hurt people. Someone molested him. Someone hurt him so he hurt us. Christ paid the price for that. He allowed all that hurt to come onto him physically so that we wouldn't have to resort to hurting others. We can be healed from that desire. We can be healed and the cycle broken for good seeking the ultimate 'rescuer', Jesus Christ.

After that revelation, I knew that if I continued to blame my parents for my problems with self-destruction, and they never changed, then that could become a way of life. I had to get past that. I needed to take responsibility for me. I didn't want to self- destruct. I wanted to get well. I was sick and I needed to rescue me, but how?

Within a couple of years, I had my own apartment. It was wonderful. I was living in the Cocoa Palms, Baby. Even the name was awesome. It was a gorgeous white, sparkling stucco apartment complex that felt like paradise to me. I lived on the 2nd story with a balcony overlooking the pool. The pool was gorgeous. I've always loved pools. Blue, sparkly, clean…I just wanted to stare at the pool for hours. It felt so good to arrange my furniture, water my house plants, decorate. This apartment was *mine*. This was me, just me. Not my family, not my parents, just me. I wanted so badly for it to go well but I found that even by myself, I still had to deal with me. One day, instead of calling 911, I called 411. "Yes, I am looking for a 12-step drug addiction recovery group." I remember my first meeting. It was refreshing to sit in a group of other people who also felt like failures. I remember a white gang member talking about the tattoos on his neck and how he'd given his whole life to this thing that was killing him. I didn't share that day but I listened a lot. I realized that I was not alone but, I didn't yet feel like I belonged. I didn't make any instant friends. But I did get a glimmer of hope along with my coffee and cookies.

BACK TO SEVEN

I was twenty-two and doing singing telegrams for a living. I was loud, proud and had twenty-six different acts. My vocabulary had a long list of foul words, and even though I called myself a Christian, I wasn't living like a good one. I was feeling less and less worthy of the name. I felt like a failure. One of the reasons I felt like a failure is because I should've been able to confront my step father but time and again, I froze up.

One day I was in the kitchen at my parent's house and two of my siblings were there. My step father comes in with a fish net and starts cornering me saying something crude about "catching a fish". My siblings didn't say anything to stop him. They just laughed and pretended it was just a joke. They had learned denial, too. I wanted more than anything to slap this disgusting man across the face but I just stood there, and put my hands up as a feeble attempt to defend myself. He tormented me and I could not stop him. "Miss Loud, Proud and In Your Face" couldn't say *anything*. This troubled me a lot. I was mad at my siblings for not knocking him out but mostly I was mad at me. What was wrong with me? Why couldn't I defend myself in that moment? I would be shaking with rage as soon as he left the room but when he was there, I seemed to check out from functioning. So, I looked it up. I knew this was not normal, and I desperately wanted to get over it so I could stop him the next time he cornered me. Now I'm not sure if the title fits exactly but at the time I felt better because I once again found a psychological reason to explain why I was repeatedly paralyzed. There was relief in just knowing another name for one of my problems. If it had a name, other people must have it and there must be a way to get better. That gave me hope.

Regression- a defense mechanism leading to the temporary or long-term reversion of the ego to an earlier stage of development rather than handling unacceptable impulses in a more adult way. The defense mechanism of regression, in psychoanalytic theory, occurs when an individual's personality reverts to an earlier stage of development, adopting more childish mannerisms.

I was going to meetings here and there, and mostly staying clean. I was working as a waitress and rent was due. I just didn't make enough money, couldn't find a decent roommate, and didn't think I was going to be able to keep my apartment. But I was using anger to keep me from being homeless. I was determined not to go back to my parent's house. My mind had not fully come to grips with the depth of how unhealthy it was there for me at that point, but pride was driving me to survive beyond them, and the past. It just couldn't be my parent's fault anymore. I was twenty-one! I'm a grown up!

I needed a miracle. I didn't go to church or read the bible regularly but I did look through it and found these verses as my hope that someday I would get clean. Someday I would get that thirty-day chip.

"The angel of the Lord encamps all around those who fear Him and delivers them." Psalm 34:7

"You are my hiding place and my shield; I hope in Your word." Psalm 119:114

"Uphold me according to your word. that I may live: and do not let me be ashamed of my hope." Psalm 119:116

Excerpt End

CHAPTER TWELVE

"Ah man they can bite it!" My son was ranting and raving about his favorite team losing a game.

"Chuck that is so inappropriate! I wish you wouldn't talk like that."

"Talk like what? It's like saying they can eat it"

"What?" I looked at him aghast.

"Mom, they can bite it is like saying they can shove it or stuff it or cram it up their...."

"What? Whoa! Whoa!" I quickly stopped his tirade, throwing my hand up to stop him, my jaw dropping.

Taking a deep breath, he started again as if he was talking to a dense third grader. "Ok Mom, here it is the way you old folks used to say it....He hesitated, thinking. "Stick it! Stick it to the man!" He exclaimed.

Feeling foolish, what he was saying finally got through to my "old" brain. "Ooooooohhhh *now* I get it!

Later that night, I handed my latest excerpt to my unsuspecting classmate. I knew they were gonna judge me after reading it. Everyone looked at everyone different. It was human nature, and we were being vulnerable, but we were all willing to take the chance anyway. I looked at this relative stranger and knew he would never see me the same after reading my story.

"Ah he can just bite it!" I thought, giggling.

Writers Group - Sharing Excerpt Eleven
Genre: Semi-Autobiographical Memoir, Christian
Author: Jo Lisa Blossom

To Myself

Can't I keep it
To myself?
Do I have to share it all?
I just want to move on
And forget I'm ill
No more doctor's appointments and forms
That would be a dream
But so far Lord
I'm still here
In a room waiting
To talk to someone
I don't want to know
Or ever see again
Can't I just leave it
Alone forever?
Be healed because I want to be
And I believe you Lord?
That's what I want
A warm wind around me
Wrapping me in love and taking away my pain.

Reprobate

He wants what he wants
The devil just taunts
Him over and again
Where he has been

He wants to go back
The horrors stack
Up in his mind
'Til he can't find
Peace in his heart
His little boy start
Was destroyed by abuse
He's grown so used
To the pain and perverse
He's under a curse
Refuses to let God heal him
So the devil will reveal him
For what he's let in
He's now a slave to sin
A sad story of unrepentance
Is now a life sentence

BOOT CAMP REJECT

I needed to overcome my past failures but they still hung on me mentally. One of those was my brief military career. A year or so earlier. I was desperately trying to come out from under the diseased wing of my life and start over. I joined the military. I figured I would join the reserves, get money for college, get out of my parent's house and live the adventure. Well, unfortunately, my adventure of cocaine the night before I left got me sent on a special field trip across the base to the "you're a blow it" office. Two weeks into boot camp, they were kicking me out. Drinking all that cranberry juice at four in the morning, two hours before checking into the induction center just didn't do the trick. But I wasn't entirely disappointed about being booted from the military. Boot camp was so enjoyable with the screaming and gross brown bathing suits for the five in the morning swimming lessons. On top of that, I had found out the day before that the recruiter had lied to me. I wanted money to go to college and reservists didn't get any. My dream of my Uncle Sam paying for my education was over and if they wanted to let me go, so be it. My parents had offered to pay for college with fifteen dollars a week so this was my grand plan to better my life, and it was over at this point. No more standing in line watching the other stressed out recruits bouncing jello on their plate, staring off into space. The suffering of that stressful environment would not be missed, but what was next?

    In spite of all the relief, being kicked out was still embarrassing so of course, I immediately began fabricating a story. I told everyone I had dislocated a shoulder during the grueling physical demands of boot camp, and was being kicked out for that. I was used to failing and lying to hide my shame. This wasn't much different.

    But this failure was especially painful because I was so desperate to get away from my bad home life. One of the only bright spots in the military adventure was that my step father had been writing me letters. He would ask me to describe my daily routine in detail. He had been in the military when he was young. I could tell that he was really interested because of his own experience in youth. He was actually encouraging and interested in something about me that didn't have to do with lusting after me. As a young woman who had longed for a normal father daughter relationship for years, this was refreshing. I had trouble admitting it, but I enjoyed that long distance, SAFE, pen pal relationship. It felt normal to have something in common, something right, something with no way to hurt me. But now I was out, and that would be the end of that.

    I was working my way up to calling and sharing the news with my parents, when I heard my name called.

    "Recruit! You need to get your blank to the

visitor's center, double-time!" My Commanding Officer, looked seriously annoyed, and as usual wanted a rapid response.

"Yes Ma'am, but where is the Visitor's Center? Do I have a visitor?"

"Do I look like I know if you have a visitor? Do I look like I give a rat's blank? Here's a map. Now move you're blank! Don't just stand there! Get your blank over there! I think your mommy is here to spank you're blank." What?! I had no time to contemplate this miserable woman's obsessive use of the word "blank". I saluted, turned away and started marching into the unknown.

Recovering from that tirade, I tried to read the map while in a state of shock. She obviously was not happy about my visitor, but was I? Was it really my mother? It turned out that it was. She was stomping on years of military tradition and didn't even realize it. You aren't allowed visitors during boot camp. A visit from Mommy is not part of the up at dawn, pride swallowing siege that's normally involved in military training. But I guess when somebody's Mom shows up at the gate to see her kid, they better let her in. This was just one example of my mom showing up at an unexpected moment when something huge just occurred. God gave her a gift. She *knew* things.

Her showing up at the base, two hours after me finding out I'm getting kicked out, was God's way of comforting me. And truly, I was sad about this new turn of events. I was putting up a tough front because, how could I feel this bad when it was my own fault? I did the drugs the night before I left for boot camp. I was the foolish girl hanging out with another questionable guy. I was the one who said yes when I should've said no. But now I was also lost again with no direction. I was the failure who was getting ready to tell another lie to her mom.

I didn't want to go home, but here was my mom to tell me she cared. It was always that way. I wanted to get away from my parents, and hate them enough to break away for good but somehow, I kept getting called back to try to fit the picture of the happy, normal family. I told my mom my tall tale about my shoulder dislocation, said goodbye, and went back to my barracks.

The next day I was moved to the base's "reject" center. That's where they put people who are being shipped out, people who didn't make it through boot camp. People like me, a drug user, a liar, a loser. People like a transvestite who was just waiting to go home where her lover was going to pay for her sex change operation. People like a sweet, chubby stripper from Oklahoma who had the IQ of a third grader, and would rather hug somebody than shoot them.

People like a beautiful girl that we would watch jog around the barracks twice a day. Except for being inside on linoleum instead of outside on blacktop, she jogged just like she did with her company. She was still in excellent physical shape but you didn't have to look very closely to notice that she had long scratch marks all over her legs and arms. This sad, beautiful girl was like me. She was coming to grips with a dream that had just died. She hadn't joined the military as a last resort to escape her life. She wanted to be there. But she had been seduced by her female superior officer, and when she tried to end the relationship, the superior officer denied it, and had her kicked out. She had two weeks left of boot camp when this happened. She reacted by harming herself with a hairbrush…and then pretending she was still part of her company. It was hard to look at her body. I would look at her and then envision kicking the crap out of that short haired, military lesbian with no conscience. That seemed like it might be a start to real justice. That poor girl was a better person than me. She never talked about vengeance. She was too nice. There was no kicking the crap out of anybody. Just an aching in my chest as I watched her every day, twice a day, jogging around and around and around…

***"Vengeance is mine saith the Lord"* Romans 12:19**

Then there was another reject, a friend I'll call "Rita". She was shy and sweet with big brown cow eyes. One day, in the chow line, she was being picked on by some bigger, more aggressive "rejects". Me, being the rescuer that I was, promptly stood up for her. We became fast friends. As it turned out, she was a lesbian, but thankfully, she appeared to have a conscience. She was soft spoken, and struggling to break free of her victim identity, too. Her step mom had molested her for years and her uncle regularly raped her. She chose females. She decided that she was going to be in charge of who she had sex with from then on. She wasn't a victim anymore but in reality, she was still a victim and I think in her heart, she knew it. She was a victim because she wasn't strong enough to say 'who cares if I never have a mom to love me'. No, she was still trying to find a mom to love her but now it was through sex. She was still living her life as a reaction to other people's twisted actions. Join the club.

There are many warnings against sexual sin in the bible. From my experience and for many people I know who've been molested, it takes a long time to feel like we can really take charge of our own purity. At that time, I felt like it was too late for me. I was already dirty and used. There was no going back, so why even bother to try to be pure? I didn't know how to say 'no', and no one ever told me I could. I didn't even know it was an option. I would just go along with whatever, and then wonder why I had done that. But I did draw the line at lesbianism. I wasn't ready to engage in that. I was still trying to find a good 'daddy' after all.

Rita got out of the military reject center about the same time I did, and then later that year she came to visit me. She stayed with me in my dreamy Cocoa Palms apartment for a few weeks but when she asked me for a kiss, she had to go. And on one particular day, a while after that, somebody else had to go too.

The gift of my Santa therapy session had taught me that I didn't have to put up with anybody's stuff anymore. I didn't have to rescue anybody, and sacrifice myself in the process anymore. My first attempt at getting over that problem was to pack up my roommate's stuff. I was mad, and on my way to go dump it all on her boyfriend's front lawn. She wouldn't pay her part of the rent and she spent all of her time at her boyfriend's house. So I angrily decided she could just live there now. The apartment was a dream come true and like everything else it was becoming a nightmare.

The nightmare had begun with two idiots, we had met somewhere, coming over with cocaine every weekend. My roommate kept inviting them over even when I told her no. She had a toddler, and I knew partying like that around a little kid was wrong, wrong, wrong. I don't know why I expected her to be healthy enough to take charge of the situation as a mother, but she wasn't. She was struggling through her own disappointments with life.

I kept complaining that these two guys shouldn't be coming over, and we shouldn't be partying like this. This isn't how I want it. etc. All of this while whiffing the cocaine of course. All four of us had been doing drugs in front of the child, and I was losing patience with it. This bad behavior, put me over the edge. Somewhere in my mind, I was worried that even though this little girl had no idea what we were doing, someday drugs would look familiar to her. She was only two but fifteen was coming. I couldn't stand by and let this continue. I didn't want to be responsible for ruining that little kid's future life. I had been objecting, and no one was doing anything different. Knock, knock, knock and I open the door and here are these two idiots again.

"What are you doing here? Get the blank out of here! I told you I don't want you coming over anymore", I said aggressively.

"She invited us." Idiot number one pointed over my shoulder towards where he imagined my roommate might be.

"She's not even here!" I planted my feet and got my pointer finger ready. Like pulling a gun out of the holster locked and loaded, I started jabbing that finger towards their faces while yelling at the top of my lungs. "You need to get the blankity blank out of here and don't come back. Take your drugs and get lost. If you come back here, I'm going to call the blanking cops! You got it?" Finally, they started backing up. Using the word "cops" was like pulling the trigger. They turned and hurried away while I slammed the door. Now I was headed in to call my roommate at her boyfriend's house. I let her have it and told her again that she needed to move her stuff out, so I could get a new roommate.

I'm sure idiot one and two also called her and told her about my freak out session. She didn't come home after that. Nobody wants to live with a morality spaz. She didn't like me freaking out over a little "fun". Party time was over, and even though she said she was moving out, she wasn't bothering to move any of her belongings out. Now, I was enjoying <u>not</u> being a rescuer by throwing it all in boxes and taking it to her. Rent was almost due and I desperately needed a new roommate and I couldn't get one with her junk in the way. I was convinced she was being completely inconsiderate and I was determined to be the new me. I also wanted to put my Cocoa Palms, sparkly white and blue dream come true, back together again. I drove over there and chucked her boxes on the lawn, yelling and screaming. I looked up just long enough to see the neighbors nodding their approval. I'm sure they were very impressed with my progress toward better mental health.

MY CAGE CALLED AEROSPACE

I eventually lost my apartment and my mother convinced me to come back home. To top it off, my parents got me a job at the large company that they both worked for. I was excited to get the job, and at the time I did not realize, or appreciate how truly valuable it was. For a person, my age, to be making that kind of money, with no college degree or experience, was pretty good. I had benefits, and it was a good company. But I also had my step father in the building. It was a large building mind you, but he found ways to make his presence known. He would send me notes through the interoffice system that were juvenile and creepy. I was very uncomfortable, and felt like he was abusing me in public. I was also very uncomfortable knowing that he was a 'perv' with other women there. He was not being held to account for his behavior, and he had a way of 'flirting' that was just plain creepy. Many women avoided him, and I was embarrassed to be his daughter. I avoided him, too….like the plague. Back then it was not labeled 'sexual harassment'. It was just 'Dick' being 'Dick'.

I did my job, and for the most part enjoyed my time there. It was my first office job, and I liked it. I only made a couple of friends, and that was mostly because of the grueling schedule. I was up at four thirty in the morning for the car pool, and that was to get to work at seven. Only once did I share the long car ride with my step-father. When he told me that my make-up looked good, but I just needed to wear red lipstick, that was enough for me. I was not ready to be emotionally abused at the crack of dawn, or on the two and a half-hour drive home every day. Road rage anyone?

Instead, I joined a car pool and spent hours and hours in traffic with four other people each week that I didn't really know. Even after a few months I still couldn't really call us friends. When you see people that early in the morning you tend to want to forget it. They would have their hair sticking up and out of place, cereal stuck to their shirt. shoes untied… it was brutal.

We all tried to start the day with pleasantries but really, we just wanted to sleep. It was still dark out, and this whole thing just felt unnatural. Then I switched to the van pool and that wasn't much better. There was a little more privacy with the big seats, and sleeping was easier but it was still a horrible schedule. The 'daily grind' is a nice way to describe a warm cup of coffee. This was something altogether different. It was grinding down my joy. It was lonely, tiring, and for a twenty one year old, who was living in fear of a stalker in the building, it was too much. I quit.

Quitting was painful. My sweet boss felt like a safe zone, and he wanted to know why I wanted to quit. He told me how smart I was, and how he would hate to lose me. I told him my step father was a child molester, and showed him the creepy notes. He cried. I didn't know what to say. He didn't know what to say. For me this was such an old situation that crying was beyond my comprehension. What I felt was rage. But I did feel sorry for my boss. He was a sweet man who felt bad for me. That was a first. No older man had ever expressed that kind of genuine concern before. He didn't want anything.

He just felt bad for me. He was a good Christian man who didn't know how to help. So, he just cried. He didn't realize but just his reaction helped me. His response felt normal. It was a relief to have that response. So much in my life felt so abnormal that having him feel despair for me affirmed that yes, I should be quitting this dream job. It was going to be better to be broke, and unemployed than to go on pretending this was normal, or acceptable. It was going to be better to say goodbye to this dear man than have to endure more sexual harassment, and emotional abuse. For eight hours a day, five days a week, I had been walking around emotionally terrorized instead of building a career. I hugged him goodbye.

    At that company, I did meet a couple of other men who fell into the same general category as my step father. I'm not saying they were molesters but one man ALWAYS looked at women's breasts, including mine. He *never* looked at our faces. Have you even met someone like that? Wow. I wanted to scream at him but never did. Perhaps a good dose of 'hey. I'm up here you piece of……" maybe that would've cured him, but alas we will never know. Thank you, good manners.
    Another man was trying to get me to do some 'modeling'. Whatever. Just another perv. Just another person to make me sad that I was pretty.

JUROR NUMBER FOUR

    "Hey do you know that Thomas guy?" It was about a month before I quit, and I was grilling another co-worker about a very cute guy down the hall. I had to know if he was taken.
    "Well, I think he just broke up with his girlfriend." She answered, while shuffling papers on her desk. Yay! I thought, perfect timing for my crush. I was

pretty co-dependent, and was searching for something to fill the hole in my heart. Something or someone to 'save' me. Jesus is the only one who can save us but back then I did not have an active spiritual relationship with the Lord. So, I was chasing a boy. He was sweet and shy and still in love with someone else. We went out on a date and he told me so. I was devastated, even though it was our first date and we barely knew each other. I went to my normal coping mechanism of alcohol and drugs. I drank a couple of beers, smoked some marijuana and got my first look inside the city jail. I had almost made the off ramp towards home, when the motorcycle cop pulled me over. He told me I was "weaving within the lane". I was actually weeping when his lights came on. I was broken hearted but that was no excuse. He did the sobriety tests which I was sure that I'd actually passed with flying colors. Then nothing. I thought he was going to let me go. "Thank you for not arresting me." I smiled at him.

He smiled back. "You're welcome." At that moment, a squad car pulled up to transport me to booking. Nice.

I decided that some people are just plain mean. It gets better. While I was being finger printed, another super nice officer told me these exact words. "You know I wouldn't worry about this. This is not even going to make it upstairs. You don't have to go to court." As he said this, he turned his head to look me in the eye. It took me a second to register what he was saying. He was telling me my latest arrest wasn't going to make it to court.

Why would he say that? Why was he trying to make my situation worse by having me end up with a warrant for not showing up? I wanted to believe him but was smart enough not to. I got a court date over a month away.

But as it happened, within the week of my arrest, I got called to the same courthouse for jury duty. I tried to tell them I hated everybody and they didn't believe me. I was picked to sit on a case, for, of all things, drunk driving. The case was against a twentyone year old, who had gotten caught at one in the morning with a keg of beer strapped into his passenger seat. The keg was his date; her name was Lola and she was trouble. He blew the breathalyzer, and was indeed very guilty. But for some reason, his enabler parents got him a lawyer to fight the charges.

For three days, this family wasted their own money, and the money of the Florida tax payers. As jurors, we got thoroughly educated on the minutia of how to fail a breathalyzer test. We ate bologna sandwiches, and wondered why we were even in the deliberation room. We convicted him in twenty minutes. We had no choice. This young, crew cut, blondie in the suit and tie was so caught. "Guilty" on all counts. I felt guilty watching his parents cry as he got carted off to jail. His lawyer should've felt guilty for taking their money and pretending he had a defense.

For me, the experience was very interesting. During the day, I was a nicely dressed, highly respected member of society. I was being called on to determine the fate of a young man my age who was also at a pivotal time in his life. As a Juror, I was treated like someone important. I had been asked to lift my right hand and swear on the bible. They trusted me to keep my solemn oath to be fair and impartial in my judgement. At night, I was struggling not to stay out too late drinking and partying with my friends so I could make it back to court in the morning.

Then a few weeks later, there I was in front of the same judge for *my* case. Yes, it did make it upstairs. My name was called and I stepped forward through the swinging wooden gate. I stood there while the Judge peered at me.

He finally said. "Weren't you, juror number four?"

I sheepishly said, "Yes."

He immediately went into kindly Grandpa mode. He told me, "I think you know how this works don't you, young lady?" Then he gave me a light sentence. I didn't lose my license or have to pay a bunch of fines. I did have a wet reckless charge on my driving record but besides that, all I had to do was go to the DMV and submit to an interview. I wasn't over the legal limit so I wasn't officially drunk driving but he could've thrown the book at me. Instead, I just had to talk to some guy with a clipboard.

I can look back now and see God's hand on my life so many times. I believe I even whispered. 'Thank you, God.' when I left the courtroom that day. It was bad but could've been so much worse. I now know that God is good all the time and all the time God is good. I don't need to dodge a drunk driving charge to show me that anymore. All I have to do now, is wake up and breathe.

Excerpt End

CHAPTER THIRTEEN

"Go crinkle cut go!" My son's teenage friend was cheering him on while he drove by popping a wheelie on his quad. I grabbed my heart in shock as he roared by laughing.

"Oh, Lord help him not to crash!" Turning around, he zoomed up with a huge smile, and turned off the engine. His friend high-fived him while I freaked out.

"Chuck! You scared the crud out of me! Where did you learn to do that?"

"The internet!" He laughed. Oh great, now I have to worry about the internet.

Later, I said "Hey Chuck, why does your buddy call you 'Crinkle Cut'?" I was double checking it wasn't some stupid pot reference.

"Ah, he used to think my name was Chip."

"What? Chip! Who's Chip?" I asked.

"He thought I was for like a year in kindergarten", he answered.

"How come I've never heard this before?" I wondered aloud.

"Oh, there's a bunch of secret stuff going on in kindergarten that you don't know about Mommy." He poked me in the ribs as I washed my hands in the sink. My menopausal brain, still wasn't making the connection to "crinkle cut". "So why does he call you "crinkle cut"?

He sighed like he had to explain chemistry to a nerd with a low IQ. "He spent the whole year calling me " Chip" and I guess I was too nice to say anything. At lunch one day, he finally asked me, 'Who's Chuck?' I said, 'I am!' Then he said, 'Who's Chip?'" He giggled remembering. So now he calls me 'Crinkle Cut' because that kind of chip is his favorite or whatever."

"Ooooohhhh. Ok, now I get it. Can I call you 'bak-ked' or 'barbeque'?" I teased him, grinning. Like usual, he looked at me like I was out of my mind.

That night, at writer's group I started to think about names. We name this. We name that. We have nicknames, first names, last names, middle names, maiden names, married names, big names, name calling. Names seemed to be really important. But what name really counts? Only the name of Jesus Christ when you get down to it. I decided to be nicer, friendlier as His ambassador in this class. I didn't *feel* like it, but as I handed over my latest excerpt to a new classmate, I reached out my hand and said, "Hi, my name is Jo Lisa."

"And there is salvation in no one else, for there is no other name under heaven given among men by which we must be saved."   *Acts 4:12*

Writers Group - Sharing Excerpt Twelve
Genre: Semi-Autobiographical Memoir, Christian
Author: Jo Lisa Blossom

Accomplice

She
Hid
The

Computer
From
The
Police.
Why?
Does
It
Matter?

Sunk
To
A
New
Low
Of
Criminal
Behavior
Why?
Does
It
Matter?

Bubble Boy

His happiness bubble is fragile.
He can only go so far
with any relationship.
If you're not in here already
he can't let you in.
New people and places
are risks
he's not willing to take.
He fought hard
to clear his area.
He was bloody and broken

for years.
Now he's healed, happy and sure
he has all he needs inside
his little bubble of joy and love.
If you pound
at the outside,
the bubble does not break.
Even if you tap so very nicely.
You won't get an
answer from him.
He can't take any more chances.
He won't even acknowledge
anyone who could
possibly disrupt his peace.
If you're outside, you are danger.
No one new is
allowed
in.
No one old is
Ever called.
No one to hurt him anymore.

DIVERSION FROM THE PAIN

"You are under arrest. You have the right to remain silent…." Wow, I thought. You really did it this time. He was clicking the cuffs on me and I was noticing his cologne. He's so handsome, I thought. I could marry one of these if I wasn't such a blow it. I thought for sure he was going to let me go. But alas, my brush with the law had just gotten more serious. He was handsome but I wasn't going to get a date. I was twenty two, and under arrest a mile from home. I was booked for driving under the influence and ordered to drug diversion classes.

Once a week I got together in a class room with

other people who'd been arrested for drugs or alcohol. We got lessons on what we were doing to ourselves, physically. There was no Jesus in the lessons. No real steps to overcoming our self-destruction. Nobody asking, "w*hy* are you using?" It was just you're killing your brain cells and foolishly harming your body.

The teacher, who was a nurse, did say that she had never met a person who'd been molested who did not struggle with harming themselves in one form or another. Nice positive feedback, and even then, I thought, no way, I will overcome this, and this will not define my life. But at that point, it *was* defining my life so I had to admit that she was probably right. I was the one who'd gotten arrested, and was still trying unsuccessfully to give up all drugs and alcohol.

I didn't get much out of the class, but I did get out of going to jail. Hey there's a plus. They also didn't take my driver's license. Even then the Lord was watching over me, giving me another chance to get it right. And when a classmate talked about a free rehab nearby, I made a mental note. With my remaining brain cells I filed away that tidbit of hope for future use.

In that class, and in the twelve step groups, people would say addicts get better, they just have to hit "rock bottom." The bible calls it a 'pit'. And truthfully that pit is very similar to a grave, isn't it? For me, back then, I always felt close to death. I felt like suicide looked pretty good since, essentially, that is what I was doing. I had been risking my health and life for years. The tendency for most of us, was to engage in risky behavior repeatedly, and eventually fall into a pit of self-destruction and depression. If we don't fight to get out, that pit becomes our grave.

Once a year or so, someone from my circle of drug addict friends would die. Sometimes it was an accident but sometimes it was not. It was always a tragedy to me when someone just gave up. But I understood the desire to just get it over with. I always wanted to know if they were a Christian. Did they go from this hell to another, or to heaven and peace? I was always relieved if I could find out they went to Sunday school. Then I knew that there was a good possibility that while they were young, innocent and open to ideas, they probably accepted Christ. They had made it out of the pit and into heaven.

I would think about that. I would remember what it felt like to be a child….to be young, and full of hope. I would remember Sunday school. We would dress up, and go to class to talk about God and how much He loved us. We would sing Jesus loves me at the top of our lungs and feel good… really, really good.

Even if it was suicide, I still believe Christians go to heaven so when my friend committed suicide, I was sad for my friend dying but another part of me was glad for them to be past the struggle, and in a better place….I am 100% against suicide no matter what, but at the time, I was trying to make sense of a the tragic loss of a twenty-three year old life.

Another

"Just another addict"…
Took a stand against reality
A little blood and brutality
He found the way out
Pushed away doubt
Pulled the trigger…
Now his pain is bigger
But it doesn't hurt anymore
Another grave dug
Covered with dirt
Green grass and hurt….

"He also brought me up out of a horrible pit, out of the miry clay, And set my feet upon a rock, And established my steps." Psalm 40:2

QUALIFIED

Now I know that God qualifies the unqualified and when someone young dies, it is a tragedy because they had potential. Everyone does. Our beautiful God even takes people who feel they have nothing to offer. People who have points against them. Not a few points. A whole lot of bad marks that make them the least likely to 'qualify' for anything worthwhile. The bible is full of people that God not only used to fulfill His purposes, but He allowed them to participate in *changing the world*. They were what society would deem "losers". Yet those are the ones that God chose to not just personally bless, but to use in a way that the world remembers. They were 'heroes of the faith'.

I have found that God qualifies us for everything we would never be able to have, or do, on our own. He qualifies us to be saved when we deserve death and, in some cases actively pursue our own demise, in one form or another. He teaches us to really live. He qualifies us for joy when on our own, we pursue strife, anger and all out hate. He qualifies us for forgiveness. We are forgiven for the things we've done, that are the source of our guilt and shame. He forgives us for the things that the world condemns us for. More than that, He qualifies us to forgive others and experience freedom from the burdens of revenge. How do I know this? He qualified me.

I sometimes think about that type of grace. A serial killer about to be executed can accept Christ, admit his need for God, ask God to forgive him and be Lord of his life. Even if his life is another ten seconds before execution, and his confession of faith is laced with expletives, God still allows him in. That is the grace of God. He has not had time to be transformed by the power of the Holy Spirit. He has not learned to listen to God's voice or pray. The demons and the habits in the flesh are still part of his life. He is still repentant because he has turned from sin…the sin of rejecting Christ, the sin of pride, and not admitting he was a sinner, the sin of doing things intentionally that he knew were wrong, the sin of looking at sinful things, saying sinful things. It's all wrapped up in the sin of rejecting the Savior. To admit he needs forgiveness is to admit all those sins. God knows he is not capable of listing every sin he's ever committed and asking forgiveness for each. He doesn't have to.

Now the Holy Spirit has a voice in his life and God has saved his soul. The devil lost another soul to the hope of heaven. But if human understanding is applied, people would say, well he wasn't really saved because there was no fruit. Or cussing proves he is still sinning and not truly repentant. Or he isn't truly changed, because there's no evidence that he's born again. But doesn't transformation take time? Is that the God we serve? Does he have to prove his heart is changed to the world, to us or just to the Lord? Doesn't the definition of grace mean that we don't have to *earn* the free gift of salvation? Is it really "free" for a serial killer? Or a child molester? Yes. We don't want it to be, but it is. That's God's grace. It's not about what we can see. It's about what we can't.

Grace- the free and unmerited favor of God, as manifested in the salvation of sinners and the bestowal of blessings, mercy, pardon

"For we ourselves were once foolish, disobedient, led astray, slaves to various passions and pleasures, passing

our days in malice and envy, hated by others and hating one another. But when the goodness and loving kindness of God our Savior appeared, He saved us, not because of works done by us in righteousness, but according to His own mercy, by the washing of regeneration and renewal of the Holy Spirit, whom He poured out on us richly through Jesus Christ our Savior, so that being justified by grace we might become heirs according to the hope of eternal life." Titus 3:3-7

    I had to face the fact that giving in to my mother's request to move back home was a bad idea. I came to realize I would soon end up dead or in jail if I didn't get out of that house. So, I put my cards on the table. Fix this Mommy or it's going to get ugly. She did what she was good at. She threw money at the symptom, and ignored the real problem. She told me to find an apartment, and she would help me move. The cheapest apartments I could find were an hour away in Vale Beach. I was thrilled to soon be living in one.

    It was an adorable apartment, built in the 1920's with a bed that dropped down out of the wall. There were built in cabinets with glass doors and a claw foot tub. It had beautiful dark wood trim all around the ceiling and the windows. It had a stairway from the front door to the second floor and a walk-in closet with a window in it. The kitchen was long and skinny with two big windows that had a view of another apartment building and the alley below. It was not the best neighborhood, but it was super vintage cute and now it was home.

    The day my step father helped me move was what I hoped would be a new start. The excitement, and joy, was almost ruined because it was him that helped me move. I was nervous the entire time, just waiting for the verbal abuse to start. But he didn't lust at me or say anything inappropriate. I'm sure my mom had told him that I'd threatened suicide. They could tell that I was serious. They had been witnesses to the weight loss, the erratic behavior and sleepless nights. He knew I was capable of killing myself because I already was.

    I wonder if he ever wished he was dead like I did. I know he was addicted to pornographic magazines. I had seen them under the bathroom sink. Somehow, they were only there while my mom was on a business trip. That year, she had been gone a lot. His life could not have been easy but I was on the edge of a breakdown. He knew that it was him who had been pushing me there.

    He was newly retired and I would come home, and he would be watching the television. I would stop and try to make conversation about something or other and somehow it would get turned around to my bra size. He was disgusting and completely unchecked. I didn't know what to say. He was a creep and I was paralyzed in front of him. He seemed to enjoy watching me squirm because he was unrelenting in his perversion towards me. I was walking on eggshells all the time at home. Moving away from that atmosphere, and his sickness, was my only chance to get well. Maybe somewhere in his heart he saw that.

    For many years I was aware that he did not have a conscience. I had taken the time to study child molesters and had found that to be the main problem. I also came to realize that there is no cure, *especially* if you are never held accountable. For many years I thought that he just didn't feel anything. Now I know that even though he had no conscience, he was capable of feelings. He was capable of feeling love. He loved me and he helped me move to get away from him, the problem. He could see the damage he was doing, and even though he refused to go to counseling or do anything in the least about it, he wasn't trying to make me stay. He helped me leave and for that I was grateful. I'm sure he was on to his next victim already. My mother had a habit of making sure children and young females were continually within his grasp.

"Though I walk through the valley of the shadow of death. I will fear no evil, for thou art with me…."
Psalm 23:4

When I read Psalm 23 it is beautiful and easy to relate it to our lives. I notice that it doesn't say we walk through the "valley of death". I think that would be hell. We just walk through the valley of the "*shadow*" of death. As a Believer I was living under the protection of Christ but I *felt* like I was dying, and I wanted to live. The only problem was that even though I truly wanted God, I couldn't seem to find Him.

In Vale Beach, I would walk over to an old church a couple of blocks away. I would go over when no one was there, and try to pray. I didn't always know what to pray for and I felt unworthy. I was so dirty and such a sinner. The church was always open during the day and was probably a hundred years old. It was very beautiful and it felt peaceful. I didn't feel like that. Every day, I had men whistle at me on the street or flirt with me. I was very pretty but I sometimes wished I was ugly. I remember dying my hair back to brown from blond to try to get less attention as a single, young girl in a sketchy neighborhood. Sometimes I got anxious being there on my own. I felt sad and hopeless. I felt alone, and sitting in church when no one else was there, didn't fill that void. It was like I just kept missing the target. I didn't know how to actually go to a service, fellowship with other believers and feel like I fit in. The only place I felt like I fit in at all, was the twelve step meetings with people talking about jail and death while dirty addicts slept on the couch in the back. But feeling like I finally belonged there hadn't helped me stay clean. The majority of the time, I felt like I was just faking everything. I was a failure and nothing made me feel any different.

Then one day, I woke up like I had never been there. I can't describe that feeling with mere words. It was as if I had a split personality and the personality who had been sleeping woke up after years of being unconscious.

It started when I was invited to a seminar, by this guy I dated for a whopping two weeks. He was into musicals and kind of dramatic. Not really my type. He was almost thirty years old, and still living at home with mom giving him lunch money. I instantly recognized he had a whole new set of problems that I didn't want to add to mine. Our relationship was basically over but he did invite me to this seminar. He was so enthusiastic about the whole thing that I thought I'd give it a shot. I had heard about weird cultish seminars a friend had gone to. She described a room kept at twenty-two degrees for hours, basically torturing people until they'd agree to anything to get out of there. I figured with the way he was talking, there was no way this seminar could be like that, so I went. I still remember the big room with the huge sign on the wall. I remember because that sign changed my life. In big, three-foot high letters the sign asked each of us. "What Am I Pretending Not to Know?"

What they wanted us to realize is that we were pretending we didn't have the three hundred dollars to attend their next seminar. They wanted us to realize that we could get that money by getting creative, you know, go wash cars in a bikini, and have that money to fork over in about two hours. I laughed at their suggestion but beyond that I didn't figure out a way to fork over any cash, or get fully brainwashed into their cult. But I did have a revolutionary awakening a couple of days later. The sleeping twin was finally awake and she was feeling strong, determined and really, really angry. The truth is that the Lord used some new age voodoo to open my eyes.

In one sitting, I wrote a twenty three page letter, to my step-father. It was a first. For years I had said nothing. I had been paralyzed in regression and trauma. I had also been waiting for years for my mom to say something. I was waiting for her to help me, while trying to keep her from having to face it, of course. For the very first time, I realized I was pretending. I was pretending she was going to help me with her husband. I was pretending she *wanted* to help me. I was pretending that she was going to do something to protect me. I was pretending that she wanted things to change. If that were true, she would've kicked him out long ago. That one sentence in big vinyl letters on the wall caused me to wake up to the fact that she *wasn't* going to help me. She wasn't *ever* going to protect me. She wasn't *ever* going to force him to get help, or divorce him, or do anything significant. If she had any intention, or was even capable of helping me, she would have long ago. On top of that, I realized I didn't *need* her to help me. I just needed me. I could handle this directly. Wow! This was a major revelation for me. I suddenly felt like nothing could stop me. I was a freight train barreling down the track with no brakes.

I let him have it like I never had. I spelled out all that he had done wrong I told him in so many words that he needed help, and he had to stop. I tried to force him into counseling. I said that if he didn't get help, all h-e double hockey sticks would break loose. I was going to keep talking about it until he did what I said. I tried with all I had to take control of this horrible uncontrollable situation. I tried to get him to care enough about the rest of us to admit his problem and get professional help.

With some letters we write, we wonder if we should mail them. You know the drill. Back and forth, should I send this? Should I not? Is this nice? Did I say too much? Do I need to say more? Are there enough stamps? With this letter, there was none of that. It was in the envelope, stamped, and out the door the same day. I did make a copy to show my siblings before I mailed it. I was so proud of myself for writing it.

I was in awe of the feeling that I was having. It felt strange and powerful. It felt scary and wonderful to finally be awake. But it didn't last. I was expecting a reaction to match the incredible breakthrough I had. I was expecting a life-changing response. After finally saying all that, things had to change, didn't they? I was expecting something huge. I got zip. Eventually my hope started to fade and my desire to self-destruct returned. My step father refused to go to counseling. My mother did nothing about nothing.

She came to see me and we walked down to the little neighborhood church and talked about it. The church was empty but we went in and sat on the old wooden pews.

"So did Dad get my letter?" I asked her.

"Yes, he got it. He said he doesn't have a problem and he's not going to go to counseling."

"What?! He needs to go!" I stared at her in disbelief.

She looked down at her hands. "I know but I don't know what to do about it."

I wanted to scream at her. "Blankin' kick him out! Divorce the blankity blank! Shoot him in the head! Do something!!!!" I didn't say anything. This was my mother after all. I didn't know how to talk to her like that.

Walking back, I looked up at the sky and suddenly remembered a film they showed us over and over in the third grade. The film was about a little girl and her red balloon. In my mind I saw that little girl letting go of her red balloon. The balloon softly floated away from her outstretched hand, up to the blue sky. We walked back in silence. There was nothing else to say.

Trying to change anything was useless. I was beginning to feel like all of our conversations were fake. She wasn't listening, and she had no desire to figure it out or face it. I felt like it was easier for her to focus on me and my problems, not him. My drug addiction was the problem, not her husband the child molester. I gave up. It had been going on so long that it felt easier to give up my new found fight, and just go back to hopeless. I didn't want to be burdened by their problems anymore anyway. I wanted to move on in a huge way. I just went back to the role of rescuer/fixer and let her keep her peace.

I decided that I would just live by myself in my adorable little apartment. I was a full hour away from them. An hour and a half, with traffic. I'd be happy living with my cat and my bird. They could live together with the elephant in *their* house. I had my own house now. The elephant that was crapping all over everything, and making everybody sick, was their problem. I wanted to be well, free, and never go back.

I enjoyed life on my own again. Vale Beach was nice. It was a cute neighborhood with all the streets named after trees. There was Chestnut, Hazelnut, Walnut, Peanut….just kidding….no Peanut. The streets were wide with big, old trees and old classic, beautiful houses mixed with new apartment buildings. There was big city sidewalks and a library with grass growing on top. I was enjoying my new home, and soon I was riding my bicycle to twelve step meetings. There were signs that this wasn't the best neighborhood but it took me some time to realize the real danger that was around me, a single, young female in a high crime area. I would go to the laundry mat and, every once in a while, some guy would come by selling steaks under his coat. They were obviously stolen from the grocery store. I should've been more scared down there but I didn't feel the way I looked. I was in a neighborhood infested with prostitutes, and junkies. I was hard on the inside, but on the outside, I was a victim waiting to happen. By the grace of God, I didn't get hurt down there.

One day, when I had about a week clean, I was minding my own business, doing my laundry, and here comes a pot smoker. I could spot them a mile away, and of course we were soon bicycling all around town stoned. I had no real resolve to make it very long clean and sober. I was lonely, and sad over my family situation. Drugs were a distraction. This fellow was a nice guy who had some problems just like me. He had been thrown out of the military because he threw a puppy out of a second story window. He had post-traumatic stress disorder. Now he was struggling because his friend who was still in the service would show up on the weekend with drugs, and even though he wanted to quit, his friend just kept showing up.

"He just keeps finding me. I feel helpless. I don't want to get high on that crap anymore." He would move, and his friend would find him again. He would cry real tears.

"I really want to quit but here he comes! Every time I move, he tracks me down. I open the door and there he is with the junk in his hand. I hate him but I am not strong enough to say no." I met his friend once. He showed up just like he said he would. Luckily, I was on my way out, and I was smart enough to keep going.

I felt deeply sorry for him especially after I became part of the problem, too. One day he introduced me to the level of drug use he was trying so desperately to get away from. First, we just smoked pot together but then it was off to the crack house on our bicycles. The first time I smoked crack I was stunned at how all-consuming it is. Immediately I became that carpet cleaner addict, scanning the floor for another rock to put in that pipe. Of course, there weren't any so we had to make two more trips on the bikes to the dealer's house until all the money was gone. I suddenly understood how this drug could completely take over your life in just one day. After several hours, and noticing way too many details about his orange shag carpet, I decided I had to quit hanging out with that guy. I never saw him again until months later.

    I had exactly zero temptation to go back to see that guy and do any more drugs with him, but being a rescuer, I did feel sorry for him. So a few months later I went back to his old run down apartment to look for him. He had moved but on a Saturday morning, I tracked him down. I asked him how he was doing, and he said he was still trying to hide but the night before his friend had shown up again. He was sick and skinny. He had lost his chubby belly, and he was living in an empty apartment with a few boxes, and empty alcohol bottles strewn around on the floor. He had long since sold off anything of value for drugs. My heart ached for him. He was going to die if he didn't get out of that city. I hugged him, and tried to encourage him to "never, never, never give up." Then I never, never, never went back.

    What can you do in the face of memories like that? He served his country and what he experienced broke him down. He had been out of the military for two years when I knew him. His friend, that showed up repeatedly, was in the military also, and always showed up while on weekend leave. What drove him to risk it all? When remembering hurting people from my past, I take great comfort in praying. If I could survive, perhaps they have too. I pray for both of them. I pray that they know Jesus and are now overcomers in the army of God.

BEACH HOUSE IN THE SHADOW OF DEATH

I was twenty-two, and living alone for the first time in my life. Well, I had my cat and my bird, but besides that it was just me in a studio apartment in Vale Beach. No roommates this time and no beautiful blue pool, unfortunately. I really missed that pool!

Before moving to Vale Beach, my mom had wanted to send me to rehab, but I refused to go. She had taken me to an outpatient center where she planned to drop me off in the morning, and pick me up at night after they shrunk my head all day long. Somehow this daily ritual was going to fix all our problems.

During the interview when we were deciding if I should go there, I showed the counselor the holes in my ears from cocaine use. He said he'd never seen those before. I thought to myself, this isn't much of a rehab. He's never seen these before? All of my friends have them. What kind of cocaine addicts has he been treating…pansies?!

They talked about the program, and how one day a week they have "family day". For most people, this weekly event is when the family gets to show up, and tell the addict what a thief, liar, and all-around scumbag they are. I was trying to imagine our family day, and I knew I wasn't ready for it. It was going to be me yelling and screaming at my mom about her molester husband. I knew she wasn't ready for it. I knew she wanted to help me but that place wasn't it. I wasn't ready to be the bad guy for my poor mom. She was still the ultimate rescue for me. My instinct was to protect her at all costs. I thought she wasn't strong enough to handle the molester problem or she would have by now, right? "Family Day" was the deal breaker. I told her that I wasn't going to that pathetic excuse for a rehab.

    One night, before I left my parent's house, some relatives came over to visit my parents. Apparently, even though we were family, and some of them were near my age, they weren't there to visit me. I felt like a fish in a fishbowl. They just stared at me, and didn't invite me into the visit or the conversation. I saw the look on their faces. I was skinny, too skinny…beautiful, perfect hair, perfect makeup but obviously strung out. The look on their faces was pity. They could see past the get up that I was hurting. They didn't come in, and talk to me or go out of their way to show me love or kindness. It's easier for the healthy non-addicted people to judge the addicted. And it's easy for addicted people to feel less than. Feeling like they didn't care enough to come in and talk to me just gave me more fuel to feel like I didn't belong, and nobody understood what was going on. The family picture was perfect except for me, the drug addict. I figured from their perspective it was simple…I was sick, they were well, end of story. I was hurt by their lack of caring and found another reason to be angry. I needed someone to ask me *why* I was so messed up. No one ever did. They knew what my step-father was guilty of but they were acting like it was fine, just like everybody else. I learned later that they were being fed lies about my siblings and I just "being mean" to our mother. She was the victim. I was unaware of this deception. I laughed when I heard that because for me, I was trying to protect my mother, and it was literally killing me.

    The excuse I had for my mother's behavior was denial. I'm not sure that fits now but what I do know is denial is what creates sins of omission. Sins of omission are when you know what you should do but don't bother. Sins of omission can be as simple as not taking the time to stop, and talk to someone who is obviously in pain. Sins of omission are what keep people from holding abusers accountable. It's easier to just ignore it than have a difficult conversation, and put someone in jail.

For the addicted person. it is easier to commit a sin of omission by not trying to get well. It's easier to say. "I'm just an addict. It's not *what* I do, it's *who* I am. Now I'm going to go get high because I'm mad at you because you don't care about me and I don't care about myself either." It's stupid but it's what self-destructive, people in pain do. Now I know that the saying "once an addict, always an addict" is not true for those who have surrendered their lives to Jesus. I am living proof of that.

***"Therefore, if anyone is in Christ, he is a new creation; old things have passed away, behold all things have become new."** 2 Corinthians 5:17*

Excerpt End

CHAPTER FOURTEEN

Another writers group and I could hardly wait. I needed this distraction from my tired middle, aged, pudgy life. I was taking mass amounts of d-3 vitamins, the "liquid sunshine" vitamin, but I was still down a lot. But tonight, was the usual poetry reading, and I was looking forward to some sing-song, ultra-sappy, try not to giggle gems from my fellow class mates. A couple macho types thought poetry was ridiculous, and took it as a challenge to try to make us laugh every time. Others were deadly serious about their poetry, and we also tried not to laugh when they were sharing. Poetry was such a personal expression, it was impossible to really label any of it "bad", but some of it was pretty close. Mine, included.

I had been teaching the kids fuzzy, wuzzy and I remembered how cute they were, with their little innocent voices all in unison. Then for fun, I had them say it louder and louder. "FUZZY WUZZY WAS A BEAR, FUZZY, WUZZY HAD NO HAIR! FUZZY WUZZY WASN'T FUZZY WAS HE?!!" That was a fun day and I smiled remembering them yelling their little heads off. Children, such a blessing to me, such a joy.

"Jo Lisa, come on up!" My instructor broke into my daydream. Here we go. Children's poetry to the right, adults to the left.

Writers Group - Sharing Excerpt Thirteen
Genre: Semi-Autobiographical Memoir, Christian
Author: Jo Lisa Blossom

Garden of Pain

I'd rather be alone
Than reap what we've sown
With our seeds of love.

I'd rather not know
What we might grow
Tall under our care.

I'd rather not harvest
The crop that our best
Together has planted.

I'd rather not see
What's not meant to be
In this garden of pain.

Frail

I remember
what 36
looked like,
so easy
it was
my favorite number
for years.
I remember
the shock
at 56,
the gray hair,

wrinkles
and sorrow.
You came
out of the woods
too thin.
I almost gasped
at the sight,
it hurt
so much.
Now at 70
the pain
is so unbearable,
I want to run.
A fixer
cannot love enough
Only God can repair
the ravages
of time.

IN THE HAND OF GOD

      While living in Vale Beach I signed up to go to a College of Business. It was a private trade school that the government would help inner city, low income people go to. I got a hundred and seventy one dollars a week to learn computerized bookkeeping. I met a few friends there and now I was visiting the home of one of them.

      "Here you can have this. It's the only thing of value I own, and it'll get stolen soon anyway." My heroin addict friend was handing me the most beautiful old medal cross necklace I'd ever seen. He and I went to business school together, and I hadn't realized he was a heroin addict until just then. The cross he was trying to give me was so intricate and old that I didn't want to take it. It was too beautiful. How could I take a gift like that?

But he looked at me with those sad eyes behind thick, coke bottle glasses and pockmarked skin, and I knew he was right. He had borrowed twenty dollars from me awhile before. Before I realized he was going to use it for heroin. Now to my surprise we were standing in an old house, on top of an abandoned building. It was a one-bedroom house built on top of an old apartment building. This is where he lived with some other junkies. No water, no electricity, no nice, cushy comforter on the old, dirty mattress on the floor. In his "room", he had pulled the cross out of a hidden area in the wall. I looked around, and felt his hopelessness. This was where some horrid landlord made an illegal buck off desperate junkies, and illegal aliens. Or they were squatters, and no one was paying anything. We snuck in and now we couldn't "stay long". I looked down at this amazing treasure in my hand, and I knew there was no arguing with him. We both knew that soon someone there would find this cross, steal it, sell it for drugs, and that would be that. He was giving it to me to repay the twenty dollars. He also knew that if he ever had that amount of money in his hand it wasn't going to make it to me. If he gave me this treasure, he wouldn't have to feel like even more of a hopeless failure when someone stole it. I wasn't a junkie. I would never be a junkie. I hugged my sad friend, and told him I would cherish it forever. I intended to.

  I think about that friend sometimes. I pray that he got into God's hand, and his life was transformed. In the flesh, I imagine that he died from an overdose. In the Spirit, I know that he was someone's baby once, and because he took that cross and tried to honor it, God noticed. Because I know my God is faithful, I believe there is a strong possibility that he's not a junkie anymore. There's a strong possibility that God intervened, he repented, God saved him, transformed his life, and gave him a testimony for God's glory.

I took that cross that day and I did cherish it. I couldn't believe how old and unique it was. It represented something to me. Hope. It also pricked my conscience. Later on, I lost it, twice. I would take it off and hang it on a motel room lamp. I would take it off because I was about to have sex outside of marriage. The Holy Spirit within me, and that cross around my neck, reminded me that this was wrong. Immorality was not what God wanted from me. He wanted more. He wanted better.

The first time I forgot the cross on the lampshade and got it back, it was a miracle. The hotel mailed it back to me, all the way from another state. But the second time, I didn't get it back. I guess God moved it on to someone else who needed it more than me.

Some people will think that it's ridiculous for people completely given over to sin to try to "honor" God. Some people will say that my junkie friend, and I were not really saved so the cross was just a valuable object to us. I would beg to differ. I know that even in my deepest, darkest struggle with depression and self-destruction, God was holding me in the palm of His hand. He was waiting for me to put the Cross on and never, ever take it off. He was waiting for me to follow the third commandment. "Thou shalt not use the Lord's name in vain." If I am calling myself a Christian, I should not be deliberately sinning. The commandment is not just about using God's name as a curse word. It is about trying to live like a Christian, not a pagan. God was waiting for me to hear His voice calling and finally surrender to His will for my life.

I'm not a perfect Christian but when I'm wrong, God has shown me the freedom in repentance. If I admit when I am wrong, apologize, and make amends; it is so much easier than just feeling badly about my mistake. Or worse yet, ignoring my sin, and having it take root and then take over becoming more sin, bigger sin. I'm not a perfect Christian but even when I do something horribly, horribly wrong, I am still a Christian. If all you heard about me was that horrible sin that I had committed, in the flesh you would be inclined to think I was not "saved" at all. You would be wrong.

    A popular 1970's bumper sticker said it best: "Christians aren't perfect, just forgiven." My mom used to say, "If you see a dead body on the road, it might be dead, but it's still a body." You can see a Christian who doesn't *look* like they are alive in the faith. They aren't producing any good fruit or living their life like a Christian should, but if they asked Christ to forgive them, come live in their heart and be their Lord and Savior when they were eight, He still did. No matter what else *we* do, God is faithful. That's what grace is.

    I'm grateful that I am no longer deeply rooted in sinful behavior but I am also much more compassionate towards those that are. They are not just sinning, they are hurting.

    I came to realize that the recovery group I was attending in Vale Beach, wasn't working. I was still lonely. I believe God made people to need two things, purpose and belonging. I had neither. Eventually, I would drive the hour back home to my old hang out, my old friends, and meth. I had a best friend then that was always there for me. She was sicker than me so we got along just fine. She wasn't a junkie but she always had a bag. I felt safe with her. That's how addicts are. We feel safe with one another, and especially if we can find someone just slightly more screwed up than we are. We know we always have some place to go where we won't get turned away. There's always an open spot on the front line of stupidity.

    This friend was stealing from anywhere she

could, but not from me. She had a reputation for being a thief, and other people couldn't understand why I was hanging out with her, but she had never done me wrong. She had a huge, generous heart, and we had started our career together on coke but we eventually tried meth, and that was now the substance we were slaves to.

    By this time, I had already been to drug diversion. That's the classes they send you to the first time you get busted. They try that small group setting before the bigger, more serious groups like rehab and jail.

    I hit a sort of rock bottom one day when I had been over one of my old freind's houses ingesting bad meth for two days. That's the other place I would visit to find company. Her roommate got some very bad dope from who knows where, and you had to do a massive amount to feel anything. That was the first clue. Of course, we missed it, and went ahead and snorted way more than we should've, and drank a lot on top of that.

    I was so sick and uncomfortable, that by the time I finally decided to go home, I decided to take my last ten bucks, and buy some weed. I had to go to this alley in Vale Beach to buy it, since I didn't know of anywhere else to get it. This was not your typical alley. It was more like a row of beat up ginger bread houses with cement in the middle. There was a lot of trim on the buildings that looked like they were inspired by Danish designs. But there were no real windows, no yards, no porches; just tall walls of fancy trim with doors, and these two guys standing there. There was only one way in, and one way out, so it was not the smartest place for a girl like me to be. But I wasn't a smart girl. I was a sick girl. I drove in, and got past the shocked look on the dealer's face, and his consequential flirting with me, to get my bag and go. I went home, and started smoking trying to get relief from how sick I felt. But that's not what I got.

    Suddenly my chest seemed to shrink. I felt like I

was being crushed, and I couldn't breathe. I was terrified. I thought I was having a heart attack. I didn't really mind dying but I didn't want to die like *that*. I knew that if I died there, it would be obvious it was drugs. I knew I should go to the hospital or call 911 but I didn't want to be embarrassed by having the last thing said about me, be that I had died from drugs. In desperation, I did the only thing I knew to do. I put my feet up, hoping it would help my heart and I got out my bible. I started begging God to save me, and started reading the bible. I don't remember what I read. I do remember that about five minutes later I felt like I was going to live. And I did.

I felt very foolish after that. I knew I had almost killed myself. I knew I had done it to myself. I knew God could help me if I could just stay clean. For a few weeks, I did stay clean. I would ride my bike downtown to the twelve step meetings, and feel like I was really on my way to getting better.

One day, I went back home to my parent's house to pick up my mail, and tell my mom how good I was doing. I walked into my parent's house, and walked in on my step-father holding a young girl down on the carpet tickling her.

"Stop, stop!" The girl was squirming, and objecting to what he was doing. She looked about ten, and I recognized her as the daughter of a family friend.

My mother said, "Leave her alone. We need to start the reading lesson." Scenes like that left me in shock. I had no response. I wish I had fought for that girl. But at the time, I said nothing. I did nothing. Emotionally, I needed relief from my pain no matter what the cost. I was overwhelmed with that feeling of powerlessness again. I was mentally traumatized seeing my step father on his way to molesting another victim, and realizing my mother had brought her over for him.

I left. Then knowing it was too late for me to speak up in the moment, was nauseating for me. What could I say that hadn't already been said? I wish I had gone to the girl's mom but how to get her phone number and address? I didn't know, and I was caught up in my own feelings of hopelessness. I didn't know what to do. On top of that, when I went home, I was sad and lonely. I gave in, and called a friend for drugs. I gave in to the temptation, and decided that even though I had almost killed myself the last time I did drugs, I would just never do "crappy" dope again. Maybe if I got high and drank enough, I could forget that little girls face, and her voice saying, "Stop, stop!" Maybe.

DINNER PARTY WITH A COOK

"Why don't you just come home and live with us? We need somebody to watch the house while we go on trips." It was over a year later and my mother had started the dreaded coercion again.

"I don't know, Mom. I'll think about it." I answered slowly. Over a year had gone by but I was already feeling like a failure back on dope. I was driving back home to visit friends almost once a week, and I still didn't have many new friends in Vale Beach. My mother kept asking me to move back home, and it didn't take long before I said okay. Big mistake, but by then it was a pattern. I justified my plan by thinking that they would be gone a lot on their "trips", so it might be alright. I could have dinner parties with my friends, and pretend I owned the place without paying rent. A twenty three-year old in paradise.

"I can't go out with you anymore."
"Why? I love you."
"I've been up for three days, and I feel great. That

means I'm turning into a 'lifer', and I just can't be your girlfriend anymore. Do you want to quit with me? I wish somebody would quit with me. We could help each other!"

"Ah I don't know. I'd have to think about that. But I still love you."

My boyfriend looked at me with his sad eyes, and turned around, walking towards his shed. That was his 'house'…a wooden shed, with no water, in his mom's backyard. Most people kept their lawn mower in there but he lived there, and dealt drugs to the neighborhood. Still the rescuer, I thought I could rescue him from his chosen lifestyle, but at that point I knew he didn't want to quit drugs. We had discussed it a few times. I was always the one talking about getting clean and ruining everybody's buzz. I just couldn't accept it. I didn't want to be a 'lifer'. I wanted to be *clean*. It felt so wrong to just give up, and accept drug addiction. This time, I had been up for three days, and knew I should feel like death itself. But I didn't. I felt good. That scared me. I couldn't do this. I knew that if I continued, and made a habit of staying up for days at a time, I would end up with a 'psychotic break'. That had happened to a couple of people I knew. They stayed up so long, that they took them away to the mental hospital.

I visited a mental hospital once, when a friend had tried suicide. I didn't like the smell. I didn't like the feeling. I didn't like anything in there. Just thinking about it made me shudder. It smelled like urine, and everybody looked like zombies on waaaay too many meds. I went once, and that was enough. I felt bad for my friend but I decided right then and there, I was never going back, not even for a visit, and certainly not because I was too stupid to go to bed.

Unfortunately, after I broke up with that boyfriend, my resolve to stay single, clean and on the right path didn't last long.

    At one of my fabulous dinner parties, I was introduced to the local meth cook. I didn't know what he was at first, but I figured it out. That didn't stop me from trying to save him. He was in love with another girl, the mother of his child. I foolishly took that as manners because he didn't want to sleep with me right away. It had nothing to do with manners, but it was the first time that had happened in a very long time. It was refreshing to me that he wasn't interested in sex right off the bat. That combined with his pathetic existence made it impossible for me, the rescuer, to resist.

    Along with a new boyfriend to save, I also had a steady stream of dope whenever I wanted it. Unfortunately, living back at home, I seemed to want it every day. I got really skinny. I was spending a lot of time hanging out with my thieving best friend, and learning to live in constant disappointment over the boyfriend. Everybody needs a best friend to whine to when your boyfriend is a meth cook.

    One day my best friend, her boyfriend, and I, went to the park to talk to a "carny" named "Tiny". He was there at the park breaking down the carnival. He was also decidedly not tiny. He was *huge*. He was about six foot, five and three hundred pounds. Apparently, he owed my bestie's boyfriend some money. There we were, talking to Tiny when he, and her boyfriend get into a spat. Of course, they did. Suddenly, her boyfriend, who was *not* large, takes off, and there we are face to face with this massive dude. Well, my best friend was loyal to her man. She starts yelling, and swinging her purse around to whallop Tiny. To my surprise, she lands one smack on the side of his head, and he falls backward like Goliath going down. A "tiny" dust cloud poofs up around him as he bounces in the dirt like a massive tree. It all happened so fast, I could hardly believe it. It would have been funny if it hadn't been so shocking. She knocked him out with her purse! What on earth was in there? I was about to ask but when I turned my head to speak, we looked at each other and then terror struck.

"We gotta get out of here!", I gasped. We realized in the same moment that when Tiny woke up, he was going to be a *little* upset. We start running as fast as our skinny legs would carry us, headed for the car. We made it about half way there, and we could hear Tiny behind us. He is shaking the ground with his huge feet, lumbering through the grass. I glance back in terror, and he is yelling, and waving his fist. "You blankity blank! I'll blankity kill you!" We never moved so fast. We got in the car, and zoomed off, with him behind us screaming and yelling. Somehow her boyfriend managed to make it to the car as we drove out of the parking lot. We had escaped! We almost wet our pants but we never laughed so hard. Tiny got knocked out by a five foot- two chick with a purse, a massively under celebrated, multi-purpose accessory.

PURSUE GOD LIKE ONLY THE DYING CAN

"You're frying your brain and you have to stop!" I was on meth everyday now and my mother was worried sick. She had come into my room and was frantic. I was showing her my art projects. "Did you sleep last night?" She stared at me waiting for an answer.

"Well, yes for a little bit. But I'm not tired!" I told her.

"You need to get some help." She said as she turned to walk out. I thought she was ridiculous of course. I mean I felt brilliant, up at three in the morning decorating.

Why I had thought coming back home would work, I will never know. Like always, I had gotten worse living at home. Coming back was a mistake, and what I was saving in rent money, I was definitely losing in brain cells and weight. I was down to a hundred and three pounds, and sinking deeper and deeper into despair. My mother still worked every day but my step-father was retired. He was there at home all day. Every day he would say lewd things to me. I don't know how I got talked into coming back to this environment, but there I was, completely hopeless again. I just never had the words to confront him. I would regress to the silence of paralyzing pain then leave, and spew hatred to my friends.

I went home as little as possible but that meant that my daily focus had disintegrated to my drug addict friends, my newest boyfriend and getting high. But I knew that wasn't what I really wanted. I remembered the free, county rehab so I decided that I should try it. I drove two hours into the mountains, and checked it out. My boyfriend, the meth cook, said he wanted to get clean, too. We had a plan…I would go to rehab, and we would *both* quit drugs. How could this not work?

Rehab was one of the best times I had ever had in my life, up to that point. It was in the mountains and it was beautiful. I had always wanted to live someplace beautiful, and this almost felt like camp. Almost. We had one long dorm with about twenty girls on each end. The guys had cabins. There was a cafeteria and classes to go to every day. There was a recreation room and tennis courts. I was excited to be there. And after the first painful few days, I started to really feel good. I started to feel like I could beat these addictions…well except for coffee and donuts.

I had several profound experiences in rehab. I met people I have not forgotten, and things I saw and heard there changed the way I view the world.

We had a talent show because you know, drug addicts are so talented. Another patient in the rehab did a modern dance routine about the torment of being a junkie. He was very talented, and the dance was amazing. Besides that, he made me uncomfortable because he was also apparently a sex addict. There was no mention of this addiction in any of our classes. Sadly. For me, it was nasty to be around that kind of blatant promiscuity. He was openly chasing other men, and definitely catching some. It was shocking and disturbing, but I'll never forget what he shared one night at a meeting.

"My Dad always told me, 'Don't ever make yourself sad trying to make someone else happy.'" That is how his father reacted to his son's life choices. I admired that father for loving his son enough to put it into *those* words to help his son. He didn't want his son to be sad, and if that's what it took, that's what it took. To me, at the time, what his father said, felt like a profound truth, and it cut me to the heart. I had been doing that all my life. I didn't know how to *stop* making myself sad trying to make someone else happy. At the time I did not yet know the technical term is 'co-dependent'. But I thought, "Yeah, I got that".

Another one, of the talent show performances, was a girl who struggled socially. She would not have survived the girls in my high school P.E. class. The vicious females in that class made a girl literally cry because she wasn't good at volleyball. Those cranky females would've eaten this chubby girl alive. She was not happy, which no one there really was all the time. But this girl was mean to other people who tried to be friendly with her. She did not shower anywhere near enough, and her clothes looked like they may have belonged to her mother. I remember sucking in my breath when she started to sing her song. I thought for sure the audience was going to make merciless fun of her because she had been so nasty to so many people. She started singing an old western song. Then she stopped, and then she started, and then she stopped, and then she started. For most groups this would've been the prime opportunity to laugh, and let human nature take its Darwinian, "survival of the fittest" course. My heart was aching for her, and I fully expected her to be shamed off the stage in record time. But with this group of tragic "losers", something truly amazing happened. They cheered her on. It was so incredibly touching because this girl wasn't their friend. She wasn't anybody's friend. She wasn't a friendly person but somehow, she had the guts to sing. She wasn't singing very well but that crowd of misfits cheered her on, and encouraged her until she almost made it through the entire song. Let me tell you it took a while. I cried. We all applauded like mad when she finally finished. This misfit girl with her head down for the entire song, lifted her head and gave us a little smile. It was a first and it was so beautiful. My faith in humanity was restored in under eight minutes. This was how humans, and especially Christians, are supposed to be… loving even when it's horrifying and uncomfortable. It's so someone else can experience true acceptance and love. I've never seen that happen before or after, anywhere else…only in a free, county rehab, with people the world had likely written off.

  There were other things that happened in rehab that indicated that God was trying to show me another way. It was the first time that I was able to put together more than two weeks clean in several years. It felt good. It felt like I might be able to make it but I didn't know how to stop doing other self- destructive things.

  I still had my meth cook boyfriend but he didn't always show up to visit me, and I was still a raging rescuer co-dependent. What else could I do? I got a male sponsor. Totally against the rules but smarty pants me, got a muscular, black haired, blue eyed, buff, good looking sponsor. It didn't matter that he was gay, and a prostitute who would go off site to visit with tricks on the weekends. He looked like a broken super hero to me. I immediately began trying to 'rescue' him from himself. Who cares about me? I decided to sleep with him, and maybe that would cure him from the sadness he seemed to be carrying around. Never mind that he was probably carrying around a deadly disease, too. It is a miracle that I did not get a disease of any kind. I slept with a practicing male prostitute who was also a recovering junkie. What an idiot. But apparently, God wasn't done with me yet.

Somehow, I thought my boyfriend back home would miraculously stop making meth, get a job, and become a healthy person while I was gone. Ninety days was plenty of time, right?

Rehab has a way of putting a mirror up in front of you, and showing you just how insane your life really is. The things I heard in rehab made me realize I wasn't the only one who was in a death spiral. One poor guy with a buzz cut was from Texas, and he shared his "moment of clarity". It happened when he realized he was chopping up the cocaine, that he had snuck into rehab, with his rehab ID card, on top of his twelve step book. He looked up from his story with a little smile, shaking his head back and forth, laughing at himself. "Ya'll my life is jus' plain out o' control! I mean what was I fixin' to do up in here anyways? I sho need help! I know it!" We all laughed because we knew *exactly* what he meant.

Then there was the charming addict with the shaved head, and the tattoo on his neck that said "mutha 13". He shared that he was out partying one night with his buddies, and the next thing he knew he was waking up half naked, alone, in the middle of the desert. When he finally caught up with his friends, they were surprised to see him alive. They told him that they had driven him out there, and left him for dead after he over dosed. They didn't want to have to explain their dead friend, to the cops, or the ambulance driver. They all shouted 'Road trip!', and off they went to drop off his puke covered body in the sand. He was hurt that his "friends" just left him like that. He wasn't laughing when he shared but of course, everybody else in the room burst out laughing. He looked up surprised, and then he threw his head back and laughed, too. "I see you guys would probably leave my broken, naked blank, too! What the blank!" It felt so good to laugh at the horror of it all, with people who truly understood the insanity.

Excerpt End

CHAPTER FIFTEEN

"What is she thinking?" I was inadvertently ease dropping on a heated conversation behind me. We were all waiting for this week's instructor at writing class. He had sent word that he would be late. Apparently, this woman needed the extra time to vent.

"I mean the woman sent her to a foreign country with her pedophile husband when she was fifteen. She set her up to get molested by him but still she thinks she's the best aunt she's ever had. Why?" Now I was hanging on every word. I glanced over my shoulder, and saw the eyes of the classmate she was talking to, get decidedly bigger.

"Wow." He said slowly before she continued her rant.

"I just don't get it. Where's the accountability? Auntie can do no wrong. She gets all the love. Gets a call every week to make sure she feels loved."

"What the heck? Your family sounds all jacked up!" The big-eyed man just read my mind.

"I know!" She continued, in a softer tone, realizing the instructor had just arrived. "I mean maybe she's forgiven her and that's a good thing. I get that, but what about the accountability? What about repentance and an apology once in her life? What about the rest of us who've never done her wrong? What are we chopped liver?"

I giggled at her expression, instantly thinking of cat food for some reason. You and me both, I thought.

The instructor had arrived and begun talking but I was distracted by the verse on the chalkboard behind him. Someone else who'd used the room had apparently left it behind and there it was. Chopped up families, chopped up liver. Sadly, we're all cat food to somebody.

"God sets the lonely in families; He brings out those who are bound into prosperity; but the rebellious dwell in dry land." Psalm 68:6

I thought, what am I Lord? Am I rebellious? Do I hold on tight to things you want me to let go? Do I need to stop to buy more cat food after class? I don't know! Ok back to reality. I tried to focus on the instructor.

"Tonight, we are going to mix it up. I want you to look around and the person sitting *directly* behind you is the person you will share your latest excerpt with! No cheating! Turn around and meet someone new!" The instructor clapped his hands, excited about his idea. I turned around and stared into the eyes of the angry woman.

"Hi", I smiled, handing her my pages. She handed me hers, apologizing.

"I know you heard me talking earlier. Sorry about that. I'm passionate sometimes." She laughed a little too loud. I smiled a little too big back at her.

"I understand," I said. "Me, too." I like her already, I thought. Mad and not afraid to say so. Tell it, sister! At that moment I remembered what the next chapter I had handed to her was. Well, I thought, here's some more to rant about.

Writers Group - Sharing Excerpt Fourteen
Genre: Semi-Autobiographical Memoir, Christian
Author: Jo Lisa Blossom

The Plank

Still waiting
for
apologies
that
never
come.

Perhaps
I
should
be
the
first
or
repeat
the
words
until
they
hear
me.

God
please
give
me
sincerity
and
love

for
the
unrepentant.

When I Die

When I die
I want to fly
Up to the sky
When you call
Let me fall
In the tall
Green grass
With birds chirping
And silver lined clouds
Above my head
When the Lord
Calls my name
And the angels
Come get me
Let me see
Eternity
Outside on a breezy day
With the warm sun
On my cheeks
And the beauty
Of flowers fresh
In my mind
God come find
Me intertwined
With you.

ONE IN TEN REMEMBER WHEN

One night in rehab, a guest speaker came in. She was tall, pretty, had glasses, a thick east coast accent and slightly graying hair. She had attended the program several years earlier. She talked about accidentally shooting up a cotton fiber and how it was floating around in her heart. She knew it could kill her at any time so her sobriety had an urgency about it. She was determined to live every day to the fullest. She should've been jumping out of airplanes or in the Bahamas with her toes in the sand working her way through a bucket list. Instead, she was there, trying to help other lost people.

She looked around the room and said, "When I was here, about twelve years ago, they told us that only one in ten addicts will stay clean. Have they told you that yet?" A couple heads nodded and she went on. "I said, that has got to be horse doo. There is no way that *only* one in ten makes it! I flat out did not believe it. So being the cynical nerd that I am, I set out to prove them wrong. I made a point to keep track of nine other people that I went to this rehab with and guess what?" We were all listening with both ears now. "Rodney, dead, AIDS brought on by IV drug use. Phil, dead, pneumonia, and we all know forty-two years olds don't die of pneumonia, unless their lungs are damaged from gee, I wonder what. Tammy committed suicide, after coming back here three more times. Marsha, in prison, drug manufacturing. Monica, in prison, drug possession for the fifth time. She still writes. Bonnie she is gone, they suspected overdose but nobody bothered to check because she died on the street. "natural causes" my blank. Um, Tony, the last time I talked to his Dad, he said he was back in the mental hospital. They found him walking down the street buck naked again. If I remember correctly, he liked to do that here, too." We laughed, and I noticed that the girl next to me was counting people on her fingers. We were on number seven. "Let me see, Danny, died in jail last year. I think he was in there for something really bad. His mom wouldn't tell me and honestly, I didn't ask much. Bad manners, anyway. Eight would be Max, and he's also passed...liver cancer." She slowly looked us each in the eye. "I am the only one still clean." I still remember the somber look on her face. What she said was hard to hear. In my foolish pride, I decided right then that she was completely full of it. But why would she lie? In meetings, they always said, "jails, institutions and death", and that's what she described.

As the days went by, and I heard more stories like those she told, I started to look at the addicts in the tv room with pity. There were several that never came to meetings. I started to realize that for some life was already over. Some of them were very vocal crack addicts who would tell you plainly that they were just "getting fat to go back out." That is a hard thing to see. They just went to chow, and the tv room. They weren't even pretending they cared. The demon was deeply rooted, and they weren't even fighting it anymore.

Another girl that had the bunk across from me, told us her story. She was a beautiful woman, and she was a severe alcoholic. She had tried to commit suicide by swallowing drain cleaner. She survived that with no after affects but eventually ended up homeless living in the park. She was found close to death, and finally got put in the hospital. She cried telling us that her dad didn't recognize her. When he was finally convinced that it was her, he never left her bedside. When she got well enough, he took her home but she ended up drinking again. Because of the care he gave her when she was in the hospital close to death, this time after relapsing, she checked *herself* into rehab. She didn't want to disappoint her dad again. She didn't want to die, and have her dad not know it was her, and wonder forever what had happened to her. Love made her keep fighting for life.

One addict was describing his relationship with his addict girlfriend. "It's not the blind leading the blind, it's the sick leading the sick!" He was right, we were all in pretty bad shape. As for my situation, it was pretty much the same. My boyfriend knew he was failing me because he was failing himself.

We got to use one of the two available phones once per night. The phones were basically pay phones outside, and we were only allowed ten minutes. They would give you your time, and call it out on the loudspeaker when it was your turn. Every night, my boyfriend told me he was clean, and looking for a job, and doing everything we talked about. Why I believed him, I have no idea. I mean why would a guy who had been using longer than me, and was basically couch surfing at the fellow cook's house, be able to get clean just because *I* was in a safe environment with no drugs? He was surrounded by drugs, and a constant stream of paying drug customers. I was the foolish one believing my own fantasy. That was my pattern. I kept trying to get men to "love me right." Just like I tried to get my step father to be a loving father all the time, and stop perpetually disappointing me. I found men that did the same thing. They were too sick to be healthy for themselves, let alone me. They continued the pattern established by my childhood.

Seventy-six days in, I asked the rehab counselor if I was ready to go home. The idiot said "yes", before doing any digging whatsoever on what I was headed home to. I was voluntarily there after all, so it's not like he could've encouraged me to wait until my ninety days was up. In case, you didn't recognize it, that was sarcasm. That professional rehab counselor didn't even try. I wish he had.

I got home from rehab, and headed over to where my newly employed, clean and sober, boyfriend was staying. I found him on the couch with the meth pipe in front of him. I just freaked out.

He was raised in a small town in Iowa by a single mom. She had faithfully taken him to church, but when I met him, he was a long way from that. Like most addicts, honesty wasn't high on the priority list, and so the "job", of cooking and dealing meth, hadn't changed. The pattern continued. It wasn't his fault. He was just another sick addict like me. But this time I had seventy-six days clean. The longest I had spent with no chemical or alcohol in my system since I was thirteen years old.

I screamed, yelled and went to a friend's house in a rage only to find them more than willing to sympathize, and get me high. Of course! I was 'not worth it'. This was more proof. I was not worth it for this guy to be honest or clean. I was not worth it for my mom to address the pervert in the house. What was the point of trying anymore? Tragically, it only took forty-eight hours out of rehab, and drugs and pain were back in my blood steam.

PREGNANT FAILURE

Less than a month later, I made another desperate attempt to get clean. I had to get away from my parents, my boyfriend, and all of the people I knew. In twelve step groups they tell you to change your play things, your play mates and your playground. I was determined. I moved to my uncle's house.

He was going through a lot and needed help with his kids. His wife had passed away from cancer and he had room. It was pretty good there for a few days, then it all went downhill.

"Your ex-boyfriend can get a sixteenth?" My uncle's new girlfriend asked. She had heard me talking about my ex the meth cook, and now she was looking at me like a starving man looks at steak. "Reeeeaaaalllly", she said. I sighed. Here we go, I thought, but now there's kids in the house. I hate this.

The rest of the story is just more of the same horror of drugs, and group stupidity. But I had nowhere else to go.

"Yep. You're pregnant", she said without even looking up. I just stood there not knowing what to do next. I felt like I was sinking into a black hole of the unknown.

I was on birth control so I really didn't expect to be pregnant. But my period was late so I looked up pregnancy tests in the phone book, and found my way to this place. It looked like it had been a clothing store. It was empty except for one lady behind a table on the outside of the dressing rooms, now converted into very small bathrooms. There was nothing medical about it but I checked in anyway. The lady behind the table gave me my little kit, and sent me into one of the bathrooms. I read the little instructions, took the test, and waited. Positive. I was in shock. I didn't know what to think. On auto pilot, I walked back to her desk.

Standing in front of her, I almost whispered. "Isn't somebody going to talk to me?" Now she looked up. The stern look on her face made it clear, s*he* wasn't going to talk to me.

"No, we don't do that here. These places can help you." She handed me a list of clinics; women's clinics. What kind of help did she think I needed? At that moment, I just needed somebody to help me process verbally. I needed to know what this *meant*. Looking at this cold, expressionless woman, I knew she didn't care about me or my emotional state. I turned and walked out. I knew who I needed to talk to next but how to say it?

"Son of a blankity blank!" My ex-boyfriend slammed his fist into the windshield, cracking it. We were sitting in the driveway of my uncle's house, and we were pregnant.

The day before this revelation, my uncle had told me that his new girlfriend, and her eight year old son, were moving in. I was going to be sharing a room with an ill-behaved little boy, whose specialty was ripping the heads off dolls. How appropriate, I thought. But why now?

I felt abandoned at the worst possible time. I had no place where I was really wanted. Except with the meth cook. Even with our mess, he seemed to want me around, and I wanted *something* in my life to work. I poured what little dignity and strength I had into that distorted relationship. Within a few days I started having morning sickness. I was also on meth every day.

Having the baby never really felt like an option. I thought that it was too late. I read about how important the first trimester was in the baby's development, and I figured I'd already done too much damage. I had a lot of justification for my decision. I was hopeless. I was a failure. I couldn't get clean or stay clean. I was homeless, and the only person who really wanted me around was a meth cook. What "choice" did I have?

Now I know that I had a lot of choice. I could've gone back to a program and gotten clean again. I had actually been clean for most of the early pregnancy, while I was in rehab. But then of course, I wasn't sure if this baby belonged to my male prostitute sponsor. The meth use alone was enough to make me give up but that little worry just put me over the edge. I wish I had been braver. I could've humbled myself, searched for help, and then accepted it. But I didn't. I was too quick to decide it was too late.

I failed at recovery, and now I had failed at not

having a baby out of wedlock. I knew being unmarried, and pregnant, was wrong. I knew having sex, and not being married was an offense to God. Somehow, in all the craziness of my life, I still cared about that.

At that point in my life, I wasn't really thinking about other people judging me. I was too busy judging myself. The accuser, the devil was immediately after my baby. He knew just what to whisper into my mind. "You are a failure. You can't get clean for yourself so there's no way you can stay clean for a baby. You're nothing but a drug addict."

"Then he showed me Joshua the high priest standing before the angel of the LORD, and Satan standing at his right side to <u>accuse</u> him." Zachariah 3:1

HOTEL HELL

I needed to fix this and NOW! I was instructed to go to the welfare office right away to get emergency medical. My appointment was in five days, next Wednesday at two. A little paperwork, a little pain, a little person lost forever to the assembly line of the abortion industry.

I had an abortion but I have no memory of it. I know I was pregnant. I know I had an abortion but I could not tell you with any certainty where I was living when it happened. I know I had moved out of my uncle's house, and went somewhere, but where? I do not know. Apparently, the experience was simply too painful because even decades later, I simply can't remember any details, except the clinic. I know which one. I know where. I know how my baby died. Part of me died that day, too.

After my abortion, I was like an emotional zombie but I tried to look at the bright side of living with my boyfriend, on our own. I had never lived with a man before. Living at hotels and paying with drug money was sordid but it felt like I was taking a step towards my own house. I really loved having a pool nearby, until the couple in the room next door started screaming and fighting for hours. Then the nest felt more like a pit. The screamers finally checked out and then just when it might've gotten better, my blue water fantasy got abruptly interrupted again.

"Hello Miss. Can I talk to you?" It was the police. I was getting laundry out of my stolen car in the parking lot. They had seen me walking by on the way back from picking up some fries. At first, I couldn't figure out why they had pulled up to talk to me. I knew I didn't look like a drug addict. I had dolled myself up like usual, and walked across the hotel parking lot, to the restaurant. I didn't really notice the black and white parked there eating a cheese burger. But they noticed me. They thought I was a hooker. All my determination to look normal with curled hair, make up, and tight pants really paid off this time.

I was obsessed with looking perfect, no matter where I went. I was wearing flowered stretch pants, and my platinum blonde hair was perfectly curled. I spent more than an hour getting made up to go get those fries. They stopped me when I was digging around in that hot red car about to go upstairs, and sleep off the vanilla shake. Of course, they immediately figured out I was also on meth.

"What are you doing staying here?" They were questioning me relentlessly, and it became apparent they thought I was a prostitute. Now the questioning took a whole new bent.

"So is your boyfriend up their cooking?" One cop looked at the other with a gleeful look. This cop thought he'd hit the jackpot. He thought we were cooking in the hotel room and running a prostitution ring. What?

"I know what you are up to! Hookin and cookin!" He was visually excited about this "big bust" he was about to make.

"What room is yours? I think we need to go take a look." I had no idea if I had any rights living there and I thought if I cooperated, maybe they'd let me go. They wanted to go search the room, and so they did. I was really sweating bullets then. The car I had was a different color than the car I owned. But they were focused on other things.

One cop went upstairs while the other stayed in the parking lot with me. Cop number one searched the room, and no meth lab. That didn't stop him. He called the number on my pager, and tried to get my girlfriend to say disgusting things to him. When she called him a pervert, he realized there was no prostitution ring either. He searched my car for something he could use to prove this was a "big fish", while cop number went to talk to the hotel security guard. I was close to hyperventilating. He found another bag of meth in the trunk. I thought it was all over. I still remember he picked it up flicked it back and forth, and then my jaw dropped when he just put it back, and closed the trunk. Normally, that would've made me ecstatic but I was in the back of that cop car having an anxiety attack because he just slammed the trunk of my stolen car.

Let me explain. My mother had co-signed on a car for me a couple of years earlier. That car was white. One night, it broke down in a friend's yard, and the gang members from across the street talked me into trading. In my friend's neighborhood, like ours, you didn't have to look far to find gang members. When the car broke down in his yard, a neighbor, aka gang member just happened to know another neighbor, aka gang member, and they just happened to have a car just like mine a couple houses away at another neighbor's, aka gang member's. It was red, and it was stolen, but it ran. The friendly neighborhood gang member, aka car salesman, convinced me to swap. He said he would scratch off all the vin numbers, and everything would be hunky dory. To prove it, he promptly went outside, and pried the metal plate from the car's doorjamb off. He handed it to me with a winning smile. It seemed like a good idea at the time. I was unemployed, broke down in the yard, and had fourteen dollars in my pocket. I thought to myself, it's my lucky day! This is a genius, fool proof plan! What could *possibly* go wrong? I drove that red car back to the hotel with my white car's license plates newly attached. I felt like hot stuff. If I had more money, I would've immediately had flames painted on the sides of my new cool, red ride.

But now, I sat in the back of the cop car, reviewing these events trying to come up with some explanation that wouldn't land me in prison. I knew the plate with the vin number from my real car was in the hotel room, hidden inside a book with the insides hollowed out. It was a real high tech criminal place to hide something. I was sure they would find that plate, and talk to the security guard who noticed that one day I had a white car, and the next day I had a red one. But both cars had the same license plate. I know he knew. But God bless that guy, he never did tell. And they never found the vin plate. Apparently, they weren't really interested in my book reading habits. After their room search, and trying to find some clue on my phone, cop number one started to get really aggravated because I wasn't the big fish they were hoping to fry.

"Blank it! No hookin' and cookin'! Two blankin' hours and nothing! I thought for sure you were hookin' and cookin'! What a waste of my blankin' time! The blankin' paperwork is hardly gonna be worth my blankin' time! I bet you're hookin' and cookin' somewhere!" I thought he must've been a sailor before he was a cop, then I noticed he *really* enjoyed saying "hookin' and cookin'". He slammed his hand on the steering wheel, and with a heavy, irritated sigh, he got out of the car.

He opened the door to the back seat and said, "Next time I'm gonna get ya." I slid out, and he removed the cuffs. Needless to say, that was the end of my dumb white girl act. Later that day, I dumped that car quicker than you can say "felony".

Even then, I could feel God watching over me but living in hotels was a low point for me. The next day we packed up, and moved to another one. I started to sink deeper into a depression. I just wanted my nightmare to be over. Birth control had failed me, I almost got arrested, my boyfriend was still making meth, and now I didn't even have a car anymore.

During this period of a couple of years, I felt hopeless. There just didn't seem to be a way out of this life. I was too sick to work, too sick to leave, too sick to do anything.

STRIPPED DOWN TO THE BONE

It was also during this time that my boyfriend convinced me to start dancing at a strip club. He was addicted to porn and would watch videos of girls stripping, and encouraged me to try it. It sounded like fun getting dolled up and dancing, and I thought I could probably use some of my singing telegram costumes. I had already done 'strip-o-grams', down to my undergarments so I thought maybe this was something I could do. I was finding it almost impossible to hold down any other kind of job so I figured, this I could handle. It seemed glamorous. I noticed that in a lot of movies, strippers and strip clubs are made out to be beautiful women living an exciting life style. In real life they are not. Most strippers and their customers are sad, lonely people. They are in a den full of inequity that *feels* dark, ugly, and leaves most people with shame. Sinners who have no place else to go, and end up in a dark room, talking to other people who are mixed up and can't handle 'real' relationships. That look that I saw on my step father's face, I often saw in strip clubs. Take the pilot for example. He looked like the all-American boy next door type, but he was trying to talk one of the dancers into urinating into his drink. He wanted to pay her forty dollars for her specimen. Of course, we all thought this was over the top gross. Which for us, was really saying something. Strip clubs are often attached to live peep shows, mini-porn booths and sex toy shops, but we had our standards! Back to the pilot. Us girls told the bouncers what this guy wanted and how gross he was. They immediately started teasing him, laughing, pointing their fingers, offering to urinate in a cup for him. "Hey Buddy, I got what you need. Give me forty bucks. I'll do it!" "Hey pee pee boy, come on over here!" They were making a public spectacle of this man, and he had *that* look on his face. He was on a mission, and didn't care that he was being openly made fun of. He did not care. When one girl turned him down, he was looking around for another girl to ask. He marched off into the dark to the other side of the club. I went to the opposite side of the club to get as far away as possible from this weirdo. But now that I think about it, maybe that pilot was actually training to be an astronaut, since they have to drink their own, you guessed it, in space.

    I think back on that and once again there is no explanation for his behavior except sin. Sin is a habit in the flesh. It is lust of the flesh that began when Adam and

Eve actually took a bite of the apple. Lust of the eyes is when we look. Lust of the flesh is when we refuse to 'take every thought captive', as the bible instructs, and we think about something until we act on it. Then those acts become habits and the door is wide open for the demonic to take control of our lives. That poor pilot, and all of us in that strip club for that matter, were actively inviting satan in, and we didn't even know it. We thought we were having fun, being glamorous, just trying to provide some poor schmuck with some company. Next thing you know he wants our urine.

I had seen "that look" on the faces of the dancers, too. Two girls in particular come to mind. One had old tights as stockings that she had cut off at her thighs. Her outfit told me she was poor. We were there for the 'contest' for new dancers, and we were all aiming to win some money. I saw her, this mousy girl, without a stitch of make-up, and this completely unglamorous outfit. I thought, "She'll never win. Look at her. Poor thing." Well, she had been a dancer there before, and she had what we did not. She had that look. She had an all-out performance that was hypnotic. She picked a song about baring your soul, and then she bared hers. She didn't care what anyone thought. She laid it all out there like all she wanted was to connect with somebody, look them in the eye, be vulnerable, and be loved for that sorrowful truth. She danced like she *needed* to dance. She won.

The next girl with that demon-driven look was getting all the men's money. Each lap dance was forty dollars. The management was also supposed to fine us forty dollars each time we broke the rules. The rules were no physical contact. That was pretty much a joke, but she was breaking the rules with complete abandon. The management fined her over and over, but she was making so much money, and was so completely given over to what she was doing, she didn't seem to notice. During the lap dances, she was not embarrassed because she was so absorbed in herself, and the men. I was embarrassed being near her. I saw her later in a different environment, and she seemed like a different person. She looked ashamed. But in that dark place, with men that didn't care who was watching either, she seemed to be in her own world. It was not about the money. It was about filling a deep need. That need was not being satisfied, so man after man would line up to have her dance on them. They had a deep need too. We all have it. But the only thing that satisfies our craving for love is God. Sex, no matter how exotic or forbidden, will not fulfill that need. Physical pleasure will not make us feel truly cared for. Only spiritual connection will fill that need. We are built to have a spiritual connection with God first, then a spouse.

  God designed sex and mankind has corrupted it. Strippers and strip clubs are an example of that corruption all under one roof. They are so far from what the movies make them out to be. One strip club was run by a man who kept two sets of books so he could rip off the IRS. I think he actually hated women, and would beat women if given the chance. He would physically assault dancers when he got angry.

  Another strip club was run by an older man and the meanest woman I have ever encountered. They would both treat the girls terribly, and then laugh if any left. They would say. "Girls turn eighteen everyday", knowing that there was a steady stream of girls at the weekly contest trying to enter into their dark world. The mean woman was the 'bad cop' and the 'good cop' was a small man who had a big rhinestone pin on his shirt at all times. The pin spelled out a derogatory name for women. Every once in a while, he would encourage us by holding open the dressing room door and saying, "Look at that? Do you see that on the floor? Do you see a twenty-dollar bill on the floor in there? No? That's right! There's no money in their girls. Get out here and make you some money!"

The old pervert who owned that strip club did plan a party for all of us that was a once in a lifetime experience. But not necessarily in a good way. We were told to dress up and come to the club on a certain day. The boss had something special planned. We got there and here come the limousines...ten in all. Ten limousines full of strippers and their boyfriends. People probably thought the long black caravan was a rock star or someone famous, but it was just us feeling fancy. The limos took us to a large boat out on the ocean, and that's where the party was. There was free food, and lots and lots of free alcohol. It was just another event where I was keenly aware of the perversion surrounding me. The strip club owner had a camera man trying to catch girls doing disgusting things on the dance floor. He didn't get much of a show. I think the girls were just glad to not be performing. It wasn't going well so he took us all out to the deck, and played a game where all the men lost their pants for minute. I think the idea was that the girls would get so turned on by the mass display of manhood that he might get the movie he was looking for. He forgot that most of these women were not interested in any sort of sexual display unless you plunked down some cold hard cash. At the party, we probably experienced something most people never would…a very fancy drive, dressed in very fancy clothes all the way to a very fancy floating pervert city. Nice.

Stripping was a difficult job unless you were a sex addict or a very good actress. I was neither. I was mentally disconnected from my physical body, and a rescuer who felt sorry for everybody. I could dress up, undress, and smile but the rest of the time I mostly just talked to the sad, lonely men who could only afford to watch.

One skinny young guy stands out in my mind. He was there almost every day. He never bought any dances. He just bought the two-drink minimum. This was all-nude so a drink was actually soda. If you wanted alcohol you had to sneak it in. Believe me lots of us were. This fellow was the intellectual type, and he told me all about the energy centers of the body and eastern mysticism stuff. I was fascinated, and very impressed with his knowledge of deep, sophisticated systems of being. Then I got a glimpse of the ten speed he rode in on.

Ninety-nine percent of the girls in those strip clubs were intoxicated. There is no doing that job without being high. My specialty was denying my drug use, so I never became friends with the other girls. They knew I was lying so they figured I wasn't worth the effort. I was very skinny, very unhappy, and acting my way through every shift. The longer I was a stripper, the more I found it almost impossible to smile. I was miserable. On my twenty fifth birthday when they had a cake for me on stage, I felt so old, I knew I was almost done. Death was clawing at me mentally, and I had no desire to do anything anymore. I wasn't celebrating anything, and it felt like my life was already over. I was so addicted to drugs I couldn't hold down a regular job and now my taste for being a stripper was gone. I couldn't fake it, anymore. It felt like abuse, and now I was doing it to myself.

Even in the midst of that, God was calling me. "Oh no, I think that guy out there might be from the church!" A beautiful dancer rushed in breathless, and was talking to me as I applied my lipstick in the dressing room mirror.

"What? What guy? What church?"

"I go to church with my grandma, and I'm pretty sure that guy is in the choir.", she said.

Incredulous, I said, "Wow, you go to church?"

"Yes, girl every Sunday. If my grandma finds out I work here, that would be bad! She's gonna whip my blank! Do you want to take my set?"

She was the only girl I knew who was not using or drinking, and now she was talking about church, *every* sunday. I noticed a light in her that I didn't feel like I had anymore. I didn't feel like I knew how to get back to where she was at. She, obviously, was on her way to being completely lost or caught by her grandma, if she didn't quit. But at that point, she had joy, and I was in so much pain I could barely function.

"Sure, I'll take your set."

Then there was the protestor. He had a bible, and he was thumping it like a mad man. He was on the sidewalk in front of the club, yelling at us as we walked in, and yelling at us as we walked out.

"You will burn for eternity! The fires of hell are in that place!" He was crazy looking with wild hair and a long green robe. He was right, but he wasn't convincing any of us, the strippers, the bouncers, the customers, of anything, except that he was crazy. He never really looked at us or talked to us, just yelled, and pointed his bony finger. He had that look too, a faraway look, only this one was full of rage and judgment. There was no concern for us, as people. No love. I'm quite sure that if one of us had gone over and told him, "You know what? You are right. I am a sinner and this is wrong. Can you help me?" He would not have done anything but continued to drive our self-worth into the ground. He would not have led us to Christ. Most of us were already full of self-loathing, and his words were condemning. What we needed was love, and a way out. His approach to saving our souls was not doing the trick. Even the demons know the bible he was waving around, and there he was with that look. It was obvious, he had the right book but he wasn't following the right guy. I wanted to follow the right guy. I was trying with my heart but my life was a mess, and I knew it.

One day a really "old" woman came in to strip. She was about sixty years old, and we were shocked that she was there. She was pretty attractive for her age, and told us she was doing this to pay for her son to go to college. Instantly, I didn't like her son. But she wanted to be there. I knew she would make money because every stripper makes money. There were girls just getting over chicken pox with marks all over, and girls eight months pregnant, that made money. It was just dark enough, and the men there were just sordid enough to pay no matter what she looked like. Even if she was downcast, twenty-five and had cake in her hair.

At that time. I had a verse that was keeping me alive. I printed and hung it around my apartment. "With God all things are possible." It gave me hope. It doesn't say some things. It says *all* things. That gave me the tiny light I needed at the end of the tunnel. By this time, I thought I would die a drug addict, but when I read that verse, I thought maybe, just maybe God would help me somehow. If God was a God of possibilities maybe somehow things could change.

One day, I discovered an out-patient rehab program. There was a doctor who was doing a bunch of research on meth and dopamine, serotonin, and all the chemicals that make the drug so addictive. He had come up with a vitamin treatment plan for meth addicts, and had a clinic offering them for cheap or free. I can't remember paying much or struggling to pay. What I did struggle with was not puking. And of course, being honest about the fact that I was still using.

There was a girl working there that I had gone to school with. She was in her scrubs and looked so professional. She *was* professional. She didn't try to embarrass me, but I was *so* embarrassed. Here she was so obviously doing well in a career as a medical assistant. It was like catching up, and sharing what we'd been doing since high school. "Yeah, I went to medical assistant school and got this great job. I get to help people. It looks like you've been busy too...uh. um.....oh yeah you're a drug addict. Bummer". She didn't say this of course, but it was in her eyes. Pity. There was no way I was going to tell her that I was still using, and so of course the vitamins won't work. I couldn't stop doing drugs, and I couldn't keep the vitamins down. My depression was getting deeper, along with my shame.

Even then, I loved Jesus. I was doing my usual pre-sex routine and taking off my new cross necklace and laying it on the nightstand.

"That's stupid" my boyfriend said. "You treat a piece of jewelry like it's God Himself. He sees what we are doing."

"I know but it makes me feel better." The cross still felt sacred.

Instead of taking the cross off to engage in sin, what I should've done is gotten my holy roller self to church. Once in a while, I did. But the devil always told me there was something wrong. For instance, an old friend invited me to a 'healing' service at his church. A guy from out of town was there, praying for people's healing. If anyone needed healing it was me. But I was too busy criticizing what I did not understand to go anywhere near the front.

I stood in the back and listened to the devil talking in my head. "Are you kidding me? This guy is a phony. You can't make an appointment with God! You can't command that God heal between six and eight on a Tuesday and that's it! I don't believe this blank!"

I didn't ask someone or investigate. I didn't realize that it was the devil putting those critical thoughts in my head. I just believed those thoughts. That was a mistake. At that point, I had no idea the devil could plant lies in people's minds. I believed the thoughts that came into my mind. I now know that some thoughts, especially those that are *accusatory* in nature, are *not* of God. But the devil was telling me that it was impossible for someone to heal people whenever *they* wanted. Of course, now I know that the bible commands us to "lay hands and pray for the sick". The results are not up to us but we, as Christians with the power of God within us, are to do what God commands and not worry about the rest. And we can do it anytime, anywhere and God *can* and *does* show up.

Excerpt End

CHAPTER SIXTEEN

It was a Saturday morning in my sluggish life and I was being highly productive. I was watching a documentary. The grandson of a notorious pedophile made a movie about his family. He told the story of what happened as the result of one man's sickness, unchecked. He cataloged all of the family members, interviewed them and they shared what the abuse had done to their lives and how they felt. It was bad. It was also difficult for me to watch. The damage in that family was deep and wide.

But as the grandfather aged, he became less of a threat and eventually ended up in a convalescent home. I watched as this brave group of siblings worked up the courage to go see their abuser, who had gone to jail, but only for a short time. He had never shown one ounce of remorse. The film showed these adult siblings filing out of the car and into the convalescent hospital. They were pleasant to the old man, who was now in a wheelchair, but all of them were quite obviously in pain. One sister said while weeping, 'He makes me want to hurt myself'. She was one of the siblings who appeared to be functioning well for the most part. Going to see him made her want to hurt herself but she didn't even go into the room. She waited in the hallway, weeping and looking terrified, while the others acted like he was just their 'Dad'. One sister even said how much she loved her

Dad. Another major rescuer completely messed up.

I read the comments left by other online watchers like myself and many of them were hostile. One said they would've 'kicked him in the face'. That's the hard thing about being abused, I thought. On the one hand the rage is so deep that it makes you want to hurt something, someone, so badly, that instead you take it out on yourself. Unless of course, you no longer have a conscience and the emotional weakness is now demonic territory. Then you become the abuser with the seared conscience. But if you are a fighter against the injustice, and God is gracious, which he always is, you can be a normal, healthy person. You can bypass the urge to hurt someone else or yourself, because you've been hurt. Hurt people *don't have to* hurt people. Looking into the eyes of Christ in my favorite picture, I realized there is just no place to lay that pain down and let go of it until you come to know Christ. Christ makes it supernaturally possible to take the pain off of ourselves and place it at the foot of the Cross. I have no idea why or how it works, but I know that when we focus on Him, and ask Him to take our pain. He does.

"Thank you, Jesus." I whispered.

I was so grateful that I had come to a place where I didn't just place my burdens at the foot of the cross, but sometimes, I was able to lift my past up to the Lord in worship. I had worked through so much of my childhood and past pain, that God had healed me. Even in my very imperfect life I could see how he took my painful past and used it for my good. He used it to develop my relationship with Him, my gratitude, my empathy for others, and so many more good things. Nothing is wasted with the Lord, I thought. Even the pain can make you a better, stronger, healthier person because you become more like Christ as you learn and grow and become more like him. You are no longer a victim but a victor! I turned down the hall to go get ready for another writers group, and suddenly I felt like singing.

"To You. O my Strength. I will sing praises; For God is my defense. My God of mercy." Psalm 59.17

Later that night, I still felt emotional but good. I actually caught myself humming. I didn't notice until one of my classmates started looking at me weird. I just smiled at her and handed her my latest excerpt. Well if she had any doubt that I was crazy, now she'll know for sure, I thought. Ah, to be at peace with who we are…just me, joy and Jesus.

Writers Group - Sharing Excerpt Fifteen
Genre: Semi-Autobiographical Memoir, Christian

Summer

Ice block
on the sidewalk
A girl and her best friend
Laying in the hot sun
Enjoying the melting fun
On the sidewalk
With an ice block
Between them
Someone came back
From somewhere
And it was there
Dropped off clear, dripping fun
They laugh and slurp in the sun
Enjoying the cold, clear goodness
In the hot, summer suburbs

Scribble

Nothing like the attraction
Of a clean page
A writer's distraction
And moment on stage
Pure, irresistible white
Ready to be painted
Words we don't write
Leave desires tainted
Touch me cry the lines
Pour out your beauty and bliss
A jot, a tittle, and time
To seal it all with a kiss
With emotions true
We scribble carefully
All of our blue
Skies and pain.

NO ROOM SERVICE PLEASE

Eventually, we made it out of the hotels. We had lived in three and I was beside myself worrying about another encounter with the police and getting arrested. It seemed like every hotel had a pancake house next to it where the cops liked to get coffee. The paranoia was taking over, and I needed an address where a maid didn't knock on the door to come inspect my dysfunction every day.

I did what I always did. I called my mom. I told her my cat was dying and might need surgery and then I told her I needed money for the first and last on an apartment. The cat was fine. I was not.

Eastman Grands…my new home. It had a pool down the way and was decidedly low income, but it was home. I was so glad to be there.

"Have you got a flute?" It was the undercover cop who frequented our apartment complex. He was looking for drug dealers and at this point, we hadn't been nearly as busy as the dealers two buildings down. He was obviously undercover and for some reason, I was just not as freaked out by this cop. I was about to figure out why. He had stopped me in the parking lot and for some reason was asking me for a musical instrument.

I said. "No. I used to play the trumpet though."
He just laughed and said. "No, I mean a flute for this."
He showed me the cocaine rocks in his hand.
I stepped back. "Ooooooh."
He was getting impatient. "So you gotta flute to smoke this with or not?"

"You mean a pipe? No. I don't have one. Sorry." This was a cop, obviously very high but nonetheless in need of assistance. If I hadn't been living in the meth addict, major paranoia twilight zone, perhaps I could have found a way to protect and serve his drug problem, but there was no way I was jumping on that paddy wagon.

I didn't get to know many people in that apartment complex. But I did get to know my next-door neighbor. He had two little boys and I eventually figured out he also had a drug addict wife. She was the bane of his existence. He would go to work and come home every day like clockwork. He was obviously trying to provide for his family and have a good home life. She would not come home every day like clockwork. She would take off and then he would come over early in the morning or late at night and ask if I'd seen her. No, but I saw the look on her face. Sorry, man. He'd ask me to take care of his boys because he had to go look for her. It was sad. But I got a look at what people go through when they aren't the ones addicted. It was a joy taking care of his little boys. I've always loved kids. Those boys and my cat were my distractions and I was grateful that I didn't think too much about my abortion. I was still thinking it was what I *had* to do. My boyfriend was still a meth cook. I was still a stripper and now I was getting a first-hand look at bad motherhood.

  I knew what drugs can do to little boys who don't understand, and babies in the womb. It was the babies who were born, that stuck with me. My cousin's best friend used meth while she was pregnant and even though her baby was born, the little girl died within the month. Another friend from high school used drugs throughout her pregnancy and her baby was born with numerous physical problems. He died, too. I had smoked meth with women while their toddlers sat on their laps. I had done big lines of cocaine after the visibly pregnant woman snorted hers and then handed me the straw. By this time, my point of reference for mothers, babies and drugs was already decided. There was no such thing as overcoming drugs during pregnancy. Only the cocaine baby lived but the mother abandoned him. I only saw that baby boy once. He was about a year old, sitting up with beautiful, big brown eyes and sandy blond hair. He looked okay at first, but then I realized that he was completely blank. He did not smile. He did not speak. He barely moved. I later learned that he grew up and became a perfectly normal person. He actually had a successful military career but I did not know that then. I only knew that women who used drugs during pregnancy had babies that were born at less than zero. I convinced myself that I had done the right thing by aborting my baby....And then I was pregnant again.

  I had gone to get more birth control and the nurse had me take a test because my period was a few days late. I couldn't be pregnant because I was vigilant about taking my pill every day, but she thought we should check. I was in shock when the test was positive. I couldn't believe it. These pills were not supposed to fail! I was devastated and she and the doctor didn't have much to say. I saw the detachment in the doctor. He had been through this with more than me. The nurse just handed me a list of 'women's' clinics. Same story different day.

I had been using meth every day and drinking regularly. I had not really tried to quit for a while. I had almost given up. I was in no shape to have a baby and didn't see that I had any other choice except to get another abortion. So back to the welfare office I went. This time was harder. It was harder to stand in line surrounded by mothers with small children and babies. It was harder because I knew I should've done better. I felt like a failure. It was harder to have the old man at the window giving me a thirty second lesson on when women ovulate. I was really interested because no one had ever told me that before. But it wasn't much help now. And why did an old man at the welfare office have to make the little chart and shove it at me when it was too late for this baby? Why didn't the doctors at the clinics do this for me? Why didn't I remember this from high school? Disgusted with myself, I smiled at the old man, took my forms and got out of there.

It was back to the abortion clinic, the green dresses and the sad girls who avoided eye contact and never spoke a word to one another.

One day my step father called. "Hey you'll never guess who showed up over here." My beloved cat had been missing for a couple of days. I had mentioned this to my mom the day before and now my step father called.

"Oh is that right." I sighed heavily knowing he had come to my apartment and kidnapped my cat. I had been living on my own in that apartment for over six months and that cat stuck to me like glue. She would follow me down the long sidewalk to the mailbox. We would slowly walk past the single story, brown duplexes. Each with a big picture window in front and a single tree surrounded by patches of shabby, yellowing crab grass and dirt. I would talk to her as we moseyed along past the fifteen doors, each with a story behind it. Mostly stories of people scratching out a life.

"You comin' Sweetie?" I would glance back every few minutes to make sure she was behind me and she always was. She would follow along past the buildings and the long chain link fence with the big blue pool inside. Around the pool, past the old, rusty, cracking, plastic blue and white lawn chairs finally reaching the row of mailboxes. We made this trip together a few times a week. She had never disappeared before and I was distraught. Now my tormentor was on the phone telling me he had her. I could almost see him holding her on his lap. Petting her soft, multi-colored fur slowly from head to tail, she had no idea he was a sick predator. She was purring while he smiled into the phone, knowing I had no choice but to talk to him. He seemed to enjoy calling me and telling me the insane story of how my cat had walked the five miles through busy city streets to go to my parent's house. He knew I wouldn't believe this horse manure but he also knew he had my cat. I had no choice. I was going to have to face him to get her back. He would have the opportunity to show me how he had the power. He had the control and he knew it.

NO ROOM AT THE MEETING

"Hey can I hang out over here for a while?" I was at an old friend's apartment and hoping it might be a safe place.

"Sure!" He said with a smile.

I had packed an overnight bag and planned to

crash on my friend's couch. We caught up and he told me all about how he had quit doing cocaine. That story gave me even more hope that he might be a potential roommate and I could get away from my meth cook boyfriend. Later that night, we decided to go to a twelve step meeting. It was pouring down rain, but we ran to the car and we went. When we got there we headed to the doorway only to find that it was so full, there was no way to get in. I'd never been to a meeting like that. There was always room to come in and sit. But not there and not that night. We stood in the rain talking to the people standing in the doorway and finally gave up. We couldn't hear and we were getting soaked.

We looked up another meeting and tried again. This one was not there. We found the address but there was no meeting. We were both disappointed. But it only took that long for the demons to attach to my friend. I hadn't done drugs since the day before and had no desire to, even though I knew the next day I would start to have serious withdrawal symptoms. He had been clean for months, but when we got back to his apartment, he got on the phone. About twenty minutes later someone came to the door and next thing I knew he was hiding in his bedroom doing cocaine. I couldn't believe it. I was crushed. How do you go from months clean and going to a meeting to using again? Demons.

I went home.

I wonder how different things would have turned out in my life if there had been someone to call or a safe place to go that night. It is not easy to say, "I need help". I could never articulate that very well, but first I needed someone safe to say it to. For me, there was no one.

One of the hardest things about addiction was the loneliness. "Friends" were easy to find but the sense of belonging was fleeting. Sooner or later, somebody rips somebody off, or cheats, or is just too disgusting to be around anymore. I felt like I was constantly searching for something that I could never quite find. I would always end up driving home in the dark by myself. I was very lonely.

Lonely- sad because one has no friends or company

ENOUGH

I had perfectly applied make up. I had my spotless white jeans and my pink fuzzy sweater. I had my perfectly platinum blond hair. I had a note from the shrink, slash voodoo healer, that my mother had paid for, explaining that going to jail was going to halt my mental progress. I had a long list of, what I thought were, excellent excuses. I had a drug charge and I was standing in front of yet another judge. He could tell that I was high. My cotton mouthed testimony pleading for mercy didn't fool him. I was licking my lips and explaining that I needed more time before I served my ninety days for under the influence. I was high, skinny and the judge knew it.

"I've seen enough! Bailiff, cuff her! Young lady, you are being remanded into custody. I see no reason why you shouldn't start serving your sentence today." My day of reckoning had come. I wasn't special. I was just like every other person. I'd committed a crime against humanity, namely myself. Even though I was already broke, it was my turn to pay.

It starts with the bus. First stop county jail. Initially, the bus reminded me of fieldtrips in third grade but it's not yellow, and nobody is singing, "ninety nine bottles of milk with your cookies." The metal handcuffs cutting into my wrists, and the metal grating on the tinted windows reminded me that this was no field trip. Metal handcuffs, metal grating, metal picnic tables, metal doors, metal bunk beds. Everything in jail is hard and cold. It's all metal and cement. All I could think about was that if I got into a fight, my face could end up knocking against all this hardness, and that would really hurt. I started thinking about accessing my inner rage, in an emergency situation. Was I angry enough at my stepfather for what he'd done to me? If confronted, could I use that rage to actually get into a physical fight with one of these rowdy prisoners? I didn't look forward to it, but I reminded myself that I'd come from some pretty scrappy roots. I didn't want to fight, but could I access enough pain and anger to give it a go? Always the answer was, "Yes!" But do I want a crooked nose and missing front teeth for the rest of my life? Always the answer was, "No!"

Jail is no fun, but it's especially no fun if you are coming off of meth. Two days in you are so tired you don't want to get out of bed, but you have to because you can smell the syrup on the pancakes. The only thing you want to do, more than sleep, is drink syrup. It didn't matter that the syrup was really runny and there was a mystery ingredient that no one wanted to guess at. It didn't matter that we had to get up at four in the morning in the freezing cold, and march without saying a word. We were monks going to breakfast. We had to have that syrup.

Then after getting jacked up on sugar, it was back to the "day room", where they had us sleeping on the floor due to overcrowding. I couldn't really go back to bed and sleep because of the noise, and the cold cement floor, and the constant threat of jail shower shoes accidentally kicking me in the face. I don't remember what started my crying but by the time I made it across the hall to the sergeant at the desk, I could barely contain myself.

She took one look at me and barked, "You need a

bed!" She got on the phone and got me a bed. She wasn't coming around the desk to give me a hug. I knew she wasn't going to be my surrogate Grammy. But I appreciated her instant compassion and get it done attitude. Finally I got real sleep in a regular dorm, in a real bed after my runny syrup….aaaaahhhhh that's better. I started to feel more in control of my tear ducts. I slept like the dead and remembered my friend who told me stories about jail. She fell asleep like that and after a couple of days, she woke up to the other girls poking her because they thought she was dead on her bunk. No such luck, now she was just pissed 'cause they woke her up.

The dorm was four rows of about twenty-five metal bunk beds. Every bed had a thin, plastic mattress, a sheet and a thin hospital type blanket. We froze at night. They had a heater but it seemed to blow cold air. The industrious inmates found a new use for feminine products. They taped them over the vents to try to stop the cold wind. I woke up and looked up at those things taped to the ceiling vents. I thanked God for these genius criminals. This is how inventions happen. If only we could invent another blanket.

If you've never been to jail. I wouldn't recommend it. But in the tapestry of life. I have to say there were things about it that were interesting and, strikingly different than the rest of the planet. I don't mean the bars on the windows or the abundance of cement. I mean the people in there. There is a camaraderie among people in bad situations that is stunning. Nobody is judging anybody. Nobody has anything to lose by just 'being'. It's the ultimate "whatever!" atmosphere. We all had nothing to lose anymore. We were caught and there were moments that it felt like a party with no drugs, no booze, but a definite sense of common adventure.

I remember being in the holding cell with

about ten other women and as much as the whole thing was depressing and sick, we actually had fun. Well, at least I did. Maybe I was the odd one in the group. But the prostitute who joyfully taught the rest of us how to earn money, without actually doing "the deed", was something to behold. She was like an energetic instructor teaching high finance. She was standing in front of us, using her hands to demonstrate. She didn't need a white board or a laser pointer because she had her trade down to a science. I had never heard anything like this. She described in detail how you would get the customer to think you were about to take him to nastyville, while at the same time, strategically ascertaining where his wallet was. She laid out every scenario like a board room presentation. Every possible wallet location came with a three-point fact sheet on what to do to get that unsuspecting scuz bucket's cash and exit the situation like a pro, unscathed, with all your clothes still on. Eyes wide and mouths agape, she had the rapt attention of at least five of us in that cell. I mean who would not want to learn how to make easy money and take advantage of a pervert? She could've been a professional head hunter trying to recruit new executives. Her presentation almost made me want to change careers...well almost. She was in jail after all.

    Then in the next holding cell, there was the prison who really took an interest in me. She had the most soulful eyes and voice. She had learned to seduce what she wanted and that was her whole game. She reminded me of a panther entirely focused on its prey, so sleek, so beautiful, so alluring. She didn't care what anybody thought or what else was going on around her. She had her laser beam eyes on me and was trying to hold my hand and look into my soul. Luckily, I was not interested in that brand of hoochie. Otherwise, she may have used that intense, smooth as silk voice to get me to embarrass myself. That would've been another totally riveting chapter in this book. Lucky you.

It is interesting how humans usually get around to similar things whether in jail or not. For example, the "store" in our dorm. A little chick ran a very successful business from the bunk bed on the end. Somehow, she had money to stock up on chips and candy. No extra shoestrings and toothpaste here, this was pure, uncut 'junk'. For most people, coming to jail means coming off drugs. The new drug of choice becomes sugar. Sudden withdrawals from drugs and alcohol are tough physically and the cravings for sugar feel almost as bad as needing the drug. Crack cocaine, meth, heroin, sugar, it's all the same in the end. We were ready to kill something for that chocolate bar.

This entrepreneur had a secret stash under her bed. She was probably doing well as a drug dealer on the outside, well except for getting arrested. Here in the can she didn't seem to be dipping into her product. She was calm, cool and collected. It's common practice for drug dealers to eat their product when about to be caught. This was so they would get the lesser charge of under the influence instead of the felony possession charge. So maybe she was the picture of cool, because if she ever got caught with the goods, she could actually eat her contraband stash and not die. That's a nice benefit of being in jail. Perhaps it was because she was in her element and her addiction was making money. Either way, this little chick wasn't going for any haggling. You mosey up, name your poison and she'd name the price.

"King size? That'll be six dollars," she'd say.
"What?! That's highway robbery!"
"No that's jailhouse cheap baby cakes. Hand over the cash or go back to your bunk and lay awake all night drooling and dreaming over the caramel and nugget you

missed out on."

"One, two, three.......six!"

About the time she had built up a real bank account, the guards would flip the whole operation. They would barge in and yell 'wristband!' That was the code command for everybody to sit on their bed with their wristband held out so they could count us. Then they proceeded to search our bunks and our cardboard boxes of meager possessions for contraband. They would look under the beds, under the mattresses, in the shoes, the socks, you name it. No mattress or blankie went unturned. And of course, they found the 'store' and we all groaned....there goes the lollipops! Back to runny syrup. Sleep, eat, wristband, sleep, eat, wristband. It was a simple recovery program but it was working.

Another interesting thing about jail is how vulnerable you feel. There is nothing like being in the company of so many people who are 'jumping off' drugs and alcohol at the same time. We are talking about some *very* edgy women. Way worse than a little pre-period crabbiness. Many times, you could feel the tension in the air and fights would feel imminent. The fights didn't usually happen but it didn't stop my mind from focusing on the surroundings. Everywhere were metal benches, metal tables, metal doors, metal bunks, cement walls and cement floors. There was no drywall, carpet or dirt to slam your face into. Some of these women were violent and if you fought, it was going to hurt and you could count on bleeding profusely. Fortunately for me, the loud mouth I was on street became the exhausted, sad girl, who didn't get excited about anything but sugar. I was growing eyebrows I didn't know I had, discovering what my natural hair color was and rapidly getting fat on the watered down jail house syrup, pancakes and candy.

"What the blank is this?" A girl we called Oasis was scooping up the syrup with her cardboard pancake.

"I think I need a straw."
Another girl chimed in, "Don't y'all know nothin'? That's rat piss, mixed with corn syrup! Ya'll lucky nobody back there can find a rat's behind to put in there!" She laughed and we started worrying. What were those mad prisoners in the back up to anyway? Almost every week there was a discussion over breakfast about that watery syrup. A lot of the food was bad but that concoction just took the hotcake. One day while I was savoring my last piece of peanut butter cup, it hit me. I *finally* figured out why the syrup was so thin. I mean this kept me up at night! Just kidding. I thought it was the prison trying to cut costs but suddenly I knew the answer. The convicts in the kitchen were downing the stuff and then adding water to cover up the evidence! I let out a deep sigh....It's not vermin, it's water!
"Oh, thank God." I said out loud.
My bunk mate stopped chewing her candybar, Looking at me sideways, she said "What?!"

The next time we were in line for the pancakes and syrup, we peered in at those plastic gloved prisoners with a new interest. Lucky blanks! They were all fat! We knew they were not only fat but decidedly happy at least a few times a month. We knew this wasn't going to change, and our only hope was being put on kitchen duty. This blatant internal sabotage continued because the guards could care less. They weren't eating those pancakes. Nobody noticed the watery syrup except us.
If we did somehow work up the guts to walk up and complain to a guard, the response was always the same. "Get back in line, and shut it, you chubby convict!"

In jail you see things that most people never do. You are in such an open environment that there is no hiding illness. Jesus is there but there is also a lot on display that is the result of life long sin. It is sad but this is the reality of incarceration. For example, there was an inmate who was eight months pregnant with baby number six that they weren't going to let her raise.

She was loud, extremely rude, mean, and in the words of my roommates, "begging somebody to hurt her from the neck up".

Another girl saw her coming and moaned, "I so want to give that dumb blank a check up from the neck up."

We laughed but it wasn't really funny. It was seriously white coat time for this woman. I remember once sleeping in my bunk, the top bunk, in a long row of bunk beds. I was rudely awakened by yelling at the end of my bed. The loud prego was once again mouthing off and actively trying to get one of the other girls to punch her in the mouth. I am normally pretty compassionate with people who are obviously hurting but in this instant another connection was made. I look over and two beds down a sleepy, rumpled looking girl was just sitting up. She sat up in almost perfect unison to when I did. We had both been abruptly awakened by this drama. She looks at me, I look at her, and we just laugh and lay back down. I'm sure we were thinking the exact same thing. Welcome to the psycho slumber party.

Excerpt End

CHAPTER SEVENTEEN

Sometimes even as a middle-aged woman, well past my addictions and after lots of therapy, I was still lonely. I looked forward to my writing class because it helped me feel like I belonged. Sitting on my porch, watching the birds in the trees, I felt comforted knowing that Christ experienced loneliness also. He spent much of His time misunderstood, even by those He was closest to, and His own earthly family. He was homeless as an adult and died a horrible death with no one protesting or fighting for His life. He was unjustly convicted of a crime He did not commit. He was separated from His Heavenly Father so we could be free. He was alone when they brought him before the crowds who yelled "Crucify him!", "Crucify him!" He laid down His life and bore the burden of *our* sin, not His…completely alone. A sparrow landed on the railing of my porch, and as if on que, a verse came into my mind.

"I . . . am as a sparrow alone upon the house top." Psalm 102:7

"I'm sorry you were lonely, Lord." I said out loud. The more I learned about Jesus, the better I felt about everything, and most of all, I knew that even if I was lonely sometimes, I belonged. Even if I didn't have a lot of church friends, I knew I was accepted in the family of God. I smiled realizing that having a relationship with

Christ has given me a good feeling deep inside that never goes away. I know without a doubt that everything is going to be all right. I am never alone.

Handing my latest excerpt to another new friend in writer's class, I smiled, suddenly feeling warm and fuzzy.

Writers Group - Sharing Excerpt Sixteen
Genre: Semi-Autobiographical Memoir, Christian

A Clenched Fist

A long list
but no reasons why.
A last kiss
and we said goodbye.

No more anger
Or record of wrong.
No more danger
if we don't belong.

A long list
but no apology.
A clenched fist
Is what I see…

As you walk away.
I hurt you again.
What you won't say
is where we've been.

Over and over I
pry open my heart,

but with no reasons why
It's ripped apart.

A long list and you say
It's "not ringing a bell".
Crushed again, I struggle away
from the fires of hell.

Spirit

Is it flesh
Or is it spirit?
I listen hard
To try to hear it
Your voice
Lord
Is what I long for.

LINE UP AND SWALLOW

    As was my habit, at that time in my life, I was continually looking for an easier, softer way, so when I heard a rumor that there was a way to go into an easier dorm in the jail, I paid attention.
    One of the other prisoners said, "If you tell the nurse you are having bad dreams, they'll let you out of here. They send you to the mental ward and there's only like thirty girls in there. Its way easier and they feed you good." Instantly, I started having nightmares.
    I was promptly moved to the mental barracks. What the rumor monger forgot to tell me is that they medicate you. Actually, they experiment on you. They made us line up, gave us pills, checked under our tongue to make sure we swallowed them but offered no further

explanation. Nobody explained how they decided who needed what. They didn't do any tests or interviews to see what our symptoms were or our medical history. They did not do anything that would be considered standard medical practice. I believe this was a revenue stream and if they passed out the "medication", they could charge the tax payers more money for "therapy" on us the crazy prisoners. They did tell us that it was dangerous to quit the medication without being weaned off of it slowly. I've never heard something so incredibly stupid. What exactly happens when you are released? When you finally get sprung from this joint, you sure aren't coming back here to be weaned and if you tried, they would promptly lock you back up for being out of your ever lovin' mind, for real. I thought to myself, well they look like doctors but it's actually an idiot parade. After my little blue pill, I better get the popcorn. This episode's gonna be a real hum dinger.

  And hum dinger it was. I was put on a mood stabilizer and the first night was the worst experience of my life. I thought I *was* losing my mind. My legs would not stay still. I felt like my body was going to explode from the inside out but there was no calling for help. I had tried several street drugs and never felt this bad. But I was not the worst off. There was another girl that the "doctor'" gave four different pills. She had three other girls trying to calm her down. The next day, after living through that nightmare, I asked about her. Had she ever been on medication before? Did they give a reason for giving her four different pills? No and no. They just decided to give her a bunch of stuff and see what happens I guess. It was horrible and really felt like concentration camp experimentation. But we adjusted eventually. No one wanted to go back to the 'big house' with the mouthy, prego inmates and the three am wristband. It was not good here in the mental ward either, but at least there were a few *less* crazy people.

But some of the prisoners truly belonged in the mental ward or at least in a program of some kind. After every meal, one girl would go in and puke. We started to notice it because the bathroom stalls are only half walls with no real privacy. So me, and the other resident rescuer asked her.

"Hey what the heck are you doing?" My fellow inmate asked her one day after she threw up again. She acted like she was expecting to be asked and she casually explained that she was throwing up her food because she was bulimic. She said she was going into treatment for it when she got out of jail. Somehow, I didn't think anybody was going to help this poor, drug addicted, prostitute to stop puking up her food. Something in the way she said it told me that she didn't think so either. She just lowered her head and gave the pat answer she had learned to repeat. My heart ached for her because it was obvious that she was on her own and had been for a long time.

I at least I had my mother, who's strategy was always, and I mean always, to throw money at problems. She would stand in line with the families of all the other inmates, for hours every Saturday just to visit me and give me forty bucks. My best friends never visited. My boyfriend never visited. My brothers never visited. My sisters never visited. My grandparents, aunts, uncles and cousins never visited. Thank God my step father never visited. My mother did. Being in that crowd of people could not have been easy for her. The people in that line with my mother were not her element, and those that were like her, probably just made her sad. Other mothers who thought they had raised their daughters better than this and yet here they were. Seeing me there and in such bad shape probably made her feel helpless to control anything. But instead of ignoring me, writing me letters telling me I deserved it, or making excuses, she was there. She was there with forty bucks, new underwear and Christian books every Saturday.

Some of what she did was undoubtedly the product of her guilt, but I was grateful then and I'm still grateful now. I didn't appreciate her enough then. I think in my heart I wanted to but I had a future to face. I wanted to stay clean and away from the life I'd come from but my options for housing were limited. I knew that no matter how nice she was, I could not go home to her husband. Although faithful, she was not truly there for me. She had to address the sins in her own life and she gave no indication that she would ever do that. I was grateful for her money and her time but I still felt that I was not worth it, in the long run. In my heart I knew that I was on my own.

I was also following her example and remained co-dependent. I thought my boyfriend was all I had. I told myself he loved me and this time when I got home it would be different. He had once again assured me that he was getting clean while I was away, simply because I asked him to.

I remember when I first met him, about a month into the relationship I decided that we were both too screwed up to have a relationship. I knew it was true. I knew I was making a mistake by staying in the relationship but he was so nice to me and I never wanted to go home.

Worrying about my boyfriend and my mother and her visits were distractions but jail day after day was a colorful way to live. One day I made the mistake of asking one girl why she was in there. She got a faraway look in her eye and said that they "accused" her of burning her children's arms with a curling iron. But she said she didn't do it. "Yeah right", I thought. I wanted to believe her but there was that look again. Demons. The rubber room is calling. Somebody missed their hair appointment.

One girl was like a female mobster redneck. She was in jail for meth dealing and it wasn't the first time, but all she could talk about was transporting more meth back to Georgia or Tennessee or wherever she was from.

She would say, "Ya'll just need to bag it up and we can holler at my cousin to meet us and we'll have that shee--it sold lickity split for the high dollah. Y'all gotta know thar's a lot of folks down home who love that white shee--it." She wanted to take a plane to Hollywood, California and then take a batch all the way to the south in the trunk of somebody's caddy.

I couldn't keep my mouth shut. "Are you out of your mind? Why are you even talking about this? Do you want to get busted again, as soon as you get out of here?" She didn't even respond. She had that faraway look too….determined and trying to recruit people to ride the crazy train with her all the way from Hollywood to Tennessee and back to prison in a cadillac.

I did make a couple of "friends" in jail. Friends in jail are people that no matter how much you like them in there, when you get out, you never want to see them again. I did not want to be reminded of jail. It felt like I was closer to going back there if I saw them. When I did see them, I would pretend I didn't. It just hurt too much.

One girl that I liked in jail really messed me up because even though she seemed kind of ignorant and stupid, she turned out to be smarter than me, the gifted child put in the special classes because I was so smart. She was a girl struggling with meth addiction too. I told her that my boyfriend was a meth cook but he was getting clean *right now* while I was in jail so we could be clean together, when I got out. She asked me if I was going back to him when I got out.

I said, "Yes. He stopped using when I got arrested and he is not going to cook anymore. We are getting clean together." It was all so very fairy tale-ish and foolish. But I believed it. She did not.

She looked me in the eye and said sadly, "If you go back to him, you are going to end up on drugs again." I was insulted! Didn't this dumb girl *hear* me? He *loves* me. He's getting clean *right now* just because he loves me! That was it! I wasn't going to share my cookies with *her* anymore.

I remembered her and what she said, when the first night I got out of jail, on the way home, I realized that my boyfriend was high. And within two hours I was high, too. The ignorant, stupid girl was me.

I regretted my foolishness but it wasn't just me that I hurt. My mom, who'd been my only visitor, braving the two-hour line of unsavory people to assure that I was loved by somebody. Then when I got out and she showed up at the same time my "clean" boyfriend did, I chose to go with him. What a mistake. But I couldn't go home to her husband. That would've been a much bigger mistake. Once again, I had no good options but I should've let her drive me to my house. I should never have let her watch me drive away like that. She deserved better. But she never complained or said anything about it. She loved me unconditionally in her own way. I think she knew how troubled I was and felt responsible, so how could she complain? Still, I knew right from wrong. And that, was very wrong. Even convicts should respect their momma's. Maybe I should've gotten 'mom' tattooed on my neck while I was in there….uh maybe not.

Before I got out of jail, I made a "connection" on the inside that was truly shocking. We were in line once, on our way to work making sock dolls and a group of jail employees walked by. One of the other girls pointed out one woman who was dressed nice, very skinny and looking down as she walked.

My discerning fellow inmate said. "You see that one? That woman is on it." I didn't believe her at the time.

"What? That's ridiculous." I thought there's no way someone would have the nerve to work in a county jail and be on drugs around that many police officers every day. Much to my surprise, skinny jail employees have incredible nerve because a couple of months later, another dope dealer friend was talking about selling dope to some lady who works in the jail. I asked what she looked like and sure enough, it was her. I was wrong again.

SHUT YOUR PIE HOLE

We had classes while in jail and in one of them, the teacher, another jail employee, was also a drug addict. Maybe just pot, maybe alcohol. I'm not sure. He drew a picture of a pie and labeled the different sections.

"This pie represents your life. This section is your family. This one is your job. This one is your health. This one is your drug of choice." What? We were paying attention now. Did he just say what I thought he said? "You see, you have to take that piece of pie for getting high and keep it as just one slice. This whole thing is your life and you have to have equal parts. You have to control it." He did say it! I was furious. This guy had no conscience. He was telling us, the students in his charge to "just control" our drug use. These were women who had sold their bodies for drugs, lost their children because of drugs, sunk to lows he could never comprehend and most were currently in jail for drugs! Apparently, to "just control" drug use was not as easy as he made it sound! I was so mad and I could not seem to get past the fury. I decided to do something about it.

I told another teacher about it and made a report. "You will have to sign your name. We can't do anything with just a verbal. It has to be a signed, written complaint. And between you and me, he should've been fired long ago. I hate that guy. He's a disgrace." This teacher was as mad as me.

"You got it." I picked up the pen and thought, what can Mr. Pie in the sky do to me? Put me in jail? Ha! To me, the teacher's pie theory was cruel. Some of these women would use it as an excuse to use again, and some of them would even *die* trying to get their drug use to fit into a multi-colored pie chart!

Then one night a dream was born for me. We went to a twelve step meeting and an outside speaker shared. What I noticed right off the bat were her clothes and her demeanor. She was dressed nice and acted calm and kind. I wanted to be like her. She talked about being where we were, in jail, dressed in green dresses and shower shoes, hopeless. She talked about being delivered from drug addiction and how she never thought she would be coming back to jail to share her story.

She encouraged us that if she could do it, we could to. "God will help you, if you let Him." Wow. I had heard testimonies before, but this time I felt real hope. I believed her. I had a tiny seed start to grow in my heart. Maybe God really can change my life. Maybe He really can help me become like her someday. Maybe someday I could come back here and encourage people, like she did. She was my inspiration to dream of myself doing something good for others. I wanted what she had. I wanted to look pretty, wear nice clothes, walk into jail and then walk right back out again.

"Follow my example, as I follow the example of Christ."   1 Corinthians 11:1

I was getting worn with being locked up. Jail was hard. It was the way time goes by so slowly. It is enough to literally drive you into depression. On the outside, we can barely keep up with all that is going on in a day, and we long for time to slow down. In jail, time goes by so slow, I literally could hardly stand it. It is a hard place to be no matter what, but I was sinking into a depression wanting to be free. I was so overcome with home sickness and longing. I experienced a longing stronger than anything I have ever felt. I was so sad one day I just couldn't shake the home sickness and the sorrow. Then a miracle occurred.

I was standing in line after lunch, waiting to head back to the dorm. I looked up at the sky, and the clouds, the blue sky and sunshine, and felt like God was talking to me. Overcome by emotion, I gazed up and talked to Him. "I want to go home so bad, Lord." Holding back tears I marched back to my bunk feeling like in that moment, God was closer to me than He had been for a long time.

"You! Pack your stuff!" Thirty minutes later I walked out free and looked up at that same sky with gratitude. I *knew* that God had heard me and let me go. He had freed me. He had mercy on me. One of the ways I knew it was a miracle was because I could *feel* it. But I also knew it because every day for that last fifty six days, lots of people were released; always in groups of three or four people at a time. That day it was *only* me.

"Happy is he who has the God of Jacob for his help, whose hope is in the Lord his God, who made heaven and earth, the sea, and all that is in them; who keeps truth forever, who executes justice for the oppressed,

who gives food to the hungry. The Lord gives freedom to the prisoners." Psalm 146:5-7

ABORTION

"If you just lay here still, you will feel a slight pinch and then the warmth will come over you and you will gently fall asleep". The nurse's voice was meant to be soothing, comforting, just like when a nurse reassured me months earlier that I could rely on the birth control to work this time. It did not and now I thought to myself, I've been here before…you don't have to tell me. I know you're full of blank.

Lying as still as I could, I tried not to move at all. Closing my eyes tight, but not too tight…so I could pretend I was sleeping already and didn't have to look at anyone. I tried to control my breathing, slow and steady, but my heart was beating out of my chest. I was afraid but thought maybe I could be invisible again.

Just as the medicine hit my brain, I got a glimpse of the man I assume was the abortion doctor. I will never forget the look on his face as he pulled a glove over his hand. What *was* that look? I've never been able to figure it out. Was it concern? Was it fear? He was about to kill a tiny human being in my womb for the twentieth time that day, so what was he concerned about? He had to be heartless to have that job. He should've had a blank, cold, beady eyed stare and that would've made more sense. I don't know what that look was, but whatever it was, it scared me for a moment. Then suddenly, I was warm and my wish had come true, I was invisible.

When I woke up, I was still on a gurney and vaguely aware of at least two other people on gurneys nearby. My abortion had mercifully happened while I was in a deep, emotionless sleep. My disconnected heart found completion in the strong sedative that allowed me to disconnect while another tragedy occurred. Oh how I longed to go back to sleep for a while longer....maybe a few years would be alright. The blanket was so warm and if I just kept my eyes closed maybe I could rest some more. But then a nurse was there, grabbing my arm, helping me to sit up and my tortured reality broke back into my dream state.

"Let's move you into the recovery room and get you some orange juice and cookies..." Oh yeah, I got it...let me just get my mind back in line with feeling nothing but blank...I can do it...ok...just a medical procedure.... a little blood, a little pain, a little paperwork...nothing more.

But if this was just another medical procedure, then why was I angry? I mean I had a medical procedure and had my bunion removed and I wasn't angry about that. No, because the doctor didn't tell me the growth on my foot wasn't human and he didn't hide the details of the procedure from me. He didn't tell me it would be quick, easy and that all I would feel was a little cramping, like a hard period, and then relief. The bunion doctor told me honestly that it would hurt, and I'd need crutches and pain pills for a while. With the abortion I needed that exact thing and nobody warned me that the crutches would last forever and the pills would never take away the pain of that day. That foot doctor gave me a diagram and told me every gory detail and I knew what was going to happen *exactly*. But the abortion was different. Nobody told me anything useful medically, and what they did tell me, when I worked up the courage to ask, was a lie.

"Are you sure it's not a baby yet?"

"No" the nurse replied. "Would you like to see 'it'?"

"Yes"...next was the jelly on my belly. The

ultrasound screen was completely fuzzy except for one small, blip, blip, blip.

"What's that?" I asked.

"That's the heartbeat". That was my cue, to jump up and run. But then that nurse let the demon speak to me.

"See, it's just a worm with a head," she said. Then the demons around my neck started screaming in my ears, "See, loser, it's too late, it's too late! The drugs, the drugs! Your baby will be born with no arms and no legs! You are a failure! It's too late!" And I knew they were right. I crawled back into my emotional emptiness. Another blank girl in a green gown, got off the table and back in line.

"Thus says the LORD: "A voice was heard in Ramah, Lamentation and bitter weeping, Rachel weeping for her children, refusing to be comforted for her children, because they are no more…" **Jeremiah 31:15**

Excerpt End

CHAPTER EIGHTEEN

Clear as a bell, I heard it. "Dad." What was that? Instantly I knew. I was in church, worshipping with everyone else, singing a song about being a child of God. I was daydreaming; watching an adorable seven year old playing the drums. I was just about to give God my standard, "Give me grandchildren or let me die" speech and then I heard it. "Dad" I knew what He was trying to say. In that moment He redeemed the word for me. "Dad" wasn't a bad word anymore. "Dad" didn't have to hurt every time I said it anymore. Raising my hands in worship, I thought, "Thanks, Dad! It's going to be a great week."

And a great week it was! At the writer's group, I felt a new found peace. Even when a new participant shared a poem about wanting to eat his cat. I was unphased. Normally, I would be the one marching up to him afterward and, telling him that I talked to someone who ate cat before and it was greasy and gamey. I would have pulled out all the stops to get this weirdo back to ground beef and, letting Fruffy live. But tonight, as I handed my excerpt over to one of the regulars, I let someone else set him straight. The blond who vacuumed naked was on him like a cat on a mouse. "Good, I thought." I can't solve the whole world's problems. And I don't have to. That's my Dad's job."

Writers Group - Sharing Excerpt Seventeen
Genre: Semi-Autobiographical Memoir, Christian

Lord I'm Listening

Lord I'm listening
For my healing
Like a freight train
Or a feeling
No more pain
Just a whisper
Blowing over me.
I'm listening with my heart
And all I have to give
Lord I'm listening
I want to hear you speak
To the hurting part in me.

Wishful Thinking

All the words
I wish had been said
Flow like rivers
In my head
All the love
I wish I'd gotten
In a childhood
Not quite forgotten

IN THE TEMPLE OF MY GOD

By this time, we had moved to a townhome. How my boyfriend talked the owner into renting to us, I will never know. But we were there and now the cooking of drugs was in my garage about once a month. I was skinny, sick, and sad all the time.

  I had to force myself to eat. I had taken some of the drug money, and gone to buy jeans. The smallest size available was one. I pulled them on hopefully, but gasped when I saw that they looked ridiculously big. Looking in the mirror in the dressing room and seeing how skinny I was overwhelmed me. I had been drinking 'weight gain' shakes for months, trying to gain weight. What happened to size seven, five and three. And now one? I felt hopeless. I sank to my knees and cried.

  My boyfriend had a gun in the closet and one day when he was out, I found myself fighting for my life. I was laying down, just being down and depressed. I just didn't feel like getting up, and doing anything. All I could think about was that gun.

  "Get up! Go get it! You know what you have to do!" The voices in my head were screaming at me, over and over. I was seeing myself getting up from the bed, sliding open the closet and getting the gun out. I could see myself holding the gun. I could see it but I didn't want to do it. I began to cry and begged the Lord to help me. The voices got louder and more insistent.

  "Get up! Go get it! Just give up! You'll never get better and you know it! You're a failure, nothing but a stupid drug addict! You are a loser! You don't deserve to live!" Sweating, I could feel something trying to force me off the bed. I gripped the sheets, trying to hold on and not get up. Desperately, I prayed again.

  "Dear God, help me!" At that moment the voices, and the force trying to pull me up off the bed, stopped. Out of breath, I rolled sideways off the bed and then fell to my knees. "Please, Jesus help me get better." I was shaken up by what I had just experienced and had to get out of the house.

      I had not committed suicide but I was beginning to think that I would never get better. I had tried rehab, jail, church, twelve step meetings, therapy and out patient treatment. No matter what I tried, I could not seem to stop using and I was so tired of trying. I knew the devil was trying to kill me.

"The thief does not come except to steal, kill and to destroy. I have come that they may have life and have it more abundantly." John 10:10

"For we do not wrestle against flesh and blood, but against principalities, against powers, against the rulers of the darkness of this age, against spiritual hosts of wickedness in the heavenly places." Ephesians 6:12

      There is a story in John Four of the bible about a woman at a well. She was deeply entrenched in a life-long habit of sin. She had been married several times, and was currently rejected by the women in her village because she was living with a man who was not her husband. I have no doubt that she had a history of not only many men, but also of being mistreated by men. I also have no doubt that she felt trapped in her sin. Other people had written her off. Jesus meets her and talks to her, cares about her, shares truth with her. I'm sure at that moment she felt deeply loved. This *man*, Jesus, rejected the societal standards of the day to talk to an outcast, foreign woman. He would undoubtedly be looked down upon just for talking to her, but he didn't' seem to care about what anybody else thought. He didn't want to sleep with her, use her or anything else. She was not invisible to him. All He does is ask for her help drawing water. He got her attention by sharing insight into her life. He offered her hope and then gently encourage her that He believed in her ability to overcome the sin that has entrapped her. He tells her "Go and sin no more." He rejects the human notion that she is beyond repair. He believes she can do better and in that gentle admonition, He encourages her that she *deserves* to do better. One of the amazing things about the story is that the woman, even though she is a "sinner", she does know something about God. She recognizes Christ as a Godly man and perceives that He is a "prophet". She is not completely ignorant about spirituality, and she is not rejecting God. She knows what is good, and what she should be doing, but she is not living it. Perhaps she felt powerless to change. Perhaps she had tried so many times that she had finally given up on her life ever getting 'good' again. Her encounter with Jesus Christ gave her hope, and that was the turning point. When we give up on ourselves. God does not.

  That was me. I knew lots about God, and loved Him, but the devil had control of my life. I needed to meet Jesus, face to face, and pretty soon I did.

  The church that was nearest my house was about a mile away, and was in a remodeled supermarket building. I started going to that church. I would get up in the morning, do my drugs, try to get the guy I was living with to go with me and then I would go by myself. None of my drug addicted friends would go with me either. I asked everybody to go with me. They all believed in God, but like me, they mostly felt disqualified or disconnected from anything God might offer, so they made excuses not to go. I didn't like going by myself but twice a month, my boyfriend's little girl was home on the weekend, and she went with me. She tried to get her Dad to go, but he always said no. We went anyway. I would take her to her Sunday school class and then I would go to the sanctuary. During worship, I would just sit in the back and cry. I tried to just sniff quietly but sometimes nice old ladies would hand me tissues.

    The Pastor was a hope peddler. He talked a lot about using what we thought in our heads to grab ahold of the blessings God promised us. I needed what he shared so bad. I had never heard anyone talk like that before. He was yelling about beating back the devil. His preaching made me feel like I could get better. He preached a lot about overcoming. He quoted scripture in such a way that I started to feel better.

    He said, "You're the head and not the tail! You are the apple of God's eye. You are above only and not beneath! You're a mighty earth shaking, history making, mountain moving, giant killing, demon stomping, water-walking Champion, Son of God, Joint Heir with Jesus!" His preaching made me feel so good. I kept going back.

    One Sunday, after going for about a year, and after taking my boyfriend's five year-old several times by myself, he finally went too. That was no ordinary Sunday.

    After worship, the Pastor said, "Today we are going to talk about the woman with the issue of blood. Let's read it."

"Now a woman, having a flow of blood for twelve years, who had spent all her livelihood on physicians and could not be healed by any, [44] came from behind and touched the border of His garment. And immediately her flow of blood stopped.

[45] And Jesus said, "Who touched Me?" When all denied it, Peter [a] and those with him said, "Master, the multitudes throng and press You, [b] and You say, 'Who touched Me?' "
[46] But Jesus said, "Somebody touched Me, for I perceived power going out from Me." [47] Now when the

woman saw that she was not hidden, she came trembling; and falling down before Him, she declared to Him in the presence of all the people the reason she had touched Him and how she was healed immediately. ⁴⁸ And He said to her, "Daughter, be of good cheer; your faith has made you well. Go in peace."
Luke 8:43-48

The Pastor continued: "This woman was sick, man! She had been sick a long time. She had tried everything to get well. It says she spent all her money and was hopeless! She could not get well."

Now I was really listening. I immediately identified with the woman. It was as if God was talking directly to me about my life.

"She was very sick for a long time. She had been to "many physicians" so we can guess that she was probably skinny and malnourished. On top of that, she was desperate. On top of all that, because she had an issue of blood, she was considered unclean. That means she was basically an outcast in that society. Then she heard about Jesus and with determination she said I'm not going to live with this anymore. She heard He was healing every sickness and every disease among the people. Faith began to grow in her heart. And she began to say to herself out loud, "If I could just touch the hem of His clothes, I can be healed." She believed it!

Let's break it down. How did this happen? She *heard* something. Then what did she do? She *thought* something. She thought, "If only I can get to Jesus and just touch his garment, I could be made well." And then what did she do? She *believed* something. She believed he could heal her. She heard something. She thought something, she believed and then what? She *did* something. She got up and *she went to where Jesus was.*

She believed so strongly that she went to where she knew He would be. For a skinny, determined, sick woman this was not easy. She had to yell 'unclean' along the way and cross the road when people walked by. But she believed so strongly that Jesus could help her. He was really her last hope, so she went! She had already tried so many things but she wasn't giving up. She was acting on her belief. She had just a little bit of faith left, maybe. She took that little bit of faith and she put it to action. Remember she *did* something. She *went* where Jesus was. She reached out to take what she needed. That woman had a *point of contact* with God. Her point of contact was his garment.

Do you need something from God today? Are you sick? That woman had faith, man! How 'bout you? Do you have enough faith today to get what you need from God?"

I was crying again. I turned to look at my boyfriend to see if he was reacting like me. I wanted to see if he felt what I did. He was stoned face, looking ahead. I pulled on his shirt.

"Did you hear that?"

He turned to look at me for a moment, "What?"

"He's talking about us! We're sick!" I looked him straight in the eyes. He knew what I wanted. He turned his face away and straight ahead again, ignoring me and watching the pastor. I turned to hear,

"You came to church today because you *need* something from God and He wants to give it to you. You just heard God can heal you. Maybe you've never heard that before. But He *can*. But you've got to do something! You've got to step out in faith. There is everything to gain, and nothing to lose! Like the woman with the issue of blood, you need a point of contact to reach out and get your healing. Maybe you've been praying for a long time. Well, today is the day! You heard it, you believed it, you got yourself here to church and now you need to reach out to touch the garment of Christ. It's *your* point of contact! He's offering it but you have to reach out and take that step of faith, believing His word enough to get up and reach out. Today up on this stage we have your point of contact!" He took duct tape and taped it to the floor. With the tape he had made a line on the stage.

He continued, while I hung on every word. "Here it is! This line is your point of contact today. If Jesus could heal all these people including this woman who had been so sick for so long and tried everything she knew how, He can heal you! If that's you, if you are sick and need healing, come on up here and walk across this line. This is the day for you to be healed!"

I was ready to run up there, but once again, I was co-dependent. I didn't want to go alone, and I wanted him to do it with me. Maybe this is why he finally came to church! It was *our* time to get healed! I turned to look at my boyfriend and begged him to go up with me.

"Come on, let's go. We need this so bad!" I started to scoot towards the end of the row.

"I'm not going," he said.

"What? Why not?" I couldn't believe he was even hesitating.

"I'm just not going. If you want to go, go for it. But I'm not going up there. I don't need to be healed of anything."

"What? Please! Please, go up there with me. Please!" I was whispering and blubbering all at once, pulling at his shirt. He just looked stone faced at me.

"No."

I slumped into the seat and cried. I watched in tears as many people went up and walked across that line. The pastor continued but I didn't hear. I was caught up in my sorrow and then it was over. I thought, "That was my chance! Now it's gone!"

I was still wiping away tears when we went out and down the hall to pick up his daughter. She looked so happy that her Dad was finally at church. She grabbed both our hands, swinging them back. She was telling us all about Sunday school and what she learned about Jesus helping people who were sick. He just stayed stone faced. I look down at her and smiled. I didn't want her to know I was distraught. But I was crushed. That was on a Sunday. Something unbelievable happened three days later.

"Pride goes before destruction, And a haughty spirit before a fall." Proverbs 16:18

GOOD COP, BAD COP

"I don't know why you just won't try. A job fair is where they help you get a job and they really need people." I was in the garage taking the trash out because my boyfriend just refused to. I was trying to convince him to look for a job. That was another thing he had refused to do for years.
BOOM, BOOM, BOOM! Now terror was streaming though my body. Before I could get a word out he said wistfully, "I'm sorry, Jo."
"What? Who is that?" He didn't answer. He knew who it was. I was frozen in place, unable to move. Someone was about to break down the door. And then they did. All of a sudden six cops rushed in. Our greatest fears were being realized. My boyfriend had been making meth in the garage and we were under arrest.
They handcuffed both of us and then took my boyfriend into his daughter's bedroom. They sat me on the couch while they searched the house. I was sitting there looking at the verse I had taped behind the

television on the wall. I put it there so I could see it whenever I sat on the couch. Now I was just staring at that verse, as the police tore apart the house.

"...*All things are possible with God"* Mark 10:27

One cop was assigned to stand there and watch me. I soon figured out he was supposed to be the bad cop, but he wasn't very good at it. He very rudely broke into my attempts to meditate on God's word.

"You, look at me! Look at me! You see this badge? You see who I am? I'm Officer Pitstak!" Apparently, he was a jaded comedian. He was looking directly at me so I could tell he meant what he said but he spit it out with sarcastic humor.

"You need to burn that name into your brain young lady! Because someday, someday you will want to thank me, Officer Pitstak." I smirked at him. I doubt it ahole. He continued, undaunted. "Now I don't want to get some tear stained thank you card to Officer DitchPile or Partsmack or Potstuck! That's Pitstak!" Apparently, kids made fun of his name when he was in school because he could not possibly have made those up, I thought. He was getting sweet revenge now. A cop with a gun and all. He pointed at his badge again and spelled it out for me, in case I couldn't spell in my intoxicated state. "P-I-T-S-T-A-K!" He paused for effect. "Did you get that? Pitstak! I'm the guy you need to send that thank you card to. And baby I know one is coming eventually. Either that or you're dead. You look too smart to end up dead!" Really? What on earth is he saying? I closed my gaping mouth again and he continued. "Don't forget little lady. It's New Heights Police Department and we are here to change your life!" He almost smiled. I giggled but then he got serious. He looked me in the eye. In a softer tone, he asked, "What are you doing with this loser anyway?" I was just about to answer but before I could, another officer called him away to another room. Apparently, they were examining the contents of my cat box.

Now a female cop walked up to talk to me. She looked familiar and then I remembered that she and the other female cop had actually talked to me about a week before, at the supermarket. I remembered because they were looking at me weird in the cat food aisle. At the time I thought, 'What's up with these two?' Always wanting to be liked, especially by weird cat owners, naturally I started talking to them. There was a split second of surprise on their faces, when I said,

"I love my cat, but she's a little picky about what she has for dinner."

"Oh…mine, too." She answered as the two of them walked away a little too quickly. Hmmm, maybe they think I'm the weird one. Nah.

Now I was staring at her remembering that day and I knew why the encounter felt different. They were watching me, and the house, trying to figure out what my role was. I think they figured out I was just a stupid girl trying to get a meth cook to take the trash out and get a job.

Now this female cop was being nice to me as her co-workers worked over my boyfriend. She was so nice that I figured out their strategy. Apparently, this female was the good cop and Pitstak was supposed to be the bad cop. He wasn't fooling me and even though she let me feed my turtle and cat before taking me to jail, she wasn't fooling me either. They didn't really care about me. How could they? They did say that my house was cleaner than any meth house they'd ever seen. That was nice.

The day of the raid was a hard day. I knew it would come. We had been living that life for more than three years by then. I was the only one obsessed with having a house and routine that looked normal. It was a constant fight trying to fool the neighbors. But it only took one friend getting busted to turn it all upside down. I was almost relieved except for worrying about who would take care of my cat and my turtle.

    I always said that if I ever got arrested, I would sing like a canary. So, I did. I told them all I knew and I signed whatever they wanted me to, but it wasn't necessary. My boyfriend was hysterical and telling them everything. He knew his daughter was about to come home from school. Luckily, his mother came to pick her up before she saw us with handcuffs on. But she saw the cop cars.

    She came home from school and the police intercepted her on the sidewalk. Ironically, it was "Just Say No to Drugs" week at school. She had just learned what drugs were. One of my deepest regrets is that day and that kid. She should not have been in the custody of two meth addicts, no matter how 'normal' our lives were. No matter that none of the meth was cooked inside the house, just in the garage. No matter that she was always at her mother's house for the weekend when the cooking happened. No matter that she had a nicely packed lunch with an encouraging note every day for school. No matter that I helped her learn to read and do math. No matter that we read stories to her every day and took her to church. No matter that we made sure she got to every one of her t-ball games. No matter that when the police asked her what her mother's name was, she said my name. No matter. That day took it all away. Sometimes there is good, but the bad outweighs it all.

    Later that day, as I walked into the cell with six other girls and four bunk beds, it struck me that once again, I was here in this cold, hard, cement and metal world. All the girls were chatty and trying to make friends but I wasn't talking. I just waited to be processed.

I was in shock. The police told me if I signed their statement, my charges wouldn't stick and they were true to their word. Just two days later, when they let me out of jail, and I was ecstatic to come home to a cat and turtle that were alive and happy to see me. The police had looked everywhere but never found a large amount of drugs. They got a confession that was enough to put my boyfriend away for over five years but they let me go. They were never after me. They wanted him because they wanted him to turn on the bigger fish. They knew I was guppy swimming in the baby pool.

When I got home, I called my Mom. Once again she showed up to help me. We put the house back in order. I was grateful that she didn't say anything. It was quite obvious that I was reaping what I had sown. She just put the dishes away, made the bed and tried to help me the only way she could without causing more trauma. I'm sure she felt like her choices had caused enough trauma for me to last the rest of my life. At that moment, I was grateful for her silence.

I was happy to be free. I also realized that my boyfriend was not going to get out of jail and I would not be able to pay the rent. I was in no shape to put together a resume, and I knew I couldn't pay the bills. I also knew I had to get out of that state, before I went to prison. I also knew where to find drugs to keep going. The police missed a couple of spots and I had no time to detox now. I had to pack and move.

YOU HAUL IT AWAY

For over a month, I cried and packed and packed and cried and packed. My friends would come over and try to help but people on meth have a lot of trouble concentrating, so it was mostly me. I was even more sad because my boyfriend was in jail and I wasn't allowed to talk to his daughter anymore. We would do three way calls with her, my boyfriend and me, but I was not allowed to speak. At least I got to hear her sweet little voice but I wasn't allowed to tell her I missed her or loved her or anything. I was just a "girlfriend", with no rights.

I grieved the loss of the two people who were most important in my life, while I tried to figure out what to keep, what to sell and what to throw away. I had a yard sale and other cooks showed up to buy some of the "equipment" we had. I promptly told them that they were idiots. I even put some stuff right into the trash. I only sold what I had to because I had to pay to move.

An old friend had been calling me and inviting me to move to where they were for several months. I would complain about my life, and they offered a way out. Finally, I felt like I could make it. I really had no choice. About a week after the raid, the police were on a call at the end of the block, and I was driving by on a bike ride. I drove up to ask a neighbor what was going on and one of the officers outside called out to me. I recognized him but I had no intention of saying hello.

"Hey Jo Lisa, what are you doing over here?" He said, turning towards me. I didn't answer, just smiled weakly and waved. My insides felt like they were shaking. I realized that he knew my name. I was petrified. At that moment, I knew I had to leave or go to prison. They recognized me now so it was only a matter of time, until I got arrested again. I was on the radar. Now my plan had an urgency and I knew where I was headed. Louisiana, the promise land.

Excerpt End

CHAPTER NINETEEN

"I was busy. I didn't know. He controlled all the money. I would've had nothing. We would've been poor. I didn't want to lose my house. My parents would never take me in with all the kids. I had nowhere to go. He had a problem with his mother, he was just hurting from that. He said he wouldn't do it anymore. I didn't like to be touched. I never saw anything. Thirty-five years and he never went for boys!" I was pulling weeds in my garden and remembering my mother's list. I had finally asked her about her truth. Instead of judging her by her behavior and naturally thinking the worst, I gave her the opportunity to speak her truth. I finally just gently asked her questions about the past. Thinking about the response I got and the list of excuses my mother gave then and over the years, I felt sad. Are they excuses or reasons, Lord? Not waiting for an answer, I answered myself, I don't know. Chucking a weed into the wheelbarrow, I realized it didn't matter. Children were still being molested and raped. Turning to get a sip of lemonade, I noticed my dog was chewing a tomato right off the vine.

"I should've never got you started on those." I said, grateful for the distraction. Luckily, she was a short dog who couldn't reach the tomatoes at the top. I loved dogs. They had a way of entertaining us and they loved us no matter what. I needed that love. Writing my story got me down sometimes, but I refused to give up. I refused to quit. I was going to finish my book no matter what.

Later that week, I met a woman new to the class. She talked non-stop but one of the things she talked about was how much she loved Jesus. She had a shirt on that said 'Smug Pug' with a picture of a pug that looked a lot like mine.

"Is that your dog?" I asked her.

"Oh yes, that's Bug the pug! She's trouble! First, she dug a hole in my begonias, and then she ate my rug."

As I handed her my latest excerpt, my poet's mind was in overdrive. 'Bug the smug pug, dug begonias and chewed the rug.' This is the stuff that keeps me up at night. Ugh.

Writers Group - Sharing Excerpt Eighteen
Genre: Semi-Autobiographical Memoir, Christian

Sleeper

He's sleeping again
Because he hurts
Where's he's been
His thoughts pervert

To make him think
That's reality
Like a wink
The fatality

Of sin trying
To take his soul
Praying and crying

Lord, please make me whole

Take away the sorrow
Of yesterday's abuse
Let me wake tomorrow
Without a noose
Of other people's sin

Choking out my joy
What happened then
When he was a boy
Was not his doing

As a man he needs to know
That what's pursuing
Him is a cunning foe
Sleeper, open your eyes

Reject that depression
Be the wise
That choose confession
Shake your fist in the air

Scream at God with rage
Why weren't you there?
Then turn the page
On what happened to you

Let Jesus grow your heart
Look hard at the ugly things
Separate the child from the part
That the man brings

To who you are
What they did was wrong
Throw it far

Into the pit where it belongs

Get up and going
Do the hard work to heal
Sleeper God is showing
You how to feel

Alive and free
You can be
Without defect
Awake and perfect

MY FRIEND PHIL

My friend Phil and another close girlfriend helped me drive the moving truck to Louisiana. It was quite a thing. The first place we stopped was the jail to say goodbye to my boyfriend. I had lost even more weight by then, and I was visibly exhausted. He was in there getting fat, and I was fading away, literally and figuratively. There wasn't much to say. I was leaving so I wouldn't die or get busted again, and go to prison. He didn't beg me to stay. He knew he had let me down, and I knew none of it mattered anymore. I had to go, and that was that.

My friend Phil and my girlfriend were relieved when I finally came out of the jail, and climbed in the moving truck. Nobody was comfortable that close to jail, especially people under the influence. We hit the road. I had never been out of the state as an adult so this trip was just a tiny bit exciting.

We had a map but luckily, we had to get on one freeway and stay there for several hundred miles. Even with this easy route, I never would have made it without my friend Phil. At midnight, we were driving sixty miles an hour over a mountain, with all the other truckers, when sparks started flying from under the truck. We pulled over to the side of this very busy freeway with big rigs zooming by very fast, in the dark. It was unnerving, and I had no idea what to do. But Phil did. He grabbed a flashlight, and crawled under the truck! I suppose he had to, because if the cops stopped to investigate, we were probably all going to jail, and I would promptly lose all my possessions to the impound yard. With a wire coat hanger, in the dark, with a flashlight, in a super stressful environment, he fixed the truck! A muffler bracket had broken, and he wired it up in less than ten minutes. We were ecstatic! He was a super hero! Thanks to Phil, we were back on the road, and out of danger in less than fifteen minutes.

    By the time we got to Louisiana, we were really exhausted. We had completed the trip in just a couple of days because we each took a shift at the wheel. I even drove that big truck. I only went over the curb a couple times, but after driving that huge truck, I sort of felt like I could do anything.

    After a couple of days of rest, I gave Phil my last hundred dollars to make it back home, and he did. When a detective called me a week later, I was surprised to learn that the truck got turned in but no trailer. Apparently, my super hero friend had stopped on the way home, and sold the trailer to some drug dealer. I tracked Phil down, and I was very mad.

    "Phil, what are you doing? They are threatening to arrest me if they don't get it back!" I felt so helpless. I was in another state. There was no way I could go get the trailer and return it. I needed him to do the right thing, and I was still in shock that he had done the *wrong* thing after I had been so impressed with his valor less than a week before. I didn't want to go to jail for something I didn't do. At that moment, I didn't care if he went to jail because I felt so betrayed. He proceeded to tell me that he thought that they wouldn't miss it. He promised to return it, and this time he was true to his word. By that time, he had only spray painted it so they dropped the case. Phil's nick name was "sticky fingers picasso" after that. Funny, but really not funny.

DETOX

When I first arrived in my new state, I had a very small amount of dope left. I remember cutting open the tiny baggy, and licking the insides. "I hate myself," I thought. I didn't like who I had become, and I knew that I had to get past this drug or I was going to die. I knew that this was my chance to really start over. I didn't know anybody on drugs, and I sure wasn't going to go find anybody. Then one of them found me.

I was standing in the backyard, eyeballing the neglected strawberry patch, in this little rented house, when some long-haired guy walks across the dirt alley towards me.

"How ya doin?" He asked casually.

"I'm ok. How are you?" I answered. I wasn't feeling super friendly. But I guess I was friendly enough, because he proceeds to tell me which houses nearby had all the action, and which one had been raided recently. Did I look like I was on drugs? I was out there looking like death warmed over, in a pair of sweatpants with cookie crumbs on my shirt. He kept talking, while I slowly realized what he was saying. By the time my exhausted brain kicked in, I was highly annoyed with my new neighbor. I did not want the information he was sharing. I had zero interest in the local druggie gossip.

Then he says, "Do you want to smoke some pot? I got some right here", as he pulls a joint out of his shirt pocket. Little did he know that at that point, drugs had just completely turned my life upside down. My annoyance rapidly turned to fury at a boiling point. I just freaked out.

"You take that blankity blank and get the blank out of here! I don't even blankity know you! And I don't blankity want to! I hate blankity drugs! Get the blank out of here and don't blankity come back! I mean it! I don't ever blankity want to see you over here again! Get the blank out of here!" I was furiously waving my arms and jabbing the air with my finger in his direction.

He took a couple steps back, closing his gaping mouth. "Hey you need to chill, Lady! I don't want to hang with you anyway. Wow. You're blankity crazy!" He walked back to his side of the alley, and out of sight. I burst into tears. My detox had begun.

I've heard people say that when you get off of meth, all you do is sleep for two weeks. And when I had detoxed in jail that is pretty much what happened but this time, that was not my experience. I was in excruciating pain. My back, and what I assume was my lungs, hurt like they were being ripped out. I could not sleep because it hurt too much just to exist. For several days, I was in very bad shape. I didn't know where to get any meth, and I had zero desire to start my train wreck life over again so I was determined to tough it out no matter how bad it hurt.

My old friend, and new roommate, was telling me 'white dope' is bad, and she didn't want anything to do with it. I didn't either. I knew that no matter what, I didn't want it anymore. I was going to get better no matter what. It was very hard. I was sick, depressed, hurting, and wanted to die, right when I was beginning to live again.

I was out of it, for a few weeks straight, but I did manage to get up eventually, and start going to twelve step meetings. They had never helped me stay clean for very long before but I was determined to try again. At least I wasn't doing this alone.

Eventually, I started to have some hope. I would also go to church, and to a biblical twelve step group. I had never tried that before. That is where I learned that when you pray for specific things you need, God will answer your prayer just to show you He can.

MY FIRST JOB

My roommate was an old friend who was a single mom. She had listened to my sob story and she understood my need to make a whole new start. She was letting me babysit her daughter while she worked, so I didn't have to get a real job right away. We were helping each other. But eventually, I started looking for a job. I had been told in church that God loved me, in spite of my sins. I was assured that He was hearing my prayers and would answer. And just like they told me He would, God immediately began answering my prayers. I applied for twelve jobs, and only actually prayed about two of them. I didn't hear anything about the first ten, but I got responses for the two I prayed about. The first one I got a card in the mail declining, and the second one, I got an interview!

My resume didn't list the fact that I had been a stripper for the past five years but it did list the singing telegram job. That intrigued the new boss. He called my past employment "interesting". I wore five-inch, hot pink heels and a pink dress to the interview because I didn't own any other business attire. He saw past all that, and decided I was worth a chance. I got the job! I was beyond happy. I had my first 'normal' job in years and the best part was that it was at a Christian apparel company. God had put me exactly where I needed to be. I was surrounded by people who followed Jesus, and I was in sales!

The boss was a man who grew to be one of my favorite people. He was awesome. He never treated me like an object. He was actually fatherly, and he must've been thinking, "Well she might not be able to type but maybe she'll bring some fun to the sales floor." He had a lot of that covered himself. He was a great sales manager. I had about sixty days clean when I got that job. God knew exactly what I needed because every morning he would gather us around for morning devotionals. He taught us what the bible has to say about being a good employee. He got excited about the Lord. He would kick up his heel and enthusiastically say 'What a God!' He was the first person I'd ever encountered who genuinely got excited about the Lord.

"Whatever you do, do your work heartily, as for the Lord rather than for men, knowing that from the Lord you will receive the reward of the inheritance. It is the Lord Christ whom you serve." Colossians 3:23-24

"Jo Lisa, come on up here!" I was being awarded for doing well at work. I had broken sales records, and I cried as I shook hands with my boss. It felt so good to be good! No more looking over my shoulder. No more worrying about what was wrong in my life. No more feeling guilty. No more feeling like a failure. Finally, I was a success!

In my opinion, drug and alcohol addiction has little to do with just randomly repeating the same behavior. It is about self-destruction. God gave us only one body, and He wants us to treat it as a temple but unfortunately, we often take our past emotional hurt and turn it back onto ourselves, physically. Addicts and alcoholics are not just using and drinking. They are not trying to let other people down, get arrested, and ruin their lives. They are trying to escape the pain of whatever got them high in the first place. They are trying to avoid everything that hurts too much. They are in extreme pain, and it's taking all of their energy and focus to try to stop that pain. Unfortunately, eventually they lose all hope of ever feeling better, and they are subconsciously obsessed with avoiding the pain, permanently. Basically, they are trying to die. At least that's what I think. But the truth is that once you combine self-destruction with chemicals that are addictive, as one of my siblings said, "you are thinking with the brain you have." You are adding another huge challenge to the mix of getting well. Now you have to face your emotional pain and you also have to get off of an addictive chemical, physically. But physical pain is only temporary, and God made the body to heal itself. For most of us, physical pain is *nothing* compared to emotional pain. (Would you rather break your leg or lose someone you love?)

    For me, when I turned toward God, I was turning away from my pain, my self-destruction, satan, my dysfunctional friends, and all the things that I had been so wrapped up in. I turned from wanting to die, to hope. I had a glimmer of hope. I started to believe the verse I had on my wall in the meth house. *"All things are possible with God."* I started to really believe it. I felt like maybe God meant it. Maybe it *was* "all" things. And maybe it was for *me*. Maybe I was *worth* it. Maybe I didn't have to live like that anymore. Maybe the crushing pain could get better. Maybe I didn't have to be sad anymore. Maybe, just maybe, *I wanted to live.*

    I was trying to be a good employee, and every day, I got to work on time. I had spent so many years hating the morning, because after staying up all night, I had dreaded the morning. I always felt so hopeless because I had failed again at a normal life. If I couldn't even sleep at night, there was no denying my life was a mess. But now, it was a whole new day. Getting up for work after actually *sleeping* all night, was pure joy. I felt alive again. I felt like I had purpose. But my body didn't always cooperate. Doing meth for six years took a toll that no amount of cheap coffee could fix. I would struggle with wanting to fall into that deep, post-meth sleep. The drowsiness was so strong, I was overwhelmed by it. In the back of my mind, I thought half-seriously that maybe I could make it look like I was praying at my desk. But that still felt wrong, so I would have to go into the bathroom and do jumping jacks to stay awake. My body took a long time to get over meth, and even though I only weighed 103 pounds when I got to Louisiana, I quickly found the cure for that is donuts.

    Working around all Christians was just what I needed but I began to realize that I needed boundaries. I had never had them before. As a fixer and a rescuer, I couldn't imagine intentionally doing things that I knew would make other people mad, or not like me. I searched my bible and quickly discovered that God invented boundaries. He was very specific about telling the Israelites not to mingle with ungodly people. It was not prejudice. It was protection from the devil. People who are not following God are following the other guy whether they know it or not. Even people who actually *are* following the one true God, can be so damaged by their past that they are subject to the devil, and unintentionally harm others. The place, patterns and behavior where they are comfortable may cause collateral damage for others. They may not be ready to address their painful stuff, and it's not our business to make them. We can pray, speak the truth in love, and then we have to love the parts that are lovable and let the rest go. If we can't accept the rest, then, we need to build the wall.

Even now, I imagine that I am placing bricks, one by one that say 'healthy boundary' on them. Every time I feel myself trying to go back to that vulnerable place, and pattern in my head, I stop. I force myself to take captive that negative, fixer thought. I can't fix it. I can't fix others. Are you a fixer/rescuer? Take a moment and imagine putting those bricks in your wall. It's a big wall. It's a tall wall. The people that make you hurt, or feel unsafe, or are unwilling to repent or change; they are on the other side of that wall. But remember that above that wall is God. He's over you and all of them. He is looking down from heaven and doing a work in you *and* in them. He will take care of them. Pray for them if you need to, but <u>do not</u> feel bad about building your wall. God invented boundaries, and for this season, and maybe forever, you *need* that boundary.

For me, once in a while, as I imagine, I lean my head against that wall and cry. I am past the place where I need to pound my fist against it. Thanks be to God, I am past self-destruction, so I won't pound *my head* against it. But once in a while, I imagine leaning my head against the cold bricks, and I cry warm tears for what is lost. Putting up a boundary, doesn't mean you feel no grief. It's ok to grieve. Then wipe your eyes, smile and thank God for that boundary. It's going to change your life. God will restore the years that have been lost to dysfunction and hurt.

"And I will restore to you the years that the locust hath eaten, the cankerworm, and the caterpillar, and the palmerworm, my great army which I sent among you. And you shall eat in plenty and be satisfied, and praise the name of the Lord your God, that has dealt wondrously with you, and my people shall never be ashamed..."   Joel 2:25-27

 # Excerpt End

CHAPTER TWENTY

"She told me that he said if she didn't let him, he'd get her little sister." I put my arm around her. The kids waited in the car while their mom stood on my porch and cried. Some days they just had to wait while this broken woman vented about her sorrow to me, the babysitter. Today I'd given them a little candy to keep them occupied. Their mom was in bad shape, and I was grateful to be able to help in some way.

"I know I need to be strong but I'm so mad! I'm furious that he did this to my children!"

"I know I want to go load my gun," I mused softly. To my surprise, she pulled back, looked me in the eye and then threw her head back and laughed. Realizing I had accidentally said what I was thinking aloud, I laughed, too. Then I got serious.

"You are the picture of inner strength for those kids Mama. You are amazing, and honestly no one could do any better. You just keep smiling as much as possible, and crying when you need to cry. If there's anything, and I mean *anything*, I can do to help you, don't hesitate to ask. Ok?"

"Ok." She hugged me again. "Thank you." She wiped her eyes, gave me a little smile, and turned towards the car. Such a good mom, I thought as I waved goodbye.

Later that night as I handed over my latest excerpt, she was still on my mind. I wish my own mother had been able to find that inner strength to divorce my step dad when we were kids. I wish she had had someone to offer whatever she needed, when we needed her to kick him to the curb. Loving my friend, and her children, and offering a shoulder to cry on was the least I could do. I knew the Lord would bless their future because she was taking a stand against evil today, and protecting her children. I was so glad to know they had a good mother. I considered it a gift from God to know her, and be able to see a mom do for her children what I'd always wished my mother had done for us.

Writers Group - Sharing Excerpt Nineteen
Genre: Semi-Autobiographical Memoir, Christian

The Melancholy

What do you do
When your mother doesn't love you anymore?
Just a kid who refused to
Zip it, click it and throw away the key.
Too much sorrow, just spills out
Every decade or so.

What do you do
When your mother doesn't love you anymore?
Get up early on a Sunday morning,
Go for a long drive in the country
With the sorrowful music up loud
And the windows all the way down…

What do you do

When your mother doesn't love you anymore?
Enjoy your Father, unseen but not invisible,
He's always been there,
Even in the melancholy,
It's a warm and beautiful spot
In the Son.

End of Story

There's nothing left to talk about
There's no way to tell the story
And make it sound better
It's hard, it hurts and it's over
Time to let it go
Wipe away the tears
Breath deep and turn away
In a new, better direction
Don't look back no matter
How much you want to
Be strong, determined and brave
It's hard, it hurts and it's over
There's nothing left to talk about
Time to let it go
Free your hands, heart and mind
For something new
Something better.

GOING TO THE CHAPEL

    After all that I had been through, I still longed for love. I was still lonely. God's love was real to me but I was still lonely. At age twenty eight, more than anything I wanted to know that I was "*the one*" for somebody. My biological father left me and never looked back. My mother was never well enough to help me. My step father put his sin first. I'd been second to many men who put drugs or alcohol first. I was still longing to be important. I was longing for the romantic part of my life to get better. I wanted to be *the one*.

"If we spend time together, we are going to be bonded. We are going to bond."

"What? Are you hitting me with psychobabble now?" I said to my date, laughing.

I met him at a twelve step meeting, and he asked me to go to church with him. He had nine years clean, had a job and looked good in a muscle shirt. I felt like he was perfect but I was still not all in, so to speak. Then he said the magic words.

"I want this more than I've ever wanted anything." It could be a pickup line to get me naked somewhere, except he would also have to be a mind reader to know exactly what I needed to hear. But God knew.

There was so much longing in his voice. I had never been face-to-face with that kind of vulnerable, deep, urgency before. He was admitting his loneliness, his longing, and he wasn't trying to get me in the sack. We were in the breakroom at his work so this was just truth with no motive. The church, the muscle shirt, the muscles, the clean and sober. There was nowhere to run. It was like he should be afraid to show that to me but he meant it so much, he couldn't help it. How can I turn this down, I thought? I was almost afraid to believe this could be real. Did I deserve this? I felt like something was missing. But maybe it's me, I reasoned. I knew I was no perfect box of chocolates. I knew I was lucky that a guy this high quality wanted anything to do with me. The conversation went on and on in my head. What am I waiting for fireworks, a lightning bolt? With my luck it would just knock me down, and burn my hair off. For a minute I giggled at the thought… bald, singed eyebrows and smoke rising from my charred scalp. Wait, that's not funny! I could see that he was wondering what was so funny.

"Ok" I said aloud. "I want it too." I remember kissing my future husband, and thinking God, please help this to work because I don't think I can handle hurting this sweet man. And if he hurts me, I'll have to pluck his eyes out and use them for earrings so nobody notices my bald, burnt head.

Sometimes love isn't like the movies…It's better.

JOURNEY TO FREEDOM

"You see that? That's your baby's heartbeat!" I burst into tears. I was looking at the child in my womb. A boy. A miracle. Words can't express the joy I felt to be pregnant. This time I had been clean and sober for nearly two years. I was married and I had been *trying* to get pregnant. God had answered my prayers.

A week before, my co-workers had all pitched in so I could walk to the supermarket next door and get a pregnancy test. I had mentioned to my friend that I thought I might be pregnant, and she immediately started a collection. It was such a sweet thing. Then when it was positive, I announced it on the sales floor, and they all cheered.

This was a very joyful season. I was happy and things were going really well. My husband and baby were my whole world. My job was going really well. I had new friends. I was clean and sober. Basically, I was living, full time, on a pink cloud. But sitting in church I often felt emotional. I was so grateful to God that I was finally free of addiction, happily married and a mother, that I would often cry tears of gratitude. But sometimes when this crying started, I could not wipe my eyes, smile, and file out to the hallway with all the other friendly church going folks. I could not turn off the faucet. I could not stop crying or hide my tears, no matter how I tried.

"You need to go to that class I told you about. You need help." I was crying again. Standing in the church hallway with my caring friend. She was looking at me with a frown on her face. This was the third time she was telling me about the abortion recovery class at the local pregnancy resource center. I was embarrassed but honestly, I just could not get a grip. I was completely losing it over my past abortions. They didn't even have to mention abortion in the sermon, just singing a certain worship song would overwhelm me with emotion. I just couldn't stop crying about what I had done. I felt like that had been another person's life. How could I have *done* that? I was so full of regret, it was overflowing. I kept thinking "I could love those children *now*." But it was too late. I had a beautiful baby that I loved more than life itself but my other three children were gone. There was no bringing them back now that I was ready to be a mother. I had been trying to get clean for so long, and I felt so good, but I could not get away from this grief. I could not get away from my pain. I was longing for my babies. There was no satisfying that empty feeling.

I knew the magnitude of the loss. I knew I had committed a sin that was so permanent, there was no making up, no saying sorry, no going to counseling and working it out with the party I'd harmed; no restitution to my victims and no paying my debt to society. There was no way to make it right with them. I was stuck. I had a gnawing at my soul. I felt frantic and lost. I felt like I was missing something…somebody. I was desperately missing…three little somebodies.

I finally made the call and took the class. I had real concerns because I was sure that I would be judged. I couldn't even imagine talking about this, the worst of sins, in front of *Christian* women. Aren't most Christian women perfect? Wouldn't they think I was the scum of the earth? A murderer?

When people say mean things about women who've had abortions, I am always struck by their ignorance. They don't need to judge the woman who's had an abortion harshly, because she is already beating *herself* up. In my experience, until a woman gets healed, and sometimes even after that, she is condemning herself much more than anyone else ever could. The accuser, the devil has a hey-day with *most* post-abortive women. For many, he is relentless at fanning the flames of guilt, and shame, in their minds. I was sure I would be judged but I mustered up the courage and went anyway.

The first night I was surprised to meet women just like me, all around the table. I was so relieved. They were just like me! They understood and there was no judgment. We were all baring our souls and it felt good. On top of that, none of us talked about being 'pro-choice' or 'pro-life' or anything like it, at that point. Those words would come much later but I was decidedly pro-life. For me, and all but one post-abortive women I have met, abortion was no longer acceptable. We were wounded by abortion in such a profound way, there was not even a question about how we felt. We were 100% against abortion.

For several weeks, I sat in a class of about eight Christian women, who had past abortions. Our healing began when we each told our stories. All of us had just done what we thought would work to remedy a desperate situation. We'd found ourselves unexpectedly pregnant and had to make a decision. I went for the quick, "easy" fix to a bad situation, just like they did. Some had trusted birth control like I had, only to find themselves pregnant in a bad situation. Some were pressured or abandoned by the fathers.

All of our stories were different but amazingly, we all basically *felt* the same. We all had deep hurt and anger. We all felt overwhelmed with grief and loss. We were all ashamed, and if the class had not been totally confidential, I doubt any of us would've had the guts to be there. We would have dealt with our grief some other way…I know why post-abortive women have a much higher risk of suicide. Don't believe me? Look it up. You will be shocked at what 'choice' has done to steal, kill and destroy people, born and unborn.

We did homework that caused us to immerse ourselves in carefully selected scriptures that showed the unconditional love of God, and the humanity of biblical heroes. We found out how we felt was not something new. It was refreshing to realize sin is commonplace, even in the bible. There is no perfect human except Jesus. The human heart is desperately wicked. We weren't unusually bad. We weren't losers and failures. We were sinners and God still loved us.

First, we admitted our sin and then it took several weeks to work through the grieving process. We studied the stages of grief. We discovered that, for the women in the class who'd also had miscarriages, the stages of grief were the same.

The first stage was denial. This is what drugs and alcohol had previously helped me achieve. Now that I was not using and drinking, grief had literally ripped the lid off of denial. It simply wasn't possible for me anymore. No more denial. Check.

Next is: anger, bargaining, depression, and acceptance. Most of my anger was at myself, but in class we made a pie graph, assigning blame. Without exception, each of us had at least one other person we blamed but the majority of our pie showed we blamed ourselves the most. We wrote scathing anger letters to those who we felt had some responsibility for our abortions.

My blame, and anger list was pretty short. I did have some anger that others never fought for my unborn children. No one ever even raised a single question. No one raised an objection. No one told me it was wrong, and I should try to find another way. Three times, three abortions, numerous people, and no one said a word in defense of the three human lives hanging in the balance. I wish with all my heart someone had. I wish someone had said, "Hey, why don't we talk about adoption." Or "Have you thought about entering a rehab home for unwed mothers, and having your baby?" But alas, "daydreaming" was not on the list of grief stages. Angry? Check.

"Bargaining" seemed pointless to me. Abortion is so final. There is no bargaining. There is no "if I do this, can I have that?" If you are grieving a relationship, you can bargain with God to get the person back, or find a better person. But with abortion, there is none of that. The only possible bargain I could make with God was to agree to never have another abortion, if He would just help me stop crying. There was no way I would ever have another abortion. I already felt like someone else had been the one to have the three I was guilty of. It felt like I'd been asleep, and had finally woken up to a nightmare of pain. Ok, bargaining…I promise to stay awake! Check.

Then there's depression. Check. Got it. This I understood. I had been living in a deep state of depression for years. I was so weary trying to get clean, and failing, that I had sunk into hopelessness long ago. I had had three abortions in five years, and any semblance of hope or joy was gone, until I'd finally moved to a new state. Now I was so sad over my foolishness, my self-destructive drug addiction, having abortions and the loss of children, that depression was like a black cloud over me threatening, and ominous. I was very emotional. The devil did not have me in a chokehold anymore but he was definitely holding me under the flood of my own tears trying to drown me. Depression, check, check, but please don't check me in. I really don't want to go to the mental hospital. I just wanted to feel better.

"You have seen me tossing and turning through the night. You have collected all my tears and preserved them in your bottle. You have recorded every one in your book." Psalm 56:8

But in my grief, I found my Savior, Jesus. He walked me through thirteen weeks of that study and I finally found peace. I also discovered I was not alone in my sorrow. We had all been foolish and we all had deep regret, that we could no longer ignore. We were strong, capable, accomplished women who could not handle this 'choice' alone anymore.

CHOICE WITH A VOICE

Pregnant women in our society have three very real options for a pregnancy…abortion, parenting and adoption. Unfortunately, they usually lean towards them in that order. Women who are unexpectedly pregnant are especially vulnerable to satan.

"And I will put enmity between thee and the woman, and between thy seed and her seed; it shall bruise thy head, and thou shalt bruise his heel." Genesis 3:15

Since the Garden of Eden, the devil has been speaking into the ear of Eve. She still listens. Sometimes he is *relentlessly* chattering into her ear, trying to convince her that she has *no choice* but abortion. He wants to pressure her into making a decision, without really considering the other options. The accuser is trying to get her to rush, and choose death over life, as quickly as possible. Pregnancy resource centers were founded generally by God-fearing Christians who, biblically speaking want to defeat the devil, and save lives made in the image of God. And generally speaking, want to help women have a safe place to investigate *all* their options.

Forty percent of all pregnancies are unplanned, and studies have shown that a large percentage of women feel pressured into abortion. This can be real or perceived pressure. It could be her own anxiety, fear, a lack of support from those around her, financial worries, a boyfriend threatening to leave her or a husband who doesn't want children. Reasons can vary, all the way to an abuser forcing her to destroy the evidence of his crime, growing in her womb.

Are we really so foolish, as a society, to think that keeping abortion legal in the case of rape or incest, is the best thing for the woman? What if she is not a woman but a girl, and she was raped by her father? What if it is him who drove her to the abortion clinic, with explicit, ominous instructions to tell them she was raped by an older school boy…or else? Well-meaning abortion clinic staff think they are helping her rid herself of the memory of a horrible crime but they don't ask her point blank, are you telling the truth? Is someone abusing you? That girl who is being controlled by an abuser does not need us to make abortion legal in the case of rape or incest. Laws that are over simplified, like that, that don't help her; they are helping *him*. And of course, the abortion industry is helping *themselves* to more money.

Allow me to make blanket statements because of the many accounts I have read and heard from women who've been in abortion clinics or worked in abortion clinics. That well-meaning staff member is trained not to ask too many questions or do anything with vigor except sell her an abortion. Did you know that some of them get paid based on how many abortions they book? You don't believe me? I challenge you to educate yourself. Read every book you can find about what goes on behind the closed doors of that industry. Go to the internet and search for former abortion clinic worker stories. Read those and tell me you are not sick for the state of humanity, and the exploitation of women. Some would say it is the height of trauma for a woman to carry a child fathered by a rapist. Every testimony I've read, from women who aborted their child, conceived in rape, says the opposite. The testimonies I've read and seen said that the trauma of the abortion far exceeded that of the rape. Two wrongs don't make a right. My God's specialty is turning terrible things into beautiful things. That is what He can do with a child of rape.

I've met several people conceived in rape, and as far as I can tell they look like people who deserve to live. They look like their mothers, and human beings made in the sacred image of God.

I once met an elderly gentlemen, I'll call Ray. He put it all in perspective.

"What about a little charity?" he asked. "Why can't a good person find it in her heart to care about the unborn child that she doesn't want? Can she offer charity for another human being and give him or her life? We are talking about less than a year of inconvenience. What about a little kindness for another human being?" Indeed, a fantastic question. What they don't realize is that they are also doing the kindest possible thing for themselves. Life is always better than death, is it not?

"I've seen it with my own eyes. I can't forget what I've seen. Now what can I do?!" The woman on the phone was describing what she felt after seeing the widely publicized photos of the atrocities inside an abortion clinic. The abortion clinic photos were horrifying and it was evident that the abortion doctor had been involved in the business of death way too long. I believe those who perform abortions are in danger of becoming homicidal. What they are doing is the killing of human life. It's hard to say the word, 'murderer' but before you freak out, and say how extreme it is for me to use that word, remember I was there, too. I was in the room for my three abortions. I can't just blame the doctor. I am as guilty as they are. However, the abortion doctor in the case we had all seen on the nightly news, appeared to have been completely infected by a drive to kill, maim and hurt. I would guess he was demon-possessed.

  When the woman on the phone said, "I've seen, I can't forget and what can I do?', I realized that is why many of us are in the pro-life arena and can't get out. We have seen, and we can't forget. It started with my own abortions, and then through my work at the pregnancy resource center I was exposed to more and more ghastly examples of the dark underbelly of abortion. We have allowed our country, who usually take pride on choosing the "moral high ground", to wallow in the business of blood for too long. If you see what an abortion really is, you can no longer ignore it. The depravity, and heart wrenching pain, of seeing a tiny human ripped apart and bleeding is worse than anything else. It is so wrong, so sad, so unjust, and so brutal that I truly cannot forget. It is only through the grace of God that I have forgiven myself for being part of that horrific act.

  Sometimes I like to imagine, how I might have reacted if I had gone to a pregnancy resource center, when I was unexpectedly pregnant. Even if I was stubborn, and didn't say anything about what my plans were. Even if I didn't say whether I was going to keep the baby or have an abortion…what if someone had asked,

"So what are you planning on doing?" Suppose I had stubbornly refused to answer. Perhaps if she just went on bravely…

"You know we have a lot of resources here so you don't *have* to have an abortion." I believe those words would have stunned me out of my trance. I felt like I had to have an abortion. I needed someone to tell me I didn't *have* to.

Hope is like an arrow shot in the heart of a demon. The demon of hopelessness would have fallen away. I would've felt like I really had a *choice*. Maybe I never would've chosen abortion. Maybe I would have birthed more babies than I aborted. Maybe I would have birthed all five. I like thinking about that. But that's not what happened.

Instead, God let me have my own sinful way, and then used that pain to make me very compassionate about this cause. He generously let me fall on my face three times, deep into the pit of sin and death. Because of His grace, I crawled out of that pit and became very determined to fill that pit with hope for people like me.

I am grateful because even though I have to endure grief on this side of heaven, in reality I serve a loving God who gave me an amazing gift in spite of my grievous sin. I don't have my aborted children now, but I do get to be with them *forever*, in eternity.

I read somewhere that the average woman takes five years to realize the magnitude of a past abortion decision in her life. I believe that. Others testify to knowing immediately, that they had made the "worst mistake" of their lives. Some don't seem to feel a thing, ever, about their abortion. Others carry the burden for thirty or forty years before ever speaking of it again. I have spoken in churches where elderly women came up and told me that they had an abortion, and I'm the first person they've ever told. I've had men come up crying asking if the pain ever goes away. I have seen the devastation to the human soul that killing our offspring causes. It's not good.

Unfortunately, with abortion there is no "fixing" it. Women who were made by God to be the helpmate, and nurturer, find that there is nothing they can do to help the child they aborted. The result of this is a profound sense of helplessness, a desperation to do something and not being able to do *anything*.

Sometimes you will see groups of women on the news with signs that say 'Keep Abortion Legal' or "Pro Choice, Pro Woman". Really? If any of them are actually post-abortive, I believe they are still in the denial stage. They chant and march insisting that women are "fine" after abortion. They'll stand behind a microphone, shaking their clenched fist and say that their abortion was the *best* decision they ever made. Liars. Liars. Liars.

Those women are lost. God still loves them in spite of their hard- hearted pride. I have prayed for them on occasion because what strikes me most is the lack of kindness towards their offspring. Don't they feel bad for their child? Don't they have any charity in their hearts for the helpless, innocent infant they killed while making the "best choice ever"? I'm sure they have shoved any glimmer of compassion for the baby way down deep into their cold heart. If they let that compassion out, they will have to admit that it was a child, *their child*, and they destroyed it. They will have to admit their sin. Then what will they chant?

I will always be grateful that I took that abortion recovery class. It literally changed my life from overwhelming hurt to peace. I am not angry. I don't have to get in anybody's face, and make sure they know abortion is not a sin, it's my choice. It's my right. Nope. I know it is a sin. I know it was my choice and my right. I admitted it. I repented. I am forgiven. I have forgiven myself. Easy stuff? No. Nothing worth anything is ever easy. It was hard, but it was worth it to avoid sinking into rage, and becoming one of those chanting, "Keep your rosaries off my ovaries." That's catchy, but no thank you.

In the class, we studied the character of God, and found out that the biblical King David, a "man after God's own heart", suffered from depression. He was deeply grieved over the sins he had committed. Just like us. His sins were murder, and adultery, to be exact. How could God call an adulterer, and a murderer, "a man after God's own heart"? Because even though David sinned, shortly thereafter, he was broken hearted over his sin, and he *repented*. He grieved because he recognized that he had sinned against a Holy God. He also suffered difficult natural consequences, and he felt deep pain as a result of his sin. God still loved him all the more. God comforted David while He let Him suffer from the mess he had made of his life. I could feel God comforting me. David's story gave us hope that God still loved us, too. We also had hope that our children would forgive us. That was a biggie.

As we finished the stages of grief, we learned that we could not stuff our grief or ignore it. We needed to feel it to be able to finally let it go. We learned that God understands grief and when Christ left the earth, He talked about sending the "Comforter". We learned that the Holy Spirit could help us endure our grief, and turn our pain into wisdom. We could learn and grow from our mistakes. We could even use our deepest, darkest sin to someday help others trying to heal.

"When I refused to confess my sin, my body wasted away, and I groaned all day long. Day and night your hand of discipline was heavy on me. My strength evaporated like water in the summer heat. Finally, I

*confessed all my sins to you and stopped trying to hide my guilt. I said to myself, 'I will confess my rebellion to the Lord.' And you forgave me! All my guilt is gone."
Psalm 32:3-5*

"Thirty four...wait....thirty six!" It was the brunette. We were back in class doing the soul ties activity. Listing all of the men we had slept with, so that we could pray to break the soul tie created when we became "one flesh" with them, physically and spiritually. I was afraid to count how many I had slept with. So many that meant so little, and now I couldn't even recall their names. A few I couldn't remember if I'd actually slept with or not. The worst was the three of my brother's friends that I slept with in only two days, when I was fourteen. Thinking about that, I felt so foolish and incredibly dirty. Then I heard that woman's number. She was laughing about it, and I smiled too, because now I only felt a little grubby.

We wrote our list of names, and if we weren't sure of the name, we put a clue, like "acid trip", "blonde idiot", "picnic table", "alcoholic guitarist", that type of thing. Gritty stuff. Then we did the only thing left to do. We prayed for our renewed purity, put our lists in a coffee can and lit them on fire. That felt good. Fire is especially fantastic when it's used to cleanse the soul. I had the urge to dance around like a native but I contained myself. It was a somber moment but because of God's amazing grace, our souls were celebrating a clean slate. This was truly exciting...much better than the sex we could barely remember.

"Come now, let us settle the matter," says the LORD. "Though your sins are like scarlet, they shall be as white as snow..."   Isaiah 1:18

We worked through the affect our abortions had had on our lives. We shared how our abortions changed us. How we had become distant from God, went numb, ashamed, felt like we deserved to be punished, how we had to keep secrets, didn't trust others, didn't deserve to succeed, or be loved by a nice guy. We worked through what we had really done to ourselves and to others…our deep emotional scars, our guilt.

"The Lord is close to the brokenhearted and saves those who are crushed in spirit." Psalm 34:18

    We asked the Lord to reveal the gender of our babies. I didn't think this would work but amazingly, it did with absolute clarity. I have never had even a glimmer of doubt that my aborted babies are two girls and a boy. I knew that I knew. Then we got the privilege of naming them….Trinity Ann, Katrina Mae and Austin Jordan. My three children have names in heaven with Christ. I know where my children are and I know who they are with. They are with the only person I completely trust to take care of them, Jesus.
    We had a memorial service and committed our lost children to God. We found peace in the reality of where our children have been since the day we had our abortions. They were with our Heavenly Father. Now they had names. It felt like we had done all we could possibly do to make this right. We had lovingly placed our babies where they've been all along, and placed our sin at the foot of the Cross. We walked away from that horrible sin and it's aftermath, and walked forward in joy toward our future in heaven with our lost children.
    With every wrinkle and creak of my aging body, I have hope. I am getting closer to my home inside the pearly gates. When I finally get to heaven someday and walk through the pearly gates, Jesus and my three

children will join me in a running hug. Can you picture that? I often do. I can feel the warm light that Jesus, the Light of the World is. I can hear the symphony of birds chirping along with the heavenly chorus of angels singing "Hallelujah!" I can hear the faint "swish, swish" of my bare feet running across the vibrant, velvety soft green grass. I can smell the sweet fragrance of all the glowing, colorful flowers around us. And I can see my Savior moving toward me, with a huge grin on his face, and His arms open wide. And I can see my three beautiful children running toward me joyfully bouncing as fast as they can toward their mother.

    Thinking about that moment takes my breath away. And I daresay it is reserved just for people who've lost children to miscarriage, abortion or some other painful, early death. Now the wrinkles and the chub don't feel nearly as bad, do they?

FATHER TO THE FATHERLESS

Years had gone by since I had really tried to find my bio-Dad. To those who aren't adopted or actually know both parents, the searching might not make sense. But for those of us who don't know our birth parents, the relentless search makes perfect sense. For me, I really wanted photos of people with the same blood in their veins. I wanted to see what my paternal grandmother looked like. I wanted to know things, and with the invention of social media, a door opened. I found another family member and asked about it. He gave me my real father's phone number. I was trembling as I dialed the phone number.

    "Hello"
    "Hello, is this George?"
    "Yes, it is. Who is this?"
    "This your daughter, Jo Lisa."

Holding the phone tight to my ear, waiting for his reaction, I was shocked by what happened next. I heard him suck in his breath before he spoke.

"Wow! You are not gonna believe this, but my wife has been *praying* for two weeks that you would find us."

"What? Wow, that is amazing." He was right, for a moment, I didn't believe him. How could that be? I was glad to hear that he was a Christian so I didn't ask much more about why his wife was praying that after so many years. The conversation continued, and most of it was more normal. He soon made an attempt at explaining his complete absence for forty years.

"I thought people just went on with the new people in their lives."

His excuse was ridiculous but he sounded so glad to hear from me. He was sad to hear that our step-father was a pedophile who hurt us. He sounded like he felt bad about that. My heart was warm with gratitude. I found him! I finally found him, my Dad!

My decades long search was over, and for several months, I felt loved by the man who was my father. I called him about once a week or he called me. I sent him a video of my young son, and he sent my son gifts for Easter. It was great, until the day it wasn't.

"Did you get my letter?" I had called, and his question was the abrupt start to our conversation. His tone sounded different.

"No. What letter?"

"Well, I sent you and your siblings a letter."

"What did it say?" I asked. My stomach was in a bunch, and my heart was pounding waiting for his reply.

"Well, I just don't see the point," he said.

"What does that mean?" I asked, incredulous. I could feel the hurt rising in my throat.

"I don't feel any connection to you, and I just

don't see the point in continuing a relationship." He answered, his voice devoid of emotion.

"Ok" I said quietly, and I slowly hung up the phone. What did I do? Why doesn't he love us? I cried then, bitter tears of disbelief, and rejection. I had lots of questions, but I didn't have the guts to call back, and ask. He had made it clear where he stood. I was nobody to him. The next day I got his letter, and with it was the video I had sent of my three-year old. It was over. No Dad for me.

I was encouraged later when my sister said she "took care of it."

"What do you mean you 'took care of it'?" I asked her.

"I wrote that blankity blank a three-page letter telling him what a piece of blankity blank he is." She answered, matter-of-factly. I wanted to hug her through the phone. She had let him have it!

"Thank you. He deserved it." I said, glowing with anger and happiness at the same time. There was no excuse for him to do that. He couldn't take an occasional phone call from his flesh and blood? But then again, what was I expecting? He did not make *any* effort to find us or communicate for decades. He lived in an apartment about three miles from one of my siblings for years, without knowing it. If he had made an effort, he could've found us. A truly loving father would've moved heaven and earth to find his children. He didn't care, and that was clear.

What I still don't understand is his statement about his wife praying that I would find them. *What was that?* I will never know until I get to heaven, and the Lord can put His arm around me, and tell me that none of it matters anymore. Only the love of God the Father means anything eternal. That was just another example of living on a broken planet. Some things just don't make sense, but this world is not my home, and I am not fatherless anymore. I know who my real father is and *that* is the point.

For ye have not received the spirit of bondage again to fear; but ye have received the Spirit of adoption, whereby we cry, Abba, Father." Romans 8:15

 # *Excerpt End*

CHAPTER TWENTY-ONE

Sitting on the porch journaling to the Lord, I was letting it all out. What do you do when you have nothing left? Nothing left to give, nothing left to say, no room to hear anything but 'I'm sorry'. Too much hurt built, and built, and built, a wall in my heart and mind. All I have left is a long list, that I want to let go, without putting anything else on it. No record of wrongs feels impossible. Please Lord let all the tears cleanse my soul. I need to stop crying, and get on with today. I want to be available for those who love me, and those who are trying to get past the past. I want to be able to try too, with a sincere, forgiving heart. I want to call back, and hear the apology…maybe. I want to be able to stop crying long enough to forgive, and start over, even without the apology that I know is not coming. Some boundaries are better torn down. Give me the strength to try again. I don't want to be vulnerable. Please Lord be my shield. Protect me from any more hurt. Help me to wipe my tears, and smile a faithful, fearless smile.

With perfect timing, a huge beetle landed in front of me on the porch railing. Sniffling, I wiped my eyes. The beetle was looking *right* at me.

"Hello little guy." The bug bobbed up, and down as if responding. Wow!. I thought, I'm making a new friend. For over three minutes, I talked to the bug while it appeared to be listening intently.

"This life sucks sometimes." I lamented. "You are actually quite lucky that you were born a bug. Sometimes, I wish I could just crawl around in the plants all day, and forget about everything else." The beetle just stared at me, while I stared back. Finally, I decided I would have to say goodbye to my little friend and go make dinner. "Thanks for cheering me up little buddy,".,

"Thank you, Lord, for bugs." I sighed.

That night I was still thinking about my amazing little friend, when I handed my latest excerpt to a classmate. Hmmm, I hope nothing about this 'bugs' you. Giggling, at my own joke, I hoped I didn't look psychotic. Oh well, wouldn't be the first time.

Writers Group - Sharing Excerpt Twenty
Genre: Semi-Autobiographical Memoir, Christian

Who

What happened in there
behind a closed door
with children inside
and
posters of dinosaurs on the walls?
Who was watching,
what was going on
after dark?
Whose fault is it
when bad things
became
every night pain,
for a little kid?
Who can I
scream at
now
that the damage is done?

Reject It!

We can do better
Down to the letter
It's too much
And such
A sad reality
Reject calamity
And find a way
To do it today
Not tomorrow
Sing away sorrow
And do it loud
You, me and a crowd
Of one mind
To work and find
Something more
Open the door
Or break it down
With worship.

MOM CALLED

"Mom called. Dad molested another kid. The kid told. Now they are trying to find him to arrest him." My sibling blurted this all out at once, and I felt like I had been hit in the face.

"What? Who called the police? Mom?" I was hoping it was my mother.

"No, the girl he molested. The police showed up and tried to arrest him, but he'd already left in the camper. Now they think he molested a little girl in another country on a mission trip."

"What the blank?" Instantly, my mouth began the verbal protest. I was falling off the moral high ground into a pit of disgust.

"Mom said they searched the house but she hid the computer. Can you believe that? What is she thinking?" She had already had some time to process all this news, and now I just kept getting hit, as she kept talking. I wasn't trying to turn the other cheek, but somehow, I kept getting emotionally smacked left and right, anyway.

"Oh no, I cannot believe that! Why? Why is she protecting that piece of blank? I am so disgusted. I cannot believe it. She's been protecting him since we were in grade school! Remember when the school called. I was in the first grade! He needs to go to jail! And honestly, maybe she does, too! Man, this stuff makes me so sick and sad." Shaking my head, I felt so overwhelmed. I had to fight the urge to run. She just looked at me shaking her head too. We talked for another twenty minutes. We cried as we hugged goodbye.

"Well at least we don't live down there anymore. What a mess!" She said, always finding the good in every situation.

"If I did live there, I'd be over there getting that blank computer, and
where he belongs.
giving it to the cops. I can tell you that! What a bunch of blank." I answered. In the moment, I completely gave up on trying to avoid foul language.

"Me, too. Love you," she said. I went home in shock. There was just no way to make it all go away. The evil had reared its ugly head again. I prayed, please, Lord, let him get arrested, *finally*. Let him go to jail

UNDER THE BLUE SKY

My step father told us that he had been molested by "several" people. I have no idea if that was true, but he refused to ever go to counseling, or admit he had a problem beyond that. He went to prison later that year because he finally pled guilty to molesting *one* child. In addition to being charged for molesting an American child, he was also looking at being extradited to another country for molesting a child, on a church mission trip. The church must not have gotten my letters, or seen the flyers I hung up and down their driveway, I thought sarcastically. He didn't want to go to jail in another country because, rumors were, it wasn't real cushy. So, he finally pled guilty and went to jail in the United States. About five years later he died there.

    God was merciful in how my step father died. He collapsed getting on the bus to go to the jail hospital. He needed heart surgery. He collapsed on the asphalt, and laid there outside, waiting for help that did not come in time. He was not alone in his final moments. I don't know for sure but I like to imagine that he had a few minutes to gaze up at the beautiful blue sky. I like to think he got to be like a kid trying to make out shapes in the clouds above. That is not a bad way to die, even in prison.

    I did not attend his service, and I still have not cried. This is one of the by-products of grieving for a long time. When death finally happened, I had no more grief to express. My grief at not having a father had been like a slow leak in a tire, taking years and years to finally go flat. Now there is just nothing left. I suppose if I feel anything it is hope. Jesus Christ gives me hope for the future. I know that my step father had accepted Christ. He was baptized in the Jordan River and he studied the bible in prison. He was saved so when I die, I will see him in heaven, and he will finally be all that he could have been here. He will be well. He will be safe. He will be free. He will be home.

I read a description once, of the effects of molestation, and the quote that sticks with me is this: "Denial is the number one offender." I think that quote sticks with me because it is a common reaction. It is simply easier not to believe, not confront, not call the cops, not get righteously angry and seek justice. It's the "easier, softer way" but only in the short term. And only for the denier. Unfortunately, relationships and justice for victims is sacrificed on the altar of denial every single day. Denial perpetuates more sin, more victims and more pain for more generations to come.

But eventually the Holy Spirit kicks the door down on evil, and it all comes spilling out, to be healed and forgiven. Most of the time, He has to kick the door down long before we open it up to accept the painful truth. We would rather just stay safely inside and pretend.

If you are a victim of sexual abuse. I strongly suggest you read the bible every day but also get educated by reading other books about the effects of abuse. Find out why you are the way you are. You are not alone, and there are many books out there written to help you. Learning that I was not abnormal for feeling the way I felt revolutionized my life. It began my healing journey with Christ. It took me a long time to get well but reading books about the effects of sexual abuse is where I first understood what was "wrong with me".

Those in a family who have not been victimized can't understand, and often don't believe, those who have. Denial is easier on the emotions. It works for a while, or forever, for some people who are not directly involved. None of us want to accept the fact that our family line is horrid. I don't. My mom talked about thinking her father was a wonderful father, and how ridiculous it was. She laughed about believing her own fantasy. She was good at denial, and for a long time, so was I. She never did elaborate on what made him a bad father. I always wondered what she meant.

The way my mother was raised must've had an effect on her. As a child and as an adult, I never stopped wanting my mother to divorce my step father and stop being part of the crimes that he was committing. She never divorced him or even threw him out of the house. Truthfully, she continually helped my step father get access to more victims. Why did she do that? I don't know, but for me that was by far the hardest truth to accept. Even though it's hard to accept, and I don't understand it, it is nonetheless, the truth. Inviting a ten-year old to take reading lessons at your home, when your husband is a pedophile, cannot be taken as anything else. Not telling the church that your husband has molested numerous children, and standing by silent, while he's sent to foreign countries, with access to lots of children, including children of missionaries, cannot be taken as anything else. Not telling the church that your husband is a pedophile, and standing by silent while he goes on trips with the junior high youth group, cannot be taken as anything else. Continually inviting young family members to visit and then leaving them alone you're your husband for hours cannot be taken as anything else. Coercing young females to live in your house when you know what your husband will do to them can't be taken as anything else.

Seeing my mother for the ill, culpable person that she is, was the catalyst I needed to erect a healthy boundary and cut ties with her. It was terribly difficult but completely necessary for my emotional health. It was a choice I had to make.

I wanted my step father to be wonderful, honorable and loving. He was not. He was a good many in many ways, but his major, ongoing sin was far too damaging not to completely eclipse nearly all the good that was present. He did teach me to read a map and change a tire. He sent me a hundred bucks once, when I was first married, and he knew money was tight. I still remember what the note said. "This was looking for a home." He was kind and generous in many ways. If it weren't for that one horrible demon that led him around to sexually abuse every available child, he would have been a good father. But for me denial of his evil side was never possible. I couldn't pretend he was a good father because over and over my denial was interrupted by his abuse. I had to face the fact that, for *me,* he was not a good father.

Embracing the ugly truth about what I don't have, here on earth, eventually translated into more and more joy at embracing the truth of what I *do have.* I choose to focus on the wonderful life and people who love that God has provided for me to enjoy every day, instead of expecting people to change and continually grieving over something that just *never was.*

"Finally, bretheren, whatsoever things are true, whatsoever things are noble, whatever things are just, whatever things are pure, whatever things are lovely, whatever things are of good report, if there is any virtue and if there is anything praiseworthy- meditate on these things." Phillipians 4:8

I went to yet another therapist in my early thirties who told me that I needed to grieve over the loss of the father I never had. Back then I still hadn't realized that I never had a real mother either. But this therapist wanted me to make a list of all that I felt I was missing, because I didn't have a father. He wanted me to write about what a wonderful father would be, and then go through all the steps of grief as if he had died or something. I refused. I told him that I had been grieving that for years. There was no way I was going to grieve anymore. I was there to put closure on that chapter. I had grieved for years, and I was done. I just didn't feel like being sad about it anymore. I wanted to finally enjoy my life *without* the grief. Instead of writing out all the things I didn't have. I directed my own 'therapy', and chose joy. I didn't get a hundred dollars an hour but for once, I knew how to help myself. I chose to celebrate. I wanted to jump up and down, and dance around for joy, because I finally knew who my Father truly is, and how blessed I am embracing that truth. In a beautiful frame I commemorated my Father God.

My Father God

My Father gives me guidance…
"For the Lord giveth wisdom, out of His mouth come knowledge and understanding."
Proverbs 2:6

My Father looks out for me…
"I will go before thee, and make the crooked places straight."
Isaiah 45:2

My Father keeps me safe from harm…
"Whoever calls to me shall dwell safely, and shall be quiet from the fear of evil."
Proverbs 1:33

My Father is always there for me…
"When you call, the Lord shall answer and when you cry, He shall say, here I am."
Isaiah 58:9

CALLED TO MORE

It was a couple of years after I had completed the abortion recovery class that I was opening the mail at work, and a pro-life newspaper came in. I was reading an article on a penny drive that a church had done. I had never done anything like that before, but for some reason, I felt like I could do that with my church for the pregnancy resource center. The Holy Spirit has to take credit for putting that thought in my head because I didn't even know what a non-profit was at that point. I'd never made a donation anywhere but church.

I called the Executive Director of the pregnancy resource center and she told me they already had a similar program. She said she had been sending letters and calling a list of local churches for a couple of years, and maybe I could start there. She gave me her list and on my lunch hour, I started calling churches.

My job at the Christian apparel company had been through a lot of transition. The company had been sold and the new owner promptly cleaned house, downsizing from about twenty-five people in the office all the way to two. What used to be a bustling metropolis of office activity was now myself and a sweet, elderly lady.

It had been very difficult to say goodbye to so many believers, that I had grown to love. The transition was difficult, and I wish I had been a more mature Christian in the way I participated. I would have prayed more. I would have used scripture out loud to beat back the devil within that company. I would've had more compassion on my superior and spent much more time in a spirit of grace, and direct communication about problems. I didn't know what I was doing, when things started going south. Then the downsizing happened. The company went from twenty-five people there every day, to eighteen, then to ten, to six, to four, and finally we moved to a new office with only two employees onsite. It was depressing. It was lonely. So having this little volunteer gig for the pregnancy center, at lunchtime, felt good.

It really started to feel fantastic when the pastors I was calling, said 'yes!' The Executive Director expressed amazement that I was getting so many to agree to participate. I laughed that off. I knew that in reality, they all thought it was *her* calling again. I wasn't anything special. I was just doing what I had learned at that apparel company. I was "working a list". I kept at it, and those "yes's, on my lunch hour began to be the highlight of my week.

A couple of months after this was happening, the pregnancy resource center was hiring a Development Director. I didn't even know what that was. But the Executive Director told me about it, and encouraged me to apply. I got a look at the requirements, and I didn't meet them. I didn't have a degree or any experience in the field. Development was fundraising, and besides the penny drive calls, I had never done that type of work. She encouraged me to apply anyway. Amazingly, the job came open just about a week after I was told my current company was closing up shop. I was losing my job.

Even though I was looking at being unemployed, I did not apply at the pregnancy resource center because I wasn't qualified. I was a college drop out after all. That list didn't say, 'warm, funny, gift of gab, able to entertain small children'. I had completely put the job out of my head.

But the future boss was relentless. She invited me to a staff meeting on my lunch hour. It was only two blocks away from my current job, so I walked over. It was then that she cornered me. She sort of, insisted, that I go into a side room for an interview. I wasn't prepared, and did not know what I was doing. But the Lord knew all the answers, and so I passed the pop quiz. Warm-check. Funny-check. Loves the Lord-check. Able to start lickity split-check.

When I actually landed the job, I got excited about it. I'd be working with believers *again*! I would be serving the Lord. Perfect! I went from one job at a Christian organization directly to another. It was another miracle. I didn't have the low cut, hot pink dress, and six inch pumps this time, but this was definitely a miracle.

Excerpt End

CHAPTER TWENTY TWO

It was spring and it was time to get out of the house and start working in the yard. My first stop was the feed store. I was there to buy fancy dog food, when I met a little girl who was apparently there to scare people out of buying ducks. It was hilarious but she was so serious it reminded me of how hard it is to be a kid. Myself and another potential customer were "oohing" and "aahing" over the baby ducks, when we encountered the former duck owner. She was about nine, and she felt compelled to share her experience.

"It's all my parent's fault," the little girl said. I hadn't noticed her before but now when she was looking up into my face, it was almost surreal. I thought, oh my heavens, this kid is Pippy the pirate's kid from that old tv show. I couldn't remember the name of the show but I did remember the red hair and freckles. This kid was her, and the serious look on her face made it feel as if there was no one else in the store. Just Pippy trying, intently, to make me, a total stranger, understand how truly despicable her parents were for letting her baby ducks die a horrible death.

Her mother joined the conversation, and the look on the little girl's face said, plain as day, that she thought her mother had some nerve to say in that sweet, it's not MY fault way…"Baby ducks are hard. We couldn't get them to survive."

Pippy almost stopped time to bore holes into my eyes to make sure I knew the truth of the matter. She very calmly, but immediately stated, "That is a lie. My mother killed my ducks...you know, just so you *know*....she's a killer *and* she's lying." It was hard not to giggle right then. I couldn't laugh because she was so dead duck serious. I glanced over at the other customer and her mouth was literally hanging open.

"Wow. I'm so sorry!" I turned my head and looked sympathetically at her mother who was now standing there with her hand on her hip, glaring at her angry, prepubescent kid. Was Pippy telling the whole story? Was her mother really a cold- blooded killer? I doubted it. I killed a lizard once. How? I have no idea. I think that lizard was eighty in lizard years and just kicked the bucket. Chuck was mad about it, until I got him a frog, which also promptly died of old age.

I was almost proud of little Pippy here. She was in public, risking the wrath of the lying murderer to make sure *somebody* knew what really happened. She looked at me again and I knew those little yellow cheepers were killed. I looked at her Mom again, and started to think she did look a little shifty. I managed to keep it together and get out of the store before Pippy shared her secret plot to get revenge by strangling her mom's gold fish.

Later that night, I was running late for my writer's class and my son was taking up all the counter space, making four peanut butter and jelly sandwiches.

"Hey, you've got to scoot. I'm going to be late. I need to microwave this!" I huffed at him.

"Yeah, whatever Lady!" He smiled at me. His eyes twinkling. "Hey we need some more bread! I think this stuff is stale!"

"Well, check in the pantry. I bought three different kinds of bread the other day." I was proud of myself that I had finally overcome the bread brain block!

Writers Group - Sharing Excerpt Twenty One
Genre: Semi-Autobiographical Memoir, Christian

Acceptance

I wish you loved me
But you don't
I can finally see
That you won't
No more trying
No more crying
Goodbye to sorrow
Happy Today, Happy Tomorrow
With joy I can
Let it be
With gratitude
I am free.

The Pedophile's Wife

She pretends she
Doesn't know what's
Going on
When
She
Really
Does.
She says I never
Abused any children
When
She
Really
Did.

MARCHING ORDERS FOR LIFE

In my first year at the pregnancy center, the Lord impressed a verse upon me. I found it in Proverbs and when I did, it seemed to be marching orders for this new journey I was on. I found it in the bible while casually flipping through it before I was to speak for the first time at a church. I was stunned by what it said. I was anxious to make sure that I was being an intelligent Christian, and not taking the verse out of context, or twisting it to what I thought it should mean. But I found that the verse stood on its own and it spoke directly to my heart.

As the Development Director I was required to tell the pregnancy center story and as part of that I told my own. That was challenging, and it was a long way from singing telegrams. But I felt that God was with me, and the marching orders didn't leave much choice, so I forged on and began speaking regularly.

The first year was difficult for me. I had already gone through the post-abortion bible study and worked through a lot of grief but I still went through depression once in a while. I was just deeply sad at the loss of my children. I realized what a gift, children are. I was so enjoying my other children that I just knew I had blown it. I had sent back more than a string of pearls, I had sent back the greatest gift a person can receive here on earth, after that of salvation. I had rejected three precious babies. I have never met them but I missed them so much.

Since I can remember so little about my abortions, one particularly dark morning I decided, that maybe, if I got my records that would help me feel more closure. I can't remember the dates or even seasons of my abortions.

I looked up the women's clinic and called to request my records. Needless to say, that conversation didn't go well.

"That will be forty dollars per record and you have to come in to make the request in person," she said.

"What? Why does it have to be in person? I can pay you over the phone with a card," I answered.

"Nope. I'm sorry but you must come in to make the request *in person.*" She repeated.

Only if I can bring my gun, I thought. Just kidding. I know that is not funny. But to even imagine going back to that clinic was like going back to where you had the worst car accident ever and having a picnic. This was not going to happen.

"Ok, well I have another question. I've requested records from my other doctors and have never paid a dime for my records. I think one of them, may have charged me ten bucks. Why does it cost forty dollars?" I asked.

"Because we have to go through thousands and thousands of records. We don't keep them on site because there are thousands and thousands of records" She kept drawing out the word thousands to make it sound reeeeeeaaaaaallllyyyyy big and she said it with such casual disdain. Like this was just a massive bother. The loss of life was overwhelming emotionally. Undoubtedly, she had given this morbid spiel to many other distraught women seeking closure. After that call I was even more depressed. I was a mess.

The next day, the pregnancy center was having a prayer gathering to pray over a piece of property we were hoping to build on. I didn't want to go. After yesterday's conversation with the abortion clinic, I was having major difficulty not crying continuously. I knew I had to go, but I didn't want to. I was thinking about quitting my job. I didn't want to spring it on the boss at a prayer event, but I felt like I could not continue in this line of work. It was too hard, and I was willing to tough it out financially, to survive emotionally.

    A few months before, I had purchased a 365 day a year bible at a yard sale for a dollar. (Can you believe that?!) Trying to work my way up to going to the prayer event, I went to that bible. I was desperate for comfort, and I knew that if I just stuck to my routine and read it, I would feel better. I opened it up, sniffling, and trying not to get snot on the pages. I read the old-testament, the new-testament and Psalms sections…then there it was. The marching orders verse.

    Of course, not having a lot of experience with God speaking to me through His Word, I called my boss.

    "Hello", she answered.

    I started rapid firing questions at her, "Hey did you plan this prayer event today because of the verse for today in the 365 day a year bible?"

    "What? No. I don't know what you are talking about."

    Of course, she had no idea what I was talking about. She was probably thinking she was going to have to fire the crazy new Development Director.

    "Oh, never mind. I'll, I'll see you there." I stammered. In that moment, I realized how silly I was being thinking that a human could've planned for that verse to be there on that particular day. It was God clearly speaking to me, encouraging me, and letting me know that I couldn't quit my job. I had my marching orders. I went to the prayer event, and I prayed, begging God to help me be strong. When everyone else took a piece of chalk to write a verse on the asphalt of the building site, I wrote mine, too…

"Deliver those who are drawn toward death, and hold back those stumbling to the slaughter. If you say, "Surely, we did not know this, does not He who weighs the hearts consider it?

He who keeps your soul, does He not know it? And will He not render to each man according to his deeds?" Proverbs 24:11-13

"An abortion is between a doctor and his patient." This is a common justification by the abortion industry. I find it odd, and wonder how many other post-abortive women do, too. I had three abortions, and not once did I meet the doctor. I couldn't tell you with certainty if there was a doctor there or if the "doctor" was a man or a woman. I did see men and women in the room, but I don't know if one of them was the doctor or not. No one introduced themselves at all. The clinic put me to sleep for ten minutes, and my pregnancy was over. No "Hi, I'm doctor so and so." No introduction to a doctor. No shaking hands with a doctor. No bed side manner or discussion with a doctor. No information about what was going on inside my body detailed by a doctor.

Abortion is considered a "blind" procedure. It's like having surgery on your heart without having any procedures and only one test to see what is going on inside there. I can't think of any other surgery that you can undergo without getting at least a diagram of the area first. I mean if you are having a hang nail removed you get an explanation about risks, with ten minutes explaining what the doctor is going to do and how he's going to do it. Then, of course, the doctor asks if you have any questions about the procedure and he answers the questions. He reassures you, invokes confidence in his expertise, puts a warm hand on your shoulder, and looks you in the eye. An abortion, at a typical abortion clinic, is decidedly *not* between a doctor and a patient. Only two people I met at the abortion clinic were actual medical professionals, and how do I know that? Well, they had smocks on so that must mean they are licensed, medical professionals, right?

More importantly, for most medical problems, invasive surgery is the last line of treatment. Most good doctors will try other ways to address the issue first. Not so with abortion. Ending a life, and destroying beautiful potential is quick, and done with as little information provided to the patient as possible. And don't forget the lies. The abortionist might use ultrasound to see where your baby is so he can quickly end its life but the industry doesn't want *you* to see. What is that?

"Doctor, please cut open my knee, and rip out the knee cap. I don't know for sure but I think that *I* know what is going on in there. It's not good and it's not necessary for you to x-ray or give me an MRI first. Just do the surgery. I'll take my chances." And that's exactly what most women who have abortions are doing. Taking their chances.

Women are not examined in an abortion clinic for ectopic pregnancies or uterus abnormalities. It's just, get as many done in a day as you can, so you can make the most money possible by exploiting women's fears, and selfish pride.

I can see now that I was full of selfish pride. I thought, after all I had already been through, I could handle this, too. I had to handle it myself, since the father was decidedly drug addicted, and no help at all. I took a chance that my decision was right. I thought I was getting a quick fix to my problem. I didn't research alternatives, and absolutely none were offered. I decided I was in charge, and I would be ok. I was not.

In addition to the sense of loss that never goes away, at 42, I had to have a hysterectomy. I had pre-cancer growing on the scar tissue from my abortions. The procedure, to unnaturally open my cervix three times, had damaged the tissue. Now cancer was growing. No more babies for me. Instead, motherhood was cut short. I'd sure like to discuss that with my abortion "doctor" now. But I don't know his or her name. I don't know what they looked like. I don't know if they were even licensed.

My quick easy fix was the height of foolishness. If I had a Q and A session with that doctor now, I would ask them how they can live with themselves, but not the unborn. I would ask them if they know Christ. I would ask them if they know they can be forgiven by God. I would tell them that I forgive them, and they have been in my prayers but not the prayers where I ask God to hit them with a mac truck.

Abortion is…. a sin.
Abortion is…. hurtful.
Abortion is…sad.
Abortion is…final.
Abortion is…forgivable.

"Rescue the weak and the needy; deliver them from the hand of the wicked." Psalm 82:4

When I was faced with that choice I was not provided with any other resources, support or options, except abortion. I was not offered, anywhere in the process, accurate information about fetal development. I was not empowered to make a well thought out, well informed, healthy decision. I was empowered to abort. I was streamlined into a system designed to take my money, or in my case, medical money from the state.

One of the things that breaks my heart about my abortions is that no one, no one, tried to stop me or get me to think about any other way. No one. Not the father. Not my family members who knew. Not my friends. Not the medical people I encountered.

To some pro-choice people, the baby's life doesn't matter in comparison to the woman's. I disagree completely with that, but if I agreed, and my life, as a woman, was the most important, why didn't anyone try to protect me? Why didn't anyone safe guard *me*? No one encouraged me to really think about that decision; no one shared about the impact abortion could have on *my* future emotional and physical health. I forgive them.

Immediately, it affected my emotional health. I fell deeper into depression and my drug, alcohol and promiscuity increased. I let my boyfriend talk me into becoming a stripper. That's what he wanted. My self-esteem sank lower and lower. Eventually I became so depressed I was contemplating suicide.

Maybe for some women it is the quick, easy solution and they have no consequences. I did not experience that.

As part of my job for the pregnancy center, I told my story for several years. During that time, I met many women, and men, who were devastated by abortion. I have never had one come up to me and say:

"You know what, you are wrong, I had an abortion and it was the best decision I ever made."

I have had women outside of church, look down and say "that was a long time ago" and "it wasn't fair to the baby…I was only 17" but that's all they can say. They are so obviously hurting that they cannot even go there.

Abortion may be my right, and your right, but it is not always *right* for every woman. For many it is terribly wrong and the hurt can last the rest of your life. For me I think about those two daughters and one son that I aborted, every day. Two girls and a boy. Three children, who would have been mine to love and care for. Three children who could have grown to have birthday parties. Three children, who, I now know, were indeed already babies when I aborted them. They already had arms, legs, hands, feet and a face. I rejected them. I did not believe in myself. I was 'not worth it' and I thought nothing good could ever come from me. I was just a loser, a drug addict, a stripper; all bad things. I had lost hope of getting better. But I chose what I chose. I can't blame anyone but I so wished someone, anyone, would have cared enough to look me in the eye and say,

"Hey have you really thought about what you are doing...*again*? Let's look up some help before you make the decision, just to be sure that is the best decision for you. Do you know how far along you are? Let's find out what that means."

BUILD A WALL OF LOVE

Abortions for me were just another symptom of my unhealthy emotional state. I was co-dependent and to cope with my childhood experiences I focused on my mother's feelings more than my own. I spent most of my life trying to 'rescue' my mother. Now I know that I was not honoring her. It was a perverse form of honor. If anything, it would have been more honoring to have firmly stood up for what was right, at the time it was actually happening, and directly to my mother. That would have been healthier for me, but that's almost impossible when you are an abused kid. But even as an adult, I only had a few conversations with her about what my step father was doing. I was too afraid to hurt her. I was convinced that if she *could* handle it, she *would* have. And since she was not 'handling it' by making an effort to stop him, it must be too much for her emotionally so I, and my siblings, bore that burden. We loved her too much.

I spent many years very angry with my mother but unable to voice my pain to her. I let unforgiveness take root in my heart, and grow to completely take over my life. The Lord tells us to 'forgive others as I have forgiven you' for a reason. The problem with unforgiveness is not only does it become all-consuming but we get used to it, and when the person isn't around, we are so comfortable with anger, we begin to get mad at ourselves. I failed over and over, and soon my unforgiveness was turned inward. I was unable to stand up for myself. I was unable to tell my mother that I needed her to help me. I was unable to tell my mother that her husband was hurting me, and so was she. I felt that I was not only "bad", but I was responsible for being sick and afraid. I began to believe that I just wasn't strong enough to get anything right. I was filled with shame for the sinful life I was living, and I continually believed that it was all my fault. I was unable to move past my long list of failures and sins. They became my identity. I didn't know who I was anymore except for a loser, failure, drug addict, stripper, liar, sinner. I became burdened by shame and self-hatred. I didn't just hate my stepfather and have a love/hate relationship with my mother, but I hated me.

Now that I am older, and am no longer involved in those sins, I can see more clearly how the Lord has used those horrible years to give me a deeper level of understanding, and compassion for others.

"He redeems my life from the pit and crowns me with love and compassion."   Psalm 103:4

Years after becoming a Christian and being free of self-destruction for many years, I found that in order to honor my mother, I needed to stay away. She had no desire to address her past and that's her choice. But when she would say certain things about how great my step father was, I cringed. Eventually, her level of unhealthiness became impossible for me to ignore, or accept. I just couldn't pretend everything was all right anymore, and since I was the child that got in trouble for laughing too loud, I found that I still couldn't keep my mouth shut. I would hear something and a week later, I would experience rage and feel unsafe. Then I would make her feel unsafe. I needed to let her go for my own emotional health, and hers. So, I did. I found that it was more honoring for me to stay away from my mother. I chose a boundary. I built a wall of love.

"Honor your father and mother so that you may live long in the land the Lord is giving you." Exodus 20:12

THE BIG THREE

One of the effects of my upbringing that I have become aware of and had to actively fight against is the tendency to feel sorry for the perpetrator. If I hear about a crime that has been committed, my first compassionate thought is for the person who committed the crime. Sometimes it is my only compassionate thought. Why? Because God built us to model Him and when we don't actively seek to do that, out of ignorance or rebellion; then we model whatever is in front of us the most. I learned as a child that the perpetrator is the one you make allowances for, the one you make excuses for, the one you coddle. My mother didn't intentionally teach me this, but nonetheless I learned it.

With what I know about God, the devil, the flesh and the world now, I don't believe every thought that comes into my head anymore. I recognize that some thoughts are the devil attempting to implant something evil. Feeling sorry for the perpetrator is evil, if the victim is ignored. Compassion for sick people, who were undoubtedly victims themselves is a good thing, but they made a choice to sin, and continue to sin. They made a *choice* to victimize someone. We cannot forget that. Those they've hurt deserve compassion. The perpetrator needs, desperately needs, accountability. Even as a victim turned perpetrator, accountability is compassionate. It is the only thing that can truly help them change for the good of others, and for themselves.

The devil cannot hear our thoughts but he has been observing human beings for thousands of years and he knows how to trip us up. He cannot "possess" a Christian but he can influence us. I have heard testimonies of those who've seen the devil in near death experiences and visions, and they relate what I already knew. Demons are relentless in speaking into our ears. Sometimes, unfortunately, we listen and if we aren't aware of it, we think it is our own thoughts.
The flesh is where patterns are built. My automatic, learned responses and repeated wrong thinking became a habit in the flesh. It wasn't truth. Essentially, it was a lie my body, my nervous system and my subconscious brain told me.
The world is the falsehoods that society accepts and promotes. The world tells me that it if feels good, do it. I'm number one, etc. Those three things - the devil, the flesh and the world are decidedly corrupt. In order to combat them, we use the 'sword of the spirit, which is the word of God'. I say <u>out loud</u>, so the devil can *hear* me, "I reject that in Jesus' name. He is the way, the truth and the life. I know that thought is not true. I reject it in Jesus' name."
Another tactic of the big three is to influence us to minimize, rationalize or flat out deny the truth of a situation. Sometimes what is really going on, hurts. It hurts to accept that some people may remain in dysfunction until they die. It hurts to accept that it is their choice.

"Do not be overcome with evil, but overcome evil with good." Romans 12:21

When I first got clean and sober after trying so hard for so many years to get well and failing, I was very, very grateful. That attitude of gratitude came naturally. I knew I was lucky to be alive, to have a home, a job, a car, all my teeth. I've noticed as the years go by that I have to work harder at gratitude. Sometimes I forget where I came from. I forget how desperate my state of mind and life situation was. I forget that I was slowly dying, and I'm still blessed to be alive. I forget that God gave me all the things that I have. Although I work hard, and try to do my best to follow Christ, even people who do that still sometimes suffer. So today I've decided to be more grateful. I've decided that even in hardship, I need to trust God. I need to remember that God is lighting my path and instead of looking down, focusing on the dirt of the path, I need to keep my head up and focus on the light, moving forward with confidence.

"Thy word is a lamp unto my feet, and a light unto my path." Psalm 119:10

My husband told me that when he was about five, his dad got him a bb gun. Like all boys growing up in the country, he started shooting stuff and tin cans rapidly became too boring. So, he would head out to the woods to shoot birds. He became an excellent shot and started going out further and further from home. He lived on an 80-acre farm so there was lots of room to roam. When he was about nine, he ventured out too far. He found himself lost in the woods. He circled around and around but could not get his bearings or figure out where he was. He had eaten the peanut butter and butter sandwich he had in his pocket, and ran out of water in his little plastic canteen. He was beginning to experience fear. The sounds of the woods that used to be alluring, now started to taunt him. He wanted to run but he didn't know which direction to go. He was tired, and after a couple of hours of this, he was almost in a panic. He realized he could be lost until after dark, alone in the woods. And a bb gun was no match for a cougar or a bear. He sniffled and tried to remain tough but he wasn't feeling very tough. Then in the distance he saw it. It looked like a straight horizontal line between the trees. He walked quickly forward, and breathed a ragged sigh of relief. It was a fence. Their fence. The fence he had walked holding his Dad's hand a few years before looking for spots to repair. At that moment that rickety, old, barbwire, fence was his very best friend. As he put his hand out, and reached for the fence, he knew he wasn't 'out of the woods yet' but he had a sense that at least he had something to follow that he knew. At least he didn't have to wander. His panic and fear began to subside. He knew this was what he needed to find his way back to the comfort, shelter and safety of home. He could not find his way home until he hit the fence line.

In our lives as we go farther and farther out to seek adventure, sometimes we get lost. Panic tries to take over and lead us into self-destruction, and away from the one thing that can really help us. The fence line of life is Jesus Christ. Not just to say 'I believe', but to really *follow*. To keep your hand out and run it along that line that takes us closer and closer to being like Him and away from fear, pain and being lost. Following that fence line always takes us home.

Excerpt End

CHAPTER TWENTY THREE

"Man! This stuff is just too darn sad. I don't think I can take reading more of this junk!" A newbie to the class was complaining to another newbie about reading other people's material. I knew he had a point. I tried to add humor to my story because I knew some people would want to go run in front of a train after reading my book. I had felt that way after reading some of the other writer's material but alas, there is the beauty. We were all suffering together, and most of us were there to grow as writers, and as humans. That meant we had to write about what we knew, our lives. It was a soap opera without the music and the super good-looking people.

Writers Group - Sharing Excerpt Twenty Two
Genre: Semi-Autobiographical Memoir, Christian

From Here

I think of
My mother
Every day.
The bond of love
Like no other
Will stay.

Instead
Of fighting
The pain of it
In my head
I set to righting
The disdain of it
Honoring her
Through prayer
Each time
And I'm sure
God is there
By design
Loving and blessing
Her life in ways
That I cannot
Today confessing
His word I praise
With all I've got
I love my mother
Best from here.

Old Things

Eventually
Trade themselves in
Somewhere
In the dark part
Of our mind
A Bell
At the
Night service window
Is ringing…

THE BEST APOLOGY EVER

In the last few years, I have found it important to keep a clear conscience and to make every effort to have a clean slate with other people. I have not always succeeded in this effort but here is an apology I sent to several people in my family to try…
 I apologize for anything I may have said or done to hurt you, or others you care about. There have been times where I was led by emotion, and did not handle it well. There were times when I did not give you the benefit of the doubt, and thought the worst of you, without asking. There were times when I was angry, and said things I should not have, unless I was speaking to you, and I was not. There were times when I said unkind things to you in anger. I apologize for those times. I'm sorry for the times I did not bother to keep in touch so that when things went awry, you'd know me. I realize that often humans judge each other by actions, not intentions. I'm sure I am guilty of that, so I apologize. I'm sorry for the times I did not care enough about how you felt, or your perspective. I'm sorry if I ever made you cry, or hurt, or get angry. I'm sorry for the times I was wrong, and did not apologize for my mistakes. This letter was written, and sent, in an effort to have a clear conscience, and be obedient to God. I don't expect reconciliation, or a response of any kind, but I do hope you can forgive me.

 There was one apology that I got to make that topped all other apologies.
 "Yes! I think I know who you are talking about. She still stands outside that abortion clinic and prays. She's the only person I know who has been doing it for over fifteen years. And she is usually just by herself." James from Operation Help had answered my call and

was giving me the good news that he knew who I was looking for. He would forward my phone number and ask her to call me back.

I already felt compassion towards the elderly woman I was looking for. I imagined that for all those years, praying alone outside the abortion clinic she probably felt so alone and powerless with so many girls walking in and out trying to ignore her. I wonder if anyone else went out there and yelled at her like I did. Remembering the look on the elderly woman's face made me cry now thinking about it... a skinny, angry, mean girl interrupting her prayers by yelling in her face.

"Why the blank are you here? Shouldn't you be down there at the orphanage helping all those kids nobody wants? Wouldn't it be better if you took your blankin time and energy and took care of children that are already blankin born? This is a waste of time and you should get the blankity blank out of here!"

Just remembering made me cringe. I am so ashamed! How could I have been so awful to a sweet old lady trying to save my baby? I so wish I could take that back. I need to take that back!

"I would be so grateful if you could give her my number and ask her to call me. I want to apologize for yelling at her back then. I was a sad, angry and on drugs. I feel terrible about that now." Then to my surprise about thirty minutes later, my phone rang.

"My name is Ruth. James from Operation Help told me you wanted to talk to me?" An elderly woman's voice was on the other end of the phone.

I just got straight to the point. "I don't know if you remember me, but about 15 years ago you were praying outside the abortion clinic in Rose Park. You know the one with a big church across the street?"

"Yes, I still pray there," she said.

"Do you usually pray alone?" I remembered her

being alone and if she wasn't, I knew this was not the woman I was looking for.

She answered, "Well, my husband waits in the car but it's just me on the sidewalk."

"Good it is you! I tracked you down because I need to apologize. I am so sorry that I yelled at you one day, when you were out there alone praying." Crying, I continued, unable to let any silence into the conversation for fear of what this woman could say…making me feel worse. "I'm so very sorry. I was a scared, angry and on drugs at the time. I should never have done that. I actually am grateful. I had three abortions at that horrible clinic and besides those three abortions, yelling at you when you were just trying to help is what I feel the most regret about in my life."

"Oh, it's all right." Ruth broke in trying to console me. "I understand. I know a lot of girls are in a terrible state of mind when they go in there. I just wish they could see into the future and see that it will be all right."

Sniffling, I asked, "Have you saved any babies? Have any of the moms changed their minds?"

With a smile in her voice, she answered, "Oh yes, some. And sometimes I don't know for sure because they go in but come back out and I don't know if they went through with the abortion or not. I can't always tell…a lot of girls are crying going in and coming out. But sometimes they drive by in their cars later and stop to show me their babies. So yes, sometimes they do keep their babies."

"I'm so glad! I want to sincerely thank you for trying to save my baby that day. Your prayers did not save my baby that day but they may have been what saved me."

"*Can a mother forget the baby at her breast and have*

no compassion for the child she has bourne? Though she may forget, I will not forget you." Isaiah 49:15

      I have had three abortions. I understand shame and loss. I have been forgiven and I know what redemption is. I have had the privilege of sharing my story many times at churches. I have had the devil try to pull me back to shame…

      "You can't say that! Three abortions? You know they are going to think you are a horrible person." And I remind myself that my children did not die in vain. I'm telling my story. I'm doing something about my mistakes. I'm using that deep hurt to help that woman listening, who has also had multiple abortions. She knows she is not alone. Someone else understands the depth of the sorrow. I do. She has hope because I am willing to let God use me. I am willing to let people judge me. I don't care. I am willing to be ridiculed, spit on and if necessary crucified to serve my Jesus, who has done so much for me.

      I am not the same woman I was when I walked into that abortion clinic. I am no longer self-destructive. I want to live, and because I want to live, I have had to live with my past.

"And such were some of you. But you were washed, but you were sanctified, but you were justified in the name of the Lord Jesus and by the Spirit of our God."
1 Corinthians 6:11

DON'T EVER, EVER, EVER GIVE UP!

      If you are in the midst of addressing the unspoken sins in your past or addressing the hurt in your family, I want to encourage you. Don't ever, ever, ever give up!

Don't let the enemy get you down. Stand up for truth, and if others believe things that are false, because it is easier for them, so be it. You don't have to try to convince everyone of who you are. Apologize when you are wrong, now, or in the past. Repent every day, and above all KNOW who you are. If you have asked Jesus to forgive your sins, asked him to live in your heart and lead your life, you are now a Child of God! You are a demon-stomping, water walking, faith-talking, mountain moving, miraculous overcomer!

Remember that you have the family of God. Be grateful for them. Try to remember the good things with your flesh and blood family but don't try to 'fix' what they *choose* to believe. People believe things about me that are completely false. I know that even if I wrote a letter to every member of my family, setting them straight on everything that's ever happened, some would still choose to believe lies about me. That is their choice.

Tell the truth without apology. Call the police if a crime has been committed. Be determined to tell the truth with love, and kindness, if possible. If not, apologize for unexpected fall out. Apologize for the method, not the message. Bake a cake, have flowers delivered, send a gift and then let it go. Move past it. You can't fix the lessons God is teaching others. Keep your own backyard squeaky clean, and take a class if you have to. Let it all out somewhere safe where people won't judge you but will embrace, and encourage you, in your spiritual growth and walk with the Lord.

Thank God for the courage to follow Him. Thank God for giving you the opportunity to try to protect other victims. Then give yourself a huge hug from Jesus, me and all the others reading this.

"Brethren, I do not count myself to have apprehended; but one thing I do, forgetting those things which are

behind and reaching forward to those things which are ahead, I press toward the goal for the prize of the upward call of God in Christ Jesus." **Philippians 3:13-14**

For me the hardest part of closing the door to other people's sin, and putting up boundaries for my own emotional health, was the lies. The lies were told by someone who has never addressed the lifelong sin in their life. Of course, they lie! And if people that I love, that have known me since birth believe that I would actually do the things that I was accused of, then so be it. That reminds me that I'm a sinner, too. I must have done things in my life that led them to believe I was capable of ill intent. I, like all of us, am a work in progress. If people believe ill of you, you are not alone. Sometimes the people, who believe ill of you, don't want to face the fact that the person they believe is lying. Maybe they can't face that. Maybe they need that person more than they need you. It's ok. I'm out, you're out, we're out! It happens. It's ok. I'm ok. You can be, too. Pray, ask the Lord to restore the brokenness and then immerse yourself in God, the bible, fellowship with your new family....the family of God. Choose joy instead of junk. Fix your eyes on Jesus and if you absolutely, have to vent, write a letter to God, a long letter. Tell Him what you want to tell others, pray over it, ask God to help you let it go and then light it on fire. Put the ugliness down on paper, then light it on fire. Let that ugliness burn in h_ll, so to speak.

Let your accusers, flesh and blood family, whoever, let them go, if you have to. If they are believers, you will see them again in heaven. If they are not, pray for their salvation. This life is short, eternal life is long, and you are headed, heaven. And guess what? There are no liars, alcoholics, drug addicts, molesters, rapists, enablers, fixers, foul words, meanness, injustice, self-righteousness, denial or idiots in heaven. This world is full of junk but this is not *our* world. As Christians, this is not our forever home, heaven is!

"He will wipe away every tear from their eyes, and death shall be no more, neither shall there be mourning, nor crying, nor pain anymore, for the former things have passed away." Revelation 21:4

    When the world turns on you for doing the right thing, you are like many in the bible. For example, Able, from the first family. His brother, Cain killed him out of jealousy because Able did the right thing, and Cain did not. Moses, at God's direction led his people out of bondage. But, when things became difficult, the people promptly turned on Moses, as the problem. Jeremiah, an old testament prophet, was one of many who shared God's warnings for the people and was killed for it. Paul was one of the first, face to face, conversions to Christ after Jesus died and rose again. He was abused and left for dead more than once. Why? For trying to share God's love with sinners. Jesus was tortured and humiliated beyond description because He preached a message of radical love. The list goes on and on. I, and many who will read this book, applaud you. THANK YOU for standing up, and stopping the abuse. Thank you for doing the right thing, and protecting other victims. Thank you for risking your reputation, and your comfort, to do what needed to be done. Thank you for your courage. Don't give up. Look to the bible to carry you through when you feel alone, sad or hopeless.
    It always amazes me when people call the bible 'an antiquated book of myths and make believe' or some other flip of the hand description. They are foolishly dismissing the most popular and life-changing book ever

written, as nothing. It amazes me because it is all in there...every struggle, every failure, every triumph, every bit of what we live every day on this cursed planet. It's *all* in there. Read it. There is a light at the end of the tunnel and it is Jesus.

To expand on the story of our creation in Genesis, we are dirty at our core. We are infused with a tendency towards sin. But why do some people just tell a lie and others abuse?

I believe it is because we are emotional beings who react to the sin happening to us or around us, and then we sin ourselves. Why, you may ask, would a God who loves us, curse us? Why would a God who teaches us to forgive one another, not just forgive us without us having to ask? Why did He even allow us to be tempted by satan in the garden of Eden? Imagine for a moment, what the relationship between God and man, His creation, would be without sin? It would be boring. Since we are complicated, creative, emotional, deep thinking beings, why would we expect God to be any different?

If you were able to create creatures in your image, like children for example, would you want them to live uneventful lives with no such thing as challenge, or struggle, or victory? Would you want them to live with nothing to cause them to grow and feel encouraged? Would you rather they go without all of the amazing, empowering emotions, just so they could avoid the pain that got them to that place of deep joy?

I think it is a lot to ask of God to create us without the tapestry and depth that makes life enjoyable. Sure, we experience pain and sin but we also have the opportunity to turn to a loving Father to assist us in overcoming that pain and sin. He has been the hand on our shoulder teaching us to ride our bike with no training wheels all along. I, for one, am grateful for that. No excuses, just a couple band aids and maybe a bruise or two. I fell off that bike several times but with God's help I dusted myself off and got back on to keep trying. I kept my eyes on the hope that someday I would get better.

    But the devil is a mud slinger. Even now I am discovering more layers of mud. I have a conversation with a relative and find out that there is yet another layer. This loveliness is made of rotten, vile, unspeakable goo and until now, I had no idea. The gut reaction…the thought that plagues my mind is "ah, just another reason to hate." But then the Holy Spirit speaks to me and reminds me that hate is no longer the mandatory reaction. I don't have to hate anymore. That way the goo doesn't stay with me. I don't have to roll around in the dirt…I am out of the pit. So now I ask myself, "Well who can I love a little more because of this?" Who can I bless with my transformation from hate, and yesterday, to love, and the now? It's not always easy, and I don't always succeed but I know things are different because the rage doesn't win anymore. I don't hate, now I love. For me, boundaries are part of healthy love.

    This book was not written to make excuses for myself, my sins or anyone else who should be held accountable. What I am hoping for is *understanding*. Why do people sin, horrible, unconscionable sins? Because as the bible says 'the heart is desperately wicked.' That is true because Adam and Eve chose themselves over God, and God then cursed the ground. We are made from the same material as dirt. According to science the fifty-nine elements found in the human body, including oxygen, carbon and hydrogen are all found on the earth's crust. Women are more refined than men because we were made from Adam's rib. We are like powdery, smooth dirt. Men, on the other hand, are chunky dirt. Of course, we are going to do stupid stuff…we're basically mud with eyeballs.

OUT OF THE ZOO

It is unfortunate that some people in the world choose not to address abuse and it continues. I dare you to *refuse* to be one of them. I would encourage you to refuse to let the elephant in the room, take over your thinking. Don't ever accept it because it's easier. Work at it! Shove that big beast out forever! If not, you are on a slippery slope to *acceptance* of sin.

Picture this...a tiny elephant sitting in the corner. Looking over you can see that he's not a cute, happy elephant but instead ugly and defiant looking. Every once in a while, the elephant extends his trunk and lets out a scream. You think, 'wow, that's disconcerting, but whatever. I'll just act like I didn't notice." The elephant begins to grow and now he's not only pushing over nearby furniture with his big body but he's starting to smell. He has gotten louder, too. His screaming is more often and is so shrill you have to cover your ears. Time goes on and the elephant is huge now. Furniture that used to provide comfort is gone. He no longer smells just a little. Now he stinks and flies are buzzing around him. He wants more attention and appears angry that you aren't looking at him all the time. Each time you turn away, he screams profanity and spits on you. You realize there may be no way to ignore him anymore. As a matter of fact, you find that you can't leave the room anymore because he is blocking the door. So, you pretend you don't see, or smell or hear, and you refuse to speak to him. A part of you knows that if you just told him to get out, he would go. But that would mean that you'd have to admit the years and years you put up with him needlessly. Pride makes you say to yourself, "Well, I don't want to appear foolish, so I can never admit that I could've been free of this big, smelly horror I'm living with. He's not that bad, really. He's actually kind of cute when he screams and flips me off." Eventually, you start to feel comfortable with him. You don't get mad at him anymore. You decide to try feeding him. Other people are shocked that you are joining in this bad behavior and try to get you to stop feeding him, but you don't listen. You don't need their help or advice! And for a while, feeding him works. He's quiet and not so demanding. Life seems easier but you notice that people who used to visit, don't anymore. Even phone calls finally stop because of his incessant screaming. Eventually, feeding him backfires completely. He's gotten so big that there's no way to move away from him in the room. You smell, too. Flies crawl on both of you. You are so crowded now that you have to embrace him just to breath. You tell yourself that it's not ideal, but hey, at least you have someone. It's just you and your elephant now and even though you are miserable most of the time, you don't have to worry about making excuses to visitors anymore. Some of them used to really put down your elephant and you had to get mad so they wouldn't hurt his feelings. They finally stopped bringing up his faults. You can't really see what they were complaining about anyway. He looks fine to you. Once in awhile, something does remind you of people you miss and freedom you used to have but when you feel down, your elephant gives you a big, smelly hug and you quickly forget again. You've come to realize that protecting the elephant in the room is all that matters after all.

    Sometimes even with understanding, God leads us away. If you have been abused, you have no obligation to continue a relationship with anyone who abused you or put you in harm's way. You have an obligation to follow God wherever He leads you and for me, that was eventually away. I had several good years with my mother. I chose to honor her in spite of the pain she was responsible for. But eventually it became apparent that I was the only one choosing to seek healing for the past. She chose to stay in it. She chose to continue to defend the abuser while at the same time denying the abuse happened. Up until that time, I thought I was in a "good space" with the situation. I felt safe with my mother. However, when she made statements admitting that she knew the abuse went on for decades. That was hard to hear. Then when she refused to believe that my step father sexually abused another gender and accused the victim of dishonesty, I could take it no longer. When that occurred two things happened internally. I no longer felt safe and within a few months, I felt *uncontrollable* rage. I was shocked at how angry I became with her. I said things that may have been true but they weren't kind. I was not prepared to accept her denial and my reaction was proof. It was apparent that I needed to distance myself from her.

    I went to counseling to work through the hurt, and grief at her loss. It was not what I wanted but it was what had to be, if I wanted to be healthy emotionally. The first counselor, a man, told me that it was the "gorilla cage" concept. Everyone knows that the gorilla is there in the cage. Everyone knows that if you get too close to the cage, the gorilla will rip your arms off. My mother was my gorilla. I could see that was true. It might have been ok for me to be in the zoo and perhaps see the gorilla from a distance but other than that, I was choosing an unsafe place for myself by getting close to the cage and continuing the relationship with her. She chose to continue in denial. That was her choice. I could not heal her. Only God can.

    The counselor also pointed out that Jesus was decidedly not a people pleaser, a fixer or a rescuer. He loved everyone but He did not "like" everyone. Jesus made it very plain that He completely objected to some people and their behavior, mostly the religious leaders of the day. He upset many people because He told the truth. Sometimes that truth bared their soul. They didn't like it. And they didn't all change. He still loved them, but He was not sugar coating the truth. He was not hiding the truth or His feelings so He could be their friend. He was our example to "speak the truth in love". He spoke. He did not pretend or deny. Because of His brutal honesty, those that were pretending to be the most moral in that society, eventually wanted to kill Him…to shut Him up.

    I accepted what the counselor shared but I had a question nagging at me. What about the verse "love keeps no record of wrongs"? I went to another counselor, a woman. I had been counseled by her months earlier, and it just worked out that I saw her too. I wasn't looking for a different answer but I was expecting her to be more compassionate perhaps. She was not. She said that this was not about love, this was about sin. Her example was a dog in the backyard of a double fenced yard. You go around one side of the house to the dog, past the fence, and you get chewed up. As a fixer, you might say, 'I've got to fix this. I'll go around another way.' You go to the other side of the house, past the fence again, to the same backyard and the same dog chews you up. Choosing to make excuses so I could continue to try to 'love' was only going to get me chewed up again. The bible tells us to turn the other cheek, but the injury was well beyond my cheeks, and I needed to heal once and for all. My mother was not healed, was unrepentant about the abuse, and was choosing to stay that way. If I wanted to heal, I needed to stay away. *And* if I truly wanted to honor her, I needed to stay away. My rage hurt her no matter how many times I apologized. I felt unsafe from abuse and I turned it around and made her feel unsafe. Now I was the abuser. Like Jesus, I told an ugly truth that needed to be told, but to continue to remind her of her sin, was not my job and it was wrong. As a Christian, I am commanded by number six, of the ten commandments, to "honor my mother and father". Sometimes the only way to do that is to stay away.

I was shocked by what both counselors said. It was hard for me to accept the loss of my mother. But the female counselor pointed out that my mother's own statements proved that she had been aware of the abuse for over thirty years, and she had ceased being my mother way back then. She said that it was foolish of me to even think of her as my mother because she had not kept me or my siblings out of harm's way, which is the basic duty of a mother. I was instructed by this sweet counselor that I would indeed be tempted by the devil to go back to my own denial; denial of my mother's actual mindset. I would go back to trying to rescue her and I would indeed be hurt again, eventually. Unless something drastic occurred the vicious gorilla/dog would continue to shred me if I got within arm's length. My homework was to pray a simple prayer for someone to share the true gospel with her and for her to be saved. I resisted the suggestion that my mother had not accepted Christ as her savior. But the counselor gently reminded me that a person can have an abundance of head knowledge of the bible but no change of heart. I still don't presume to know whether my mother is saved but I did my homework. She carefully instructed me to pray no more and no less. She encouraged me to do it out of obedience to God and nothing more. I did but I was reminded that many people would've said I was unsaved when I was a suicidal stripper on drugs, but I was saved. I loved God. I just didn't love me.

For me, and many women I've met, abortions leave a lasting grief. We can work through it and forgive ourselves but sometimes that sense of loss stays with us. I also had a loss of other family members because of moving and deaths. I knew that if I followed the advice of the counselors, I would be losing my mother. With a boundary there would also be other family members who would not understand my actions, and would not bother to ask. I would lose them, too. I kept thinking, "what about the grief?' If I did as both counselors instructed, I would be grieving *again*. The counselor advised me to change my focus. Instead of dwelling on the loss of family, focus on the wonderful *gain* that occurred by being part of the family of God. She reminded me that the family of God will last forever. It's only forever, right? God chose a bigger, better family for me that is not perfect but seeking to be more like the One who is. I purposely dwelt on this truth, and God comforted me through this transition. It wasn't easy but it was necessary. It may be for you, too.

  Years from now, I will not remember the wild assumptions, complete falsehoods and utter abandonment of my extended family during that difficult season. What I will vividly remember is the hope, joy, truth, laughter and love that Christ gave me, to carry me through. What I will remember is how in the midst of my loneliness and grief, the Lord never left my side and He gifted me with a new perspective on family. Now I seek to love those who love me well, stay grateful and open to new family relationships and continually keep my eyes fixed on my loving Father.

  Looking to Christ as my Comforter makes it easier to accept that I will never have a "home" on this planet to go to. I have to remind myself that I can make my own home. I'm a grown up after all. People whose parents live in the same house for forty years have no idea how good they have it. If you have your original parents and can go home to the place you grew up without an anxiety attack or a full-blown mental breakdown, consider yourself lucky. Give your mom and dad an extra hug for me. Thank them for being there. Mow their lawn. Eat their potato salad and if you find a gray hair in it, smile and blame the cat.

Excerpt End

LAST CHAPTER

"I feel like we are going to be ok," she said. I was looking into the eyes of the best Mom I'd ever met. I felt so blessed to know her. Her children were so much happier lately, and I could tell she was stronger than ever. Babysitting her children was already a joy but this was just icing on the cake. I could tell that no one would ever harm her children again without her fierce intervention. I could tell that she was going to be hyper-vigilante, and would call the police in thirty seconds flat if she suspected anything. I knew that she wasn't going to make excuses or accept abuse of any kind in her life, or the lives of her precious children. Another cycle of abuse broken for another family. Yay God!

That week in class as I handed over my excerpt to the dark poet, I said,
"Hey guess what?"
"What?" He looked curious, but morose.
"I'm almost done with my book!" I said with a bit of glee.
"What? That is so sad!" He looked confused by my glee. That's not unusual, I thought.
"Yes! It's not sad! It means that God is bringing this part of my journey to an end." I said trying to comfort him.

"That's an odd God." He answered slowly.

Putting my arm around him, I said, "You know what He is a deliciously odd God. He does whatever He wants, and it's always good."

Writers Group - Sharing Excerpt Twenty Three
Genre: Semi-Autobiographical Memoir, Christian

In order to break the generational curses that have tried to destroy my family I have to exercise my authority over the devil, and reject sorrow. Accepting other people, that are unrepentant, into my life, makes me sad. I long to hear them say, "I'm sorry. I was wrong. I'm never doing that again." I spent so many years just going along with the abuse that I am just not able to do that anymore. For me, that is a self-destructive pattern that leads to depression. I don't want to sink into despair over other people's choices. Those are their choices, not mine. I am grateful for what once was. It used to be easier to ignore what was really going on. And truly, we are likely surrounded by people who are fully involved in the struggle with sin. We just don't know. For my family, I do know. It makes me sad because they are my family and I still love them.

But how to love those who are unrepentant? When I'm able, I want to encourage and love those who struggle with sin. But with family, it just hurts so much because there is a bigger picture with a lot of ugly details. There are things I know, that I wish I didn't. There are a lot of things that have been told to me that I have never repeated. I have to bear those burdens in confidence. I wonder why the Lord let me know such hard things. But He did. I know, and I'm not saying what I know, but it also makes it hard for me to encourage and love. I feel like, emotionally, I have to let the unrepentant go.

I love my mother but she is not someone I can have in my life. I tried to find a way to continue the relationship. I've had the hard conversations and provided opportunity for repentance. I tried again and I still got none. As a healthier person than I've ever been, I'm proud of me. I bit the bullet. I faced the music. I mustered the courage. I stood up to the abuser. I refused to pretend. I refused to neglect the important conversation. I've said what I needed to say. Now I can let it all go.

"Take heed to yourselves. If your brother sins against you, rebuke him; and if he repents, forgive him. And if he sins against you seven times in a day, and seven times in a day returns to you, saying, 'I repent,' you shall forgive him." **Luke 17:3-4**

"If it is possible, as far as it depends o you, live at peace with everyone." **Romans 12:18**

"When my father and my mother forsake me, the Lord will take me up" **Psalm 27:10**

My family's story may be similar to the story of Hosea in the bible. Hosea was a prophet who God told to marry a prostitute. God told Hosea to marry the prostitute, and to love her, and love her children. It was a picture of God's love for Israel despite her unfaithfulness; God still loved her. So, if my great, great grandmother was the "town prostitute", and my great grandfather married her, perhaps he is like Hosea. And if my grandfather was the only child that my great grandfather knew was his, out of all fourteen that my great grandmother gave birth to, and he chose to love her, and them, anyway, perhaps he is like Hosea. Perhaps God is determined to redeem the painful history of every family, including mine. But God only has us to use as tools. It's like saying,

"Well, I want to make this beautiful building but I only have hand shovels. It will take generations to make it happen, and I can only get one small section done at a time. It will look like it will never get done for most of the way. It will be a big mess on the outside but the inside will see steady progress. But I've got to start somewhere."

Perhaps God started with my great grandfather. He married the town prostitute, and had a son. That son knew who his father was so he held his head a little higher than the rest. Then that son got married to my grandmother, and they had a son and three daughters. Those daughters were victimized by someone, and those daughters didn't get it all right, and some of the victimization continued. Then those daughters had children, and again some of the victimization continued. But those children had children, and the victimization once again began to repeat, but it was stopped. Only a few of those children were victimized, and although their parents struggled with self-destruction early in life, Jesus healed them. This time when the victimization reared its ugly head again, they handled it right. They fought and sacrificed, and spoke out as loudly as they could to make it right. They were vigilant, and endured all the times their children whined because they weren't allowed to go to slumber parties. They endured when they were called "hyper vigilant", "over protective", "paranoid". They endured because, in their hearts, they were sure. Jesus gave them strength, insight, and determination to take the offense against sin and the devil. And it worked. Those children grew up feeling safer, and because their parents were outspoken about sin, and the healing love of Jesus. They *were* safer. They were free.

The building is finally built. It's beautiful. It took

many generations and a lot of pain, blisters, dirt and tears but it is now a monument to the love of God. And it started with my great grandfather who married the "town prostitute", just like Hosea.

"The word of the LORD that came to Hosea son of Beeri during the reigns of Uzziah, Jotham, Ahaz and Hezekiah, kings of Judah, and during the reign of Jeroboam son of Jehoash king of Israel. When the LORD began to speak through Hosea, the LORD said to him, "Go, marry a promiscuous woman and have children with her, for like an adulterous wife this land is guilty of unfaithfulness to the LORD." [3] So he married Gomer daughter of Diblaim, and she conceived and bore him a son."   Hosea 1:1-3

If we look closely, every day, we can see how God blesses us over and over. For example, my favorite flowers are zinnias. I've tried to grow them a few times with no real success. I lovingly look at them, fondling them at the store, but never can justify spending any money on flowers, instead of more practical things. But I've always wanted a huge bunch of zinnias. One day I noticed that there were four, count 'em, four, big patches of zinnias outside of my work building. Every morning I walked in there, and got to enjoy my favorite flowers. Do you think that is a coincidence? No, that is God telling me that He knows what my favorite flowers are, and wanted to make sure I have some to enjoy. I am so grateful for a loving father that knows me so well, and cares so much. As Christians we are so blessed to know who our heavenly Father is. The Creator of the universe loves us, not just in the big things but the tiny, everyday things.

Sometimes I think about how fortunate I am, and

I am just in awe of how God blesses us, in spite of ourselves. I think about how my husband is so perfect for me, and if you had asked me in the first year of marriage, I wasn't so sure, but looking back I can see that God picked him especially for me.

  I remember going to counseling that first year, and being asked to provide one word to describe marriage. My word was 'compromise', and my husband's word was 'commitment'. I remember being shocked at his word. I had never expected that word. I didn't know exactly why his word surprised me. Looking back, I can see that it was because I had been waiting, working, longing for someone to be 'committed' to me my whole life. I was the kid that somehow got the message that I was 'not worth it'. And this man just said I was. He said he was 'committed' to loving me. That was new to me, and after twenty-five years of marriage, it still is. When my husband tells me 'You're the one', I feel like it is such a privilege to have him. Even though I don't feel very attractive as I age, and I have a couple crooked teeth and more wrinkles every year, he still says, "You're the one". Wow. Do I deserve this, Lord? Apparently, I do, in spite of myself. In spite of a sordid past, and so many mistakes. Another human being thinks I'm 'worth it'.

  My husband is the *second* human to say I'm worth it. Truly. Jesus Christ, told all of us that we are 'worth it' when He died on the cross for us. He proved our worth in that wonderful gift. He didn't have to leave His Father or His home in heaven, but He did…for us. He endured homelessness, hatred, torture, pain, all of our sins, guilt, shame, and death, just to show us we are worth it. But He proves our worth again, and again, in so many other ways beyond that. In writing this book, there have been times when I almost let the devil talk me out of finishing, but God kept me going. I believe that God is reaching out to someone that is reading these words right now. Someone who feels disqualified, not good enough, too bad or otherwise unwanted. God wants you. Repent of your sins and accept true love. Accept the greatest love that has ever existed... Jesus Christ.

"You have changed my sadness into a joyful dance; you have taken away my sorrow and surrounded me with joy." Psalm 30:11

"And we know that all things work together for good to them that love God, to them who are called according to His purpose." Romans 8:28

"I shall not die, but live and declare the works of the Lord." Psalm 118:17

THE END

AFTERWARD

So maybe you are a new Believer and you don't know how to have a "relationship" with Jesus. People in relationships, loving relationships, listen to one another. They get to know each other. If one of them writes a very lengthy love letter to the other, they read it. They read it again, and again, savoring the love behind the words. They talk to each other and they spend time with other people who support their relationship, and help them grow closer. There it is! Read the bible, pray, journal your thoughts, and see what God has to say. Listen with your spirit, get an education on spiritual warfare, and everything else Christian...read lots of Christian books. But always, *always*, read the bible first, and do your very best to follow the example of Jesus that's in the new-testament. Spend time with other Believers...fellowship. Make your life about love. Turn away from everything else, and start walking towards God. All the old, yucky stuff will stay behind you because you are going in a new, fresh, beautiful direction. Have fun, and do what Jesus did...serve others before yourself.

I've learned some tools along the way to stay spiritually healthy and I hope they help you, too.

Personalize scripture- I learned this from an eighty nine year old woman, at a women's conference. She was amazing. She shared how she had taken her favorite Psalm and personalized it. She took the promises of God and made them hers. She wrote in her bible and read the verse daily until she had those promises hidden in her heart. Here's what I mean. The bold is the personalizing. What's in parenthesis is what's actually in the Bible.

MY PSALM 91

I (He) who dwell in the shelter of the Most High
will find rest in the shadow of the Almighty.
I will say of the Lord, He is my refuge,
My God in whom I trust

Surely He will deliver **ME** (you) from the fowler's snare
and the deadly pestilence.
He will cover **ME** (you) with His feathers
and under his wings **I** (you) will find rest.
His faithfulness is **MY** (your) shield and rampart.

I (You) will not fear the terror of the night,
    nor the arrow that flies by day,
⁶ nor the pestilence that stalks in darkness,
    nor the destruction that wastes at noonday.

⁷ A thousand may fall at **MY** (your) side,
    ten thousand at **MY** (your) right hand,
    but it will not come near **ME** (you).
⁸ **I** (You) will only look with **MY** (your) eyes
    and see the punishment of the wicked.
⁹ Because **I** (You) have made the LORD **MY** (your) dwelling place—
    the Most High, who is my refuge[b]—

¹⁰ no evil shall come near **ME** (you),
   no plague will come near **MY** (your) tent.

¹¹ For he will command his angels concerning **ME** (you)
   to guard **ME** (you) in all **MY** (your) ways.
¹² With their hands they will lift **ME** (you) up,
   lest **I** (You) dash **MY** (your) foot against a stone.
¹³ **I** (You) will tread on the lion and the cobra;
   the young lion and the serpent **I** (you) will trample.

¹⁴ "Because **I** (he) holds fast to **God** (me) in love, **HE** (I) will deliver **ME** (him);
   HE (I) will protect **ME** (him), because **I** (he) know **HIS** (my) name.
¹⁵ When **I** (he) call to **HIM** (me), **HE** (I) will answer **ME** (him);
   HE (I) will be with **ME** (him) in trouble;
   HE (I) will rescue **ME** (him) and honor **ME** (him).
¹⁶ With long life **HE** (I) will satisfy **ME** (him)
   and show **ME** (him) **HIS** (my) salvation."

     Study scripture, <u>not</u> evil- Have you ever had a dream that turned into a nightmare? For hours after you are awake you think about it? What did that mean? Why was it so fun and light and then turn into blood, gore and hearing demons talking? I don't know the answers. But I do know that demons are real and we need to be prepared to stomp on them whenever they try to enter into our journey following God. And they will. You don't need to know much about them. You don't need to study paranormal activity, crime, or watch shows about witchcraft. As a matter of fact, you need to *avoid* those things like the plague they are. The devil would love it if you spent all your time studying him and his plan instead of studying God's word and His plan. Don't get lured in by anything evil.

Read at least one book on spiritual warfare and praying scripture. Use scripture as your 'Sword of the Spirit' against the devil. If you are struggling with negative thoughts, tell the demons, "Shut up and leave me alone! I am a child of the Most High God! You have no influence over me!" Use scripture verses in your prayers. For example, if you are unsure of yourself in a situation, say *"I can do all things through Christ who strengthens me."* (Phillipians 4:13) Demons flee when Christians speak the Word. The name of Jesus is also very powerful to stop evil in it's tracks. Say it out loud even if it has to be a whisper under your breath, *say it out loud* so the demons can hear you. They can't hear your thoughts but they can hear your voice.

Take The Authority God Has Given You- If you have repented and accepted Christ into your heart you are a vessel of the Holy Spirit. The Holy Spirit is the most powerful authority on earth in the spirit world. The devil is like a bug and you can squash him before he bites you. If you became aware that a poisonous insect was crawling on your arm, would you stop and study it? "Oh my, this is fascinating! Look how scary it is! Look at those teeth!" No, you would knock that thing off and stomp on it with relief that you got it before it got you. It's the same with the devil. If you are struggling with bad thoughts, tell him out loud, "In the name of Jesus Christ, I command you to leave me alone! Devil you go back to the abyss! You have no power here!" Remember as a Christian, with the Holy Spirit living inside you, you are a giant in the unseen world. A giant with a mission of love!

Memorize Scripture- Read the bible and take the verses that mean the most to you and memorize them. The Bible is called the "Living Word" because God can speak to you through it. I have experienced and heard so many people say, "The verses were glowing and jumping off the page. I just knew God was talking to me in that verse." Memorize those verses as a way to "hide them in your heart." When you are going through something hard, remember them. Allow God to comfort, lead and guide you through His Word.

Guard Your Mind- Be careful about what you let in to your eyes and ears. Listen to Christian music/radio regularly. Many songs are actual scriptures put to music and listening brings a much better feeling into the room than songs about sex, drugs or alcohol.

Worship!- Singing to the Lord is a very powerful weapon against depression, confusion and anger. Even if you don't know the words, just opening your mouth and singing, "I love you, Jesus!" will bring joy back into your heart. Don't be embarrassed, be happy!

Look to God to Be Enough- No matter what other people do, the love of God has to be enough. Don't ever forget how much you are loved. You are loved by the Creator of the universe! People will let you down, because they are people, going through their own stuff. They are not going to meet your needs. Lift your hands up to God and ask *Him* to meet your needs right now. Forgive those you resent for not caring more and thank God He cares enough to meet your every need. I wish I had known, *really known*, God when I was younger but I was confused and hurting for a long time. Sometimes, I still fall back into the patterns of the flesh but sometimes I am aware of it now and can say out loud, "God I forgive them! You are more than enough!"

Work Through Your Stuff- If you get mad, don't let it consume you. There is 'righteous anger' as described in the bible, however there is also unhealthy rage and the flesh. If things come up that still hurt and make you seriously mad about your past or things that happen today, go get some counseling. Do not let a resentment build inside you because one becomes two, two becomes three. Next thing you know what the bible calls a 'root of bitterness' is growing inside and soon a tree of rage will take over your life and ruin your peace and take your joy. Don't let it. Go get some help when you need to.

Remember God Created Boundaries- If it is unhealthy for you emotionally, spiritually and/or physically to be around certain people, even in your family, don't go around them anymore. Pray about keeping a boundary with that person or persons. You have the right to say what you can and cannot allow in your life. You don't have to feel guilty about wanting to nurture your peace and joy. God also created peace and joy and you deserve to have them. It is better to stay completely away from others that refuse to address their own issues. The first person you need to keep healthy is you. You don't allow dysfunction or abuse into your life anymore. Your life is a gift from God, live it well.

"Be angry, and do not sin, do not let the sun go down on your wrath, nor give place to the devil."   *Eph. 4:26*

"And we know in all things work together for good to those who love God and are called according to His purpose."   *Romans 8:28*

"Then Jesus spoke to them again, saying, "I am the light of the world. He who follows Me shall not walk in darkness, but have the light of life."   John 8:12

"Jesus replied: 'Love the Lord your God with all your heart and with all your soul and with all your mind." Matthew 22:37

"For ye were sometimes darkness. but now are ye light in the Lord: walk as children of light."   Ephesians 5:8

ABOUT THE AUTHOR

Jo Lisa currently lives in the south with her husband of over twenty-five years. To share your thoughts on her writing, please email blossomjolisa@gmail.com , (or jolisa_blossom@yahoo.com).
She would love to hear from you!

Made in the USA
Monee, IL
07 February 2024

775af2a5-bf44-42e7-ba89-b20bd4ddf00dR01